Investing in Children
Policy, law and practice in context

Christine Piper

WILLAN
PUBLISHING

Published by

Willan Publishing
Culmcott House
Mill Street, Uffculme
Cullompton, Devon
EX15 3AT, UK
Tel: +44(0)1884 840337
Fax: +44(0)1884 840251
e-mail: info@willanpublishing.co.uk
website: www.willanpublishing.co.uk

Published simultaneously in the USA and Canada by

Willan Publishing
c/o ISBS, 920 NE 58th Ave, Suite 300,
Portland, Oregon 97213-3786, USA
Tel: +001(0)503 287 3093
Fax: +001(0)503 280 8832
e-mail: info@isbs.com
website: www.isbs.com

First published 2008

ISBN   978-1-84392-324-4 paperback
       978-1-84392-325-1 hardback

British Library Cataloguing-in-Publication Data

A catalogue record for this book is available from the British Library.

Project managed by Deer Park Productions, Tavistock, Devon
Typeset by GCS, Leighton Buzzard, Bedfordshire
Printed and bound by T.J. International Ltd, Padstow, Cornwall

With thanks to Derbyshire County Council
for investing in me

Contents

Preface   xi

Part I: Remodelling the components: children, families and risk

1   The 'problem' of spending on children   3
A paradox   8
Barriers to change   9
Hurdles to investment   11
Constructing the problem: 'trouble'   14
The future: perceptions of risk   18
A discourse of children's rights   21
The investment theme   25

2   Transforming Parliament's children   28
The 'child'   28
The 'birth' and 'death' of childhood   32
An effective image: the child as 'victim'   35
The 'innocent' child   39
The child as offender   44
The responsible citizen-child   47
The child in current policy   50

3   Upgrading risk-based investment in children   54
The importance of economics and science   54
Investing in democracy: the education of children   55

Investing in defence and commerce: health and nutrition   58
Investing in law-abiding adults   60
Investing in inclusion   62
Change for Children   67
Risk and early intervention   70
Limiting investment expenditure   73
Investment as problematic in practice   75

4   **Reconstructing parental responsibility**   **80**
The parent: problem or partner?   80
Keeping children (and their mothers) at home   84
Keeping children 'moral'   87
Safeguarding children from sex   88
Protecting children from harm at home:
    the beginnings of accountability   89
Parental partnership with the state   91
Intervention in parental partnerships   94
Parenting responsibly: a widening remit   96
Ensuring children behave responsibly and achieve
    the five outcomes   100

Part II: The mechanisms for, and success of, investment policies

5   **The science of prevention: constructing and
        assessing risk**   **107**
The science of effective parenting   107
Concepts of risk in child protection and youth justice   110
Risk factors, actuarial science and crime pathways   113
Assessment tools   121
Conclusions   129

6   **Law's role in investment**   **132**
Law and children   132
Enforcing or denying duties   135
Explaining the law's stance on local authority duties   144
The weight of the child's views   146
A role for rights   149
Law as a giver of mixed messages?   154

7   **Investing in early intervention: addressing
    risk factors**   **163**
    Evidence-led interventions   163
    Targeting the subject   169
    Non-intervention   170
    Assessing key programmes   174
    The answer is in the detail?   187
    Conclusions   191

8   **The right mix of parents, policy, science and law?**   **194**
    The investment approach to legitimating expenditure   195
    The problem of problematic science   198
    Images of children: 'time to stop knocking the young'?   199
    A more proactive role for rights?   202
    Parental autonomy: thus far and no further?   203
    The law and order agenda   207
    No linear progression?   210

References   *215*

Index   *241*

Preface

The thread which runs throughout this book is that of investment in the lives of children and young people. To be more precise, the question the book seeks to answer is why, historically and in the present, it has proved so difficult for successive governments to spend sufficient public money on services and support for children and their families, such that children have happy childhoods and become healthy, wealthy and wise adults. To try to answer this question, the book brings together insights from a range of disciplines, including law, sociology, criminology and history, to identify the complex and interrelated factors which help the state to 'invest' in children and young people, or hinder it from so doing. The challenge is to explain why, once governments expanded their remit – from a relatively narrow focus on the defence of the realm and the maintenance of law and order – to include social and welfare policies, policies to directly benefit children have proved so contentious and difficult to implement.

To do this, the book reviews, within the context of investment in children, a range of issues around past and current policies and practice. So, whilst the book discusses the *Every Child Matters*, social inclusion and youth justice policy agendas, focusing on notions of risk and responsibility, early intervention, the role and limitations of law, and the importance of 'science', the aim is to shed light on the apparent difficulty in achieving public investment in children and young people.

The argument of the book is that the 'intangibles' – ideologies, social constructions and moral precepts – are at least as important as the role of science and law, and indeed may be more important, in obstructing or encouraging the passage and full implementation of legislation, policy and practice which hope to improve the lives and prospects of children. That is why the first half of the book focuses on notions of family and parental responsibility, assumptions about what children and young people 'are' and the extent to which they should be held accountable, as well as the current preoccupation with risk and the role of state investment against future risks. The second part of the book then seeks to understand the role of science and law – two major sources of authority and 'truth' in modern society – in formulating and implementing an investment in children programme. It critiques the over-reliance on science, and it points up the limitations of law as an enforcer of policies.

The final chapters examine the results of research so far undertaken on relevant selected intervention programmes and identify promising developments. However, the last chapter also draws attention to the alternative agendas around children and young people which are competing for government money and the public's support, and warns that there are dangers in a child-focused policy whose justification relies so heavily on future cost savings stemming from the production of healthier, more employable and law-abiding adults.

I have, necessarily, been very selective in the aspects of policy on which I have chosen to focus because, as argued in Chapter 1, it is only the detail of historically contingent developments which sheds any meaningful light on why it is so difficult to achieve proper investment in children. So there is an emphasis on the prevention of youth offending because that has always been so important in driving social policy both now and in the past, but there is less discussion of education and health in relation to children and young people. However, as the first part of the book shows, the production of healthy and well educated adults has regularly been the motivation for investment at times of economic and military weakness or when a particular health problem, now obesity, threatens to overwhelm state resources.

Investing in Children is, then, essentially an exploration, by a socio-legal scholar with an interest in history, to find out why the UK does not come higher in the league tables of child well-being and, in the light of that, to work out what would have to happen to ensure more investment in children and young people. This is not a book by an expert in criminology, the sociology of childhood, public law, human rights, or youth studies, but what I have aimed to do is to make the law accessible to non-lawyers – because I think it is crucial to understand the boundaries as well as the potential of law as an agent of change, to place the science of crime prevention and early intervention in a wider context, and to fit together the thinking of several disciplines into what I hope is a coherent whole around the concept of investment.

Part I

Remodelling the components: children, families and risk

Chapter 1

The 'problem' of spending on children

There can be no dispute that the UK's position in the league table of child well-being in the EU is lamentable and that there is a need for more effective investment in services to support children, young people, their families and communities. (Hallam Centre for Community Justice 2006:1)

Our aim is to make this the best place in the world for our children and young people to grow up. (Ed Balls in DCSF 2007: Foreword)

A paradox

A vast amount of legislation affecting the lives of children and young people has been passed in the UK over the course of the last two centuries. At one time or another, Parliament has decided, amongst other things, that children must be educated, their employment forbidden or regulated, their diet supplemented, their health checked, their age of entry into sexual and marital relationships laid down and the sources of their financial support defined. Parliament has also specified the circumstances in which children can be removed from their parents, punished for their wrongdoing and, more recently, not only who should count as their parents when reproduction has been assisted but also how, legitimately, children can be 'made'.

Further, as a collection of individual parents, grandparents, brothers and sisters, aunts, uncles and friends, we spend millions of pounds

3

on 'our' children. The total spend on Christmas presents in the UK is around £15 billion, working out at about £300 per person in 2005, rising to £390 in the run-up to Christmas 2006,[1] with another £500 or so on food, cards and accessories (Deloitte 2005), and much of this is child-driven (Tremblay and Tremblay 1995). In surveys some years ago, 35 per cent of respondents said that the most expensive presents they bought would be for children (PR Newswire 2003), with a fifth of all parents and grandparents saying that they would be spending more than £300 on presents for their children or grandchildren (AITC 2003). For those choosing private education, the current 'typical' total cost over 16 years of sending one boy to preparatory and senior schools, followed by university, will be around £300,000.[2]

The UK also has what appears to be a noble history in relation to child-focused legislation. There are well-known pieces of 19th century legislation, such as those concerning children climbing chimneys, going down mines or working in factories, and in the 20th century important Children Acts were passed in 1908, 1948 and 1989, dealing with issues as diverse as the establishment of local authority Children's Departments, the legal criteria for care orders, inspection of foster homes and nurseries, juvenile courts, child employment and the death penalty. In addition to this child protection legislation, free compulsory 'elementary' education was introduced by legislation passed 1870–91 and free universal secondary education by the 1944 Education Act, whilst the National Health Service Act of 1948 impacted at least as much on children as adults, notably in relation to the previously very poor health and safety of mother and child during childbirth (see, for example, Titmuss 1938). Some of this legislation legitimated expenditure on children by bodies accountable to the taxpayer, such as inspectorates and local authorities, whilst other Acts mandated private individuals and businesses to help protect children – with economic costs for employers or parents. All were the result, at least in part, of attention being drawn to the deprivations endured by children and, as noted at the start of a book entitled *A Better World for Children*, 'Little in life arouses moral indignation and demands moral judgements and action more than the suffering of children' (King 1997: 1).

Negative attitudes to children

Yet, despite all this, the contention of this book is that the British, as a nation, have, historically, been 'dead mean' in relation to our children. Perhaps surprisingly, the history of much child-focused legislation is one of tardiness, reluctant acquiescence and incomplete implementation. Governments have, in practice, been reluctant to promote measures which require new or increased expenditure on children; parliaments have sometimes proved similarly reluctant to pass such measures and the courts have often shown timidity when interpreting legislation about children and families. For example, one of the most famous child protection acts, the first 'Cruelty Act' (the Prevention of Cruelty to and Better Protection of Children Act), passed in 1889, was preceded by a series of failed bills over several decades, whilst Part III of the Children Act, passed exactly a century later in 1989, did not, it is argued, establish readily available children's services. According to Munro and Calder, 'The 1989 Children Act set out a clear agenda on both family support and child protection, but it did not lead to the desired rebalancing of priorities and the use of resources' (2006: 440).

The apparent reluctance of the state and its agents to intervene in the lives of children and their families or an inability to sanction sufficient expenditure is in contrast to what sometimes appears as a more willing propensity to punish the 'wrong-doing' of children. It is easy to find quotes which evidence a derogatory view of children and young people. The following are a sample of headings for news items in July 2007, a month in which Professor Sir Albert Aynsley-Green, the Children's Commissioner for England, is reported to have told the General Synod of the Church of England that 'Britain is one of the most unfriendly countries for children in the world' and one with a 'creeping criminalisation' of young people through the use of anti-social behaviour orders (ASBOs) (Petre 2007).

'Council uses web to fight yobs' (Kablenet News 2007; Kable is a public sector IT company and this was a serious news item)

'Sheds burned as vandals go on rampage' (Fraser 2007; a news item in the *Edinburgh Evening News* referring to the work of the youth action team)

'Yobs turning cities into No Go Areas' (Sky News 2007; a news item on a report by the House of Commons Public Accounts Committee)

One contributory reason could be prevalent public attitudes in the UK to children 'en masse'. Lister (2005), surveying child-focused policies, has concluded that the UK has 'a culture unsympathetic to children'; Qvortrup notes that he 'would not hesitate to use Kaufmann's notion of "a structural indifference" towards childhood and children on the part of corporate society' (Qvortrup 2005: 7; Kaufmann 1996) and Vaughan (2000) goes further to argue that public responses to children who offend or behave anti-socially are evidence of an attitude akin to 'child-hate'. Indeed, there appears to be some truth in the notion that the British have a higher regard for animals than for people and, to quote a newspaper headline, 'The public worry more about Spanish donkeys than child poverty' (Toynbee 2007a). A survey conducted in England by the National Children's Bureau (NCB) found that 33 per cent of adults agreed that 'the English love their dogs more than their children' (Madge 2003), and a survey by Petplan in 2005 found that one in five pet owners in the south-west of England 'love pets as much as their children' (although respondents in the north of Scotland gave a much lower priority to the needs of their pets).[3] Ferguson has highlighted a more alarming manifestation of public ambivalence to children – a 'systematic distancing from children' by professionals in child protection work which he considers to be 'severe and dangerous' and resistant to change (2004: 216). He sees this as arising, at least in part, from the 'legacy of poor law attitudes where children are not seen as the deserving poor' (ibid). One contention of this book will be that historical 'bequests' do indeed influence current policy.

Childhood 'deficits'

Whatever the reasons for the apparently ambivalent status of children in the UK, it is accepted that children and young people in the UK have in the recent past experienced more material disadvantage than children in many other western countries. According to HM Treasury, 'Child poverty increased dramatically in the last two decades of the twentieth century. By 1998, the UK had the highest child poverty rate in the EU' (2005: para. 5.5). The increase was fourfold in the 20 years after 1979: the proportion of children living in households with an income lower than 50 per cent of the average increased from 9 per cent to 35 per cent (Freeman 2000: 522) and, in a 1995 UNICEF analysis based on 25 countries, 'the UK had the third highest poverty rate after Russia and the United States' (ibid). The number of households accepted under the UK housing legislation as 'homeless' increased year on year for Britain (excluding Northern Ireland) from 1980 to 1991, whilst the decreases in the 1990s were not uniform (Quilgars

2001: 105) and the trend is again upwards (Bradshaw and Mayhew 2005). Indeed, the homelessness charity Shelter launched a poster campaign in London in the spring of 2007 in which it publicised the fact that one in seven youngsters in Britain, with 400,000 in London, 'trapped in squalid conditions', are 'desperate to escape homelessness and bad housing'.[4] Many of the homeless are initially placed in temporary accommodation, and a study in 1987 showed that three-quarters of such homeless 'units' contained children and that couples with children spent on average 70 weeks in such accommodation (Quilgars 2001: 112).

In response to emerging evidence of these trends, the Labour Government, in power since 1997, set a target of halving child poverty by 2010 and ending it by 2020. Using a relative measure of child poverty, child poverty rates have been declining since 1999/2000 (Bradshaw and Mayhew 2005) and, so far, 600,000 children have been lifted out of poverty. However, the latest figures show that, whilst the proportion of children living in households with a relatively low income 'fell between 1998/99 and 2004/05, from 24 per cent to 19 per cent on the before housing costs measure', there was a small rise in 2005/06 to 20 per cent (DWP 2007a: 13) and, according to the definition used, as many as 3.6 million children remain in poverty (NSPCC et al. 2005: 15). One in four children in England, Wales and Scotland lives in poverty, 'of which 16 per cent live in persistent poverty' (ibid), and government policies have, therefore, 'stalled rather than reversed the increasing levels of child poverty over the last 30 years' (ibid). More recently, the Save the Children charity, in a report briefing entitled *Living Below the Radar,* stated that one in 10 children, amounting to 1.4 million, is living in severe poverty, with a couple with one child living on an average of £7,000 per year after housing costs (Save the Children 2007: 1). This has prompted the question as to why a 20-year programme was planned rather than, say, a 10-year programme. If it is an urgent issue, it is argued, the cost should not be spread over 20 years (Bradshaw 2001: 9; Hendrick 2003: 211).

There are other indicators that many children and young people are not experiencing happy periods of childhood and adolescence. A study based on interviews with 7–11-year olds in primary schools showed that children are anxious about global warming and terrorism and are stressed by national tests (Alexander and Hargreaves 2007). Whilst the infant death rate has continued to drop, as has the rate of death and serious injury from child pedestrian traffic accidents,

'A range of health indicators for children and young people have taken a downward trend' (Bradshaw and Mayhew 2005). The gap in infant mortality rates between the children with a parent classified as a 'routine' or 'manual' worker and children in the overall population has 'narrowed very slightly' in recent years but there has been a general widening of this gap since 1998 (DWP 2007a: 14). There has also been a much publicised sharp upward trend in the prevalence of obesity among all children aged 2–10 (ibid).

School exclusion rates are also on the increase, more children are now born to drug-using parents, more children are drinking alcohol in harmful quantities, and there is no reduction in the rate of suicides in the under-14 age group (Bradshaw and Mayhew 2005). ONS statistics showed a steady rise in suicides for the 15–24 age group from 9.9 per million of the population in 1977 to 20.4 in 1996 (Higate 2001: 179), an increase driven by the rising rate for young men, whose methods of suicide are more 'aggressive' and so more 'successful' (ibid: 180). More recent figures from the National Statistician show no clear trend in the UK over the period 1996–2005, with 0–3 children under 13 committing suicide in each year but with 16–39 children under 16 doing so in each year, with a latest figure of 20 for 2005.[5]

Bradshaw and Mayhew conclude that, 'While overall the UK can claim that life is getting better for children, child well-being continues to be mixed: the list of improving indicators is more or less equal to the list of deteriorating/no change indicators' (2005: Key trends: 4). Children in poverty, and their parents, suffer a variety of linked disadvantage. In particular, the economic and employment status of' the household in which a child lives affects his or her well-being. Further, processes of polarisation and residualisation in social housing in the 1990s in the UK impacted on the schools attended as well on the housing lived in by children (JRF 1999): policies such as the 'right to buy' council houses and more choice in selecting schools have led to estates and schools with a much narrower class base. Research by the Institute of Education as part of the Millennium Cohort Study showed, for example, that many children from disadvantaged backgrounds are up to a year behind more privileged youngsters educationally as early as the age of three (Ward, Sullivan and Bradshaw 2007; for the full study see Hansen and Joshi 2007). Multiple disadvantage has become concentrated in particular geographical areas and the inhabitants are more likely to experience social exclusion.

All of the above issues were given a high profile in 2007 when UNICEF published another report on the well-being of children in

21 industrialised nations which put the UK bottom of the table and generated the following headlines in national newspapers on 14 February:

'Betrayal of a generation' (*Daily Mail*)
'British children: poorer, at greater risk and more insecure' (*The Guardian*)
'Britain's children: unhappy, neglected and poorly educated' (*The Independent*)
'British youngsters get worst deal, says UN' (*The Daily Telegraph*)
'Britain's children are unhappiest in the Western world' (*The Times*)

In response to the report, the Children's Commissioner for England, Professor Sir Albert Aynsley-Green, is reported to have said, 'The findings are disheartening but not surprising as they echo what children tell me on a daily basis' (Womack 2007).

Barriers to change

The poor life experiences of children, catalogued above, are well documented. These findings are rarely contested and few would disagree that 'There is no question that the biggest cause of poor outcomes for children is poverty and social exclusion' (MacLeod 2000: 14). One of those poor outcomes – because crime is rarely a good career choice – is offending by young people. There is ample research evidence that minors imprisoned for serious crimes are very likely to be seriously disadvantaged with abusive backgrounds, and Chapter 5 will review some of this evidence. However, a widespread acceptance of these links by politicians, academics and professionals does not mean that there has been a shift in political and public thinking large enough to countenance a much greater expenditure directly on children, an increase in targeted interventions in families or, indeed, more 'time' spent listening to children and considering their needs and rights. This book sets out to explain why such a shift is so difficult to engineer and examines whether new political agendas can turn round a national Scrooge-like approach to state resources for support and services for children. In particular, it assesses, in Chapter 3, whether the social inclusion agenda of the New Labour governments, the importance in policy and practice of early interventions in children's lives, the changes wrought by the 2004 Children Act, with its 'safeguarding' agenda and new children's trusts, and the proposals in the Children's Plan published in December 2007 (DCSF 2007) will have more success in promoting and ensuring more investment in children.

To start to answer this question, we need to focus on the 'components' of our thinking around children and family policy which, historically, have encouraged or allowed specific forms of expenditure and intervention. In particular, the focus will be on three sets of ideas and ideologies: about the child, about the family and about 'the future'. The 'child' focus is on childhood itself and how particular influential 'images' of children and their 'needs' are constructed and 'used', socially and politically. The focus on 'family' is on how and why assumptions are made about what parents 'should' do and what the state should not do, who should be responsible and who should be held accountable. A focus on the 'future' raises questions about the ways in which social and political ideas about the future are changing: what do we consider to be the biggest risks the UK faces and can those risks be reduced by 'investment' in children? This leads to other issues for this book to address, notably beliefs around the utility of investment and the role of the two major 'truth' producing systems: science, which may or may not support the idea that investment in children will produce the desired returns, and law, which may be instrumental in implementing or frustrating child-focused legislation. Searching for answers to these questions will reveal continuities and change over time but the exact configuration of those components at this point in time illuminates why our current policies are politically possible. However, this quest also points to less welcome developments that logically flow from approaches taken to childhood, parenting and the authority of science and law.

The focus will be on the UK and England in particular. This may appear very parochial and insular, especially as some of the issues and developments discussed are also ones to be found in countries around the world. For example, Jenson, writing from the perspective of Canadian policy, postulates the development there of an 'investing-in-children' paradigm to explain shifts in thinking around family responsibility, state benefits, labour force participation by parents and early childhood initiatives (Jenson 2004: 176–80). All this is very familiar; there are 'world-wide inter-generational problems' but there are different understandings of the problem and solution (King 2007: 868). So Muncie, while noting global trends in responses to youth offending, argues that there 'remain marked and significant global (as well as European) variations in policy, extent of adherence to UN Conventions and resort to custody' (Muncie 2006: 64). It is the detail of the developments in a culturally and politically distinct jurisdiction which illuminates the generalities and starts to make some sense of what is – or is not – happening. The aspects of policy on child welfare and development which will be reviewed in this book will, therefore, of necessity be limited: there needs to be room for detail. This will inevitably mean that some aspects of child-focused policy, notably health and education, will not be given the attention they deserve, whilst there is an emphasis on the prevention of youth offending because that is so important in driving policy both now and in the past. It also brings out different issues and perspectives in a way that the more technical areas of health and education do not.

Hurdles to investment

> All laws [affecting children] are made by adults in order to create the kind of society that adults wish to have. (Guggenheim 2005: 47)

Child-focused proposals for legislative reform face the same hurdles as any proposed reform of the law in a liberal democratic society: both the proposals themselves and any expenditure or administrative changes they will entail must be politically acceptable to the government and, ultimately, legitimate in the eyes of the electorate. There must be sufficient political and popular support for the type of proposed intervention by the state in the life of the individual or family and there must be support for the increased expenditure that proposed changes would entail. These basic hurdles have, however, proved particularly problematic for reform aimed at minors and, in practice, these political hurdles act as rationing devices for child-focused legislation.

Legitimating change

There are specific reasons for these difficulties and the apparently mundane issue of school dinners provides one of the best examples to illustrate them. The Provision of School Meals Act – to improve the health of children by better nutrition – was passed in 1906 after much opposition. It gave local authorities the power to spend money on providing free school meals, yet by 1940 only half of local authorities were doing so. A century after the Act was implemented, the government's role and the level of resources to be allocated to school dinners has again become a publicly debated issue (see Chapters 3 and 4). So why has the idea of an education service using public money to feed children been so contentious? The reasons are essentially very simple. The norm in modern society has been for children to be brought up in a family. That family decides on the child's up-bringing, taking account of available resources and beliefs about what constitutes a child's best interests. Consequently, what counts as a legitimate state intervention has depended historically on two sets of ideas: dominant ideas about the family, notably the rights, duties and responsibilities of family members, and the strength of particular ideas about what is good and appropriate in the rearing and education of children. It would, however, be difficult to find two concepts that are more fluid and contested than 'family' and 'the child's best interests', or two concepts which carry such ideological or moral 'baggage'.

These concepts, themselves the subject of a wealth of analysis from a range of diverse academic, scientific and political viewpoints,[6] are crucial to long-held beliefs in the importance of the family in a liberal democratic society. The family 'manages' the socialisation of the young into productive law-abiding adults such that social stability is maintained without compulsion. Historically, and in the present, the belief that there needs to be a parenting unit with the independence and authority to carry out this function has influenced policy. It is reflected in the priority still accorded to the status of marriage which is perceived as a more stable unit (see, for example, *Supporting Parents* (Home Office 1998)), in the upholding of the rights of parents over their children (evidenced by the lack of sufficient political will to outlaw smacking in the UK), and in the presumption that parenting, by and large, should be left to parents. This attitude is strengthened by the fact that the general public in the UK does not consider child poverty and structural disadvantage – linked to poor outcomes and the need for interventions – to be a social problem (i.e. it is not an issue that warrants state action). The reasons lie in strongly held notions of parental responsibility for creating and then maintaining children: 'People should not have children if they cannot look after them properly' is a recurring comment in media stories. So the father with 17 children who receives, it is reported, £508 per week in benefits is referred to in the media as 'shameless Mick' and 'Britain's biggest scrounger' (Jepson 2007),[7] although he might, in a different time and place, be viewed as a cost effective producer for the state of 17 new workers of the future.

What we have here is another paradox: in a liberal society the family is both too important to meddle with and too important to be left alone. Yet investment in children inevitably involves – for most children – intervention in the family or, at the very least, an enforced sharing of responsibility for facets of the child's upbringing and well-being. In practice, this means that state intervention in the lives of children is seen as necessary and justifiable only if there is too high a risk that the care the family provides will not ensure whatever minimum standards of child welfare and socialisation of the young are acceptable to society at that time and in that place. The lines drawn are dependent on notions of the child and ideas about the importance of parental autonomy, on the content of 'truths' held about the child's needs, and on attitudes to risk generally and specific risks in particular. And all these factors are contingent on context.

Remodelling the components

The first part of this book is essentially about the shifts in all these concepts and ideas and, consequently, how compulsory or voluntary sharing of parenting with the family to invest in children has historically and in the present been possible – or not. In these shifts, the concept of the 'best interests' of children has been very important: it operates as a legitimating concept by encompassing diverse moral agendas to improve the lives of children and young people. Investment is more likely to be achieved if the construction of best interests rests on ideas that are widely held and 'taken-for-granted'[8] and if there is a sufficient measure of consensus about the priority needs of children.

There is, therefore, an interplay with images of children, and constructions of childhood and family, and successful change requires the compatibility of all these components. As James and James point out, from the perspective of a cultural politics of childhood, it is social policy which regulates the relationship between the 'cultural determinants' of childhood – the moral discourses, the structural and social factors, the economic and political conditions (2004: 7). Yet social policy can only regulate the components which exist and – whilst there are reflexivities and interconnections which work to modify the components – there are limits to change at any point in time. The formulation of historically contingent policy is constrained by the nature of existing components and, notably, by ideologies and concepts. For example, adoption reform was delayed for at least 15 years after the Children Act 1989 because of the strength of particular moral and ideological discourses around 'family' and the needs of children. Until the (very contested) passage of the Adoption and Children Act in 2002 there had been no consensus to legitimate any alteration to the welfare principle to downgrade parental rights, or the removal of a ban on same-sex couple adoption which cut across dominant conceptions of the heterosexual family, or the qualified promotion of continuing contact with birth parents which undermined ideas about the autonomy of the 'replacement' family.

Legitimating increased expenditure is a related hurdle: new expenditure requires cuts elsewhere or increased income in the form of higher taxation and the question of taxation levels has always concerned politicians. The most famous example, that of the Tea Act 1773, one of a series of statutes which led to taxation-induced problems in the American colonies that ultimately led to independence,[9] is a long-lasting reminder to politicians of the dangers raised by tinkering with taxation in unpopular ways. Rationing resources is, therefore, integral to political life, though the nature of the state's justifications for expenditure are contingent on time and place and, in particular, on dominant ideas about the state's role, constructions of childhood and whatever other issues are most pressing at that point in time. For any new form of intervention – however acceptable to the electorate – the increased expenditure must independently be justified as being proportionate to the desired outcome of the intervention. In some political and economic climates, this justification takes the form of explicitly 'proving' cost savings.

Constructing the problem: 'trouble'

All this of course begs the question as to the content of the new policy to be justified and legitimated. There is a chicken and egg scenario here or, rather, there are several chickens and eggs. A particular view of childhood and children's needs – or of the role and rights of parents – will encourage the belief that a particular state of affairs is a problem to be addressed. Yet, where there is more than one view of children and families, the situation constructed as a social problem will prioritise a particular view of children and families. How future risks and current social and political anxieties are conceptualised will likewise affect, and be affected by, all the other constituent components. A growing body of work in sociology has also examined the mechanisms which link structural issues with the agency of children and so allow space for children themselves to influence constructions of the child and formulations of policy (see, in particular James and James 2004: 24–5). How children experience and react, as social actors, to the way they are treated is, consequently, another factor in promoting both structural and discursive change.

Within the constraints set by these intangible factors, policy is constructed for political reasons. An analogy is sometimes drawn with policy in relation to deaths and injuries arising from accidents involving cars. Such accidents have economic and psychological costs at the level of the individual and the state. If the problem is constructed as that of the reckless or unskilled driver, the solution will focus on the driver (to be trained or punished); if the problem is construed as that of unsafe vehicles (in contrast, say, to the low rate of fatal accidents for racing cars) then the solution will focus on the manufacturer. Political and economic factors will determine whether the state would prefer to regulate manufacturers or car drivers, and the selection and construction of those factors will be influenced by the context of the prevailing political ideology.

For the decade after New Labour came to power in 1997, the basic political ideology has been the 'Third Way' (see Parton 2006: Chapter 5). It is an ideology which was espoused by the then Prime Minister Tony Blair and his governments, as well as by the then President of the United States, Bill Clinton, and by several European leaders. Defining the Third Way has proved difficult: 'One observer described it as the Loch Ness Monster of British politics – everyone's heard of it, there are occasional sightings but no-one is sure the beast really exists' (Dickson 1999). It is a 'third' way in that it rejects the other two main 'ways' of socialism and neo-liberalism (see Giddens 1998) and, therefore, of necessity holds a somewhat ambivalent position with regard to both the free market and state management of economic and social life. It is argued that New Labour is 'strong on values' (Jordan 2000: 1) and much of the analysis has been concerned with those values. Le Grand (1998) outlines four core values underpinning the Third Way: Community, Opportunity, Responsibility and Accountability (CORA); others have listed them as equality (of worth and opportunity), autonomy, community (individual responsibility and social inclusion) and democracy (see Jordan 2000: 20).

However categorised, there is a clear emphasis on reciprocal responsibilities and accountabilities, with a focus on personal responsibility set alongside ideas around social justice. There may be an acceptance that structural factors affect life chances but there is also a focus on what the individual must do to take responsibility for improving those life chances. So, to return to the analogy above, the problem may well lie in the manufacture of the motor car – and there might be some attempts to improve the standards of manufacture – but that does not absolve the bad driver from responsibility.

These changing political conceptions of the citizen and his or her role in the life and health of the state will also influence those ideas about children which are 'picked up' by policy makers. Hendrick's research, for example, has categorised the fluctuating importance *over time* of different notions of the child to justify, explicitly or implicitly, a particular expenditure on children or a politically risky intervention in their family lives (see Hendrick 1994 for the period 1872–1989). Some of those historical notions are still important and there are also newer images of children available to reformers and politicians. Some of these current images legitimate what Haydon and Scraton (2000: 228) have referred to as a 'politics of adultism' which seeks to exclude children; others legitimate a tough approach to those constituted as 'dangerous youth'. In contrast, in the 19th century and well into the 20th century, successful child-focused campaigns – concerted efforts to introduce new legislation – drew profitably on images of children as innocent, dependent, vulnerable, and needing adults to give them a 'voice'. If an unequivocal picture of the needy child could be presented, one where 'need' is a socially accepted construction underpinned by a compelling image of the child, that it would be 'immoral' to ignore – and that of course is the rub – child-friendly policies have more easily harnessed support and legitimacy and become law. Recent legislation, notably in relation to sex offenders, has also drawn on such images of innocence.

A useful case study about the flexibility and co-existence of divergent images – with implications for policy responses – is that of the discursive use of the word 'trouble' in relation to children and their behaviour. 'Trouble' is one of those words that we take for granted. Only when we stop to think about it do the nuances, the ambiguity and breadth of meanings emerge. The uses can range from the ridiculous to the tragic with, for those of us old enough to remember, Frank Spencer's euphemistic 'spot of trouble' in the TV comedy 'Some Mothers Do 'Ave 'Em' in the 1970s at one end of the continuum and, at the other end, the 'Troubles' in Ireland, denoting the two periods of extreme and sporadic violence in 1919–21 and the late 1960s to the mid-1990s. Over more than two centuries, in reference to minors, 'getting into trouble' has usually implied 'in trouble with the law', specifically infractions of criminal law and the involvement of the police. Indeed, the White Paper of 1968 setting out the proposals for reform of the juvenile justice system was entitled *Children in Trouble* (Home Office 1968); a more recent report by Allen (2006) was similarly entitled *From Punishment to Problem Solving: A New Approach to Children in Trouble*, and *Youth Matters*, the consultation paper, refers to the young person who 'gets into trouble' or who 'drifts into trouble' (DfES 2005: paras 12 and 15; see also ibid: pp. 5, 9, 21 and 64).

Yet being 'in trouble' has had other and wider connotations. For example, 'Children in Trouble' has been a permanent but changing display area at the Victoria and Albert Museum with specific displays focusing on Victorian children at work and childhood diseases of the past.[10] The child in trouble may then be the child with a range of problems, not just relating to his or her behaviour or morals. This links up with the 'troubled child'. For example, the web page for Children's Hearings in Scotland states that it is 'our duty, along with our partners, to safeguard the needs of the most vulnerable and troubled children and young people in Scotland' and to 'make a difference in the life of a child at risk or in trouble'.[11] Here, the children referred to encompass those in need, at risk of abuse or who have offended. Similarly, a Barnardo's publication about community-based services 'for young people at risk of entering care or custody' in Northern Ireland is entitled *Troubled children or children in trouble?* (Gorman and McGeough undated), and 'Children in trouble are troubled children' was the message given by the founder of the Michael Sieff Foundation at a conference on juvenile crime prevention (Haslam 2002).

More recently, 'troubled' and 'troublesome' have come to refer to children who have emotional and behavioural problems. 'What works for troubled children' is the title of a publication about a project aimed at a variety of issues including bullying, bereavement, aggressive behaviour and depression (Buchanan and Ritchie 2004). Generally, these concerns are seen as the province of mental health professionals. So, for example, a recent American text is entitled *Taming the Troublesome Child: American Families, Child Guidance and the Limits of the Psychiatric* (Jones 2002), definitions of Attention Deficit Disorder can include reference to the troublesome child,[12] and BUPA publishes a parenting guide with information on how to deal with 'troublesome tots'. Sometimes, however, troublesome children are seen as the province of more punitive regimes. For example, in October 2005, when the Government announced plans for what the media referred to as 'basbos' (baby anti-social behaviour orders for the under-10s), *The Telegraph* explained that 'The Basbo may see, for example, a troublesome child barred from verbally abusing neighbours or from entering parts of an estate' (Hennessey 2005).

This use of words is not an irrelevant issue. The choice of the particular version of 'trouble' to be used is significant as such words have iconic status and are pointers to the preferred solution to the problem being constructed. Whether or not the solution is better mental health services, recreational facilities, civil orders or criminal punishments depends on how the child or young person is constructed. These different connotations have, for example, legitimated the integration or differentiation of youth justice and child protection systems in the UK (see Hill *et al.* 2006). At one end of the range of images is the youth who is 'trouble' and a danger; at the other is the 'normal' mischievous bundle of trouble. Currently, our perceptions of children often fall at the 'danger' end of the continuum with the result that we have a very high rate of custodial punishment for young offenders.

Given that there has occurred what has been referred to as the 'politicisation of youth justice', and given the high media profile of failures in child protection, what is crucial for the electoral success of governments – and parties who would be governments – is how the children are perceived and how problems are constructed in relation to children who are at risk of abuse, of failure to thrive, or of committing crimes. Yet, how the problem is conceptualised is contingent on time and place. The extent of scientific knowledge about children and the causes of, notably, abuse and offending will probably be a contributory factor but it may not be determinative if particular cultural, religious, economic or political issues predominate at a point in time.

The future: perceptions of risk

How the 'problem' of children is constructed is crucial, but it often hinges on another factor – our notions of what the future holds and, more specifically, what the future is likely to hold if nothing is changed. Here, then, the notions of risk and investment are central and particularly so in what has been termed the risk society: 'The idea of a "risk society" might suggest a world which has become more hazardous, but this is not necessarily so. Rather, it is a society increasingly preoccupied with the future (and also with safety) which generates the notion of risk' (Giddens 1999: 3). This focus on the future might be seen at odds with another trend to which attention has been drawn – the growing importance of the child in late modernity as a symbol of nostalgia, the child envisioned as 'a longing for times past, not as "futurity"' (Jenks 1996: 106-7). The child, it is said, 'is the source of the last remaining, irrevocable, unexchangeable primary relationship' (Beck 1992: 118), and the love and loyalty that was previously invested in, for example, marriage or class solidarity is now invested in the child (Jenks 1996: 107). Yet this personal investment only points up the importance of feelings of insecurity in social and personal thinking and the importance of confronting personal and social fears – those risks of dangers that 'must' be reduced or averted.

With child policies, then, the notion of investment has become crucial in managing the risk of unwanted outcomes in the adulthood of today's children. That investment might, as Hendrick has pointed out, be an investment in the mind or the body of the child (Hendrick 1994), and the sources of 'evidence' to support pressure for specific investments in children may be found – and have been found, historically – in morality or religion, in economics, and in scientific knowledge (see Chapter 3). The choices about the sort of investments to be made will depend on which concerns about our insecurity we prioritise at any point in time: 'What is it that we fear most: the exploitation and inequality of the market, the arbitrary authority of the state, the erosion of the nuclear family, neighbourhood crime, the day-to-day violence that occurs in the home? Every society will prioritise one set of insecurity concerns above another' (Ainley 1999: 8). As Hendrick points out, 'New Labour may be the first government to put children at the *centre* of a social investment programme, but it is by no means the first to use children for its own – and the Nation's – ends' (Hendrick 2005: 8). Investment in practice may be direct expenditure on services to and for children, it might be expenditure to pay for 'monitoring' their lives (for example by the establishment of health and safety or school medical inspectorates or via Health Visitor schemes), or it might be the loss to the economy through outlawing child employment. There are, therefore, issues around the importance of historically contingent notions of investment and constructions of morality.

The notion of investment is rooted in a particular set of ideas about childhood which construct it as a period of preparation for an economically active and useful working life and for a lifetime of law-abiding and making positive contributions to the society. It has, historically, proved easier to justify expenditure which can be presented as having a direct influence on specific future costs and losses related to war, economic growth and reduced criminality. The objective would be to prevent future loss of productive workers (or effective military personnel) and future expenditure on, notably, the penal system, social security payments and the health service. An early 20th century example of investment for national security was legislation to mandate medical inspections of school children:[13] recruitment for the Boer War (1899–1902) had alerted Parliament to the poor physical state of the nation's young men. The Provision of School Meals Act 1906 was another example of investment for future prosperity. Similarly, the prevention of civil disorder can legitimate expenditure by state or charitable bodies to reduce future criminality. The reformatory and industrial schools in Victorian England set up 'for the children of the perishing and dangerous classes'[14] would be an example in the 19th century. Chapter 3 will return to these themes in more detail.

However, not all those pressing for child-focused reform would subscribe to such a view of investment. They might wish to promote the happiness of, and respect for, children during their childhood or wish to improve their chances of developing happy and fulfilled adult lives in senses wider than those encompassed by the imperatives of law and order and economic growth. Such wider views may themselves be underpinned by a variety of contrasting perspectives. In the 19th century, the explicit aim of 'giving children a childhood' entailed removing them from places of daily employment which were perceived to be morally or physically harmful. In the 20th century, those constructions of children as innocent and vulnerable have been joined by children as rights-holders, or by sociological constructions of children as agents – as 'being' rather than simply 'becoming', and as citizens of the present as well as the future. Social policy has also compartmentalised children, and professional involvement and academic interest have often followed these distinctions.

It is, therefore, significant that the current *Every Child Matters* agenda for children from birth to the age of 19 aims to provide joined-up services for children. According to the government website, 'every local authority will be working with its partners, through children's trusts, to find out what works best for children and young people in its area and act on it', whilst the Children's Fund, launched in November 2000, aims 'to tackle disadvantage among children and young people', 'to identify at an early stage children and young people at risk of social exclusion' and to 'make sure they receive the help and support they need to achieve their potential'.[15]

Current policies of social inclusion and investment in children who are 'at risk' of becoming adults with a range of disadvantageous life situations would appear to herald a different approach to children. On the face of it, these policies speak of children and young people in new ways and aim to break down the distinctions between compartmentalised interests. Consequently, they should provide the means to improve access to resources for children and young people and so challenge what, historically, has been a *de facto* rationing of expenditure on minors. However, they are predicated on calculations and assessments of 'at risk' children, families and neighbourhoods, and those notions of risk, though crucially important, are shifting and amorphous, and so Chapter 5 will focus on the construction and assessment of risk. In practice, policies based on them may not yield the intended investment outcome.

But there is a further issue – the notion of investment is itself predicated on ideas about the effectiveness of investments and their returns. Investment is only undertaken in expectation of rewards of some kind, and so investment in children depends on new ideas about the utility of the proposed intervention in the lives of children. Here, the current importance of 'early interventions' is a prime example. The investment agenda is heavily dependent on the notion that investment put in place early in the children's lives, or early in their dealings with the state, will reap better dividends than later – or no – investment. There is, consequently, a significant reliance on the findings of scientific research which have suggested that early interventions are indeed 'worth' it. Yet, as we shall see in Chapter 7, researchers are advising caution in interpreting results; criminologists, for example, can no more give a certainty of prediction that intervention will prevent crime than can those who have been trying to predict whether a child will be abused by parents. All 'experts' can only make the best assessment of what is most likely to occur on the basis of what research has suggested but, in order to sell to the electorate the costs of investment, the government needs to give the appearance of certainty of outcome.

A discourse of children's rights

The 20th century saw increasing colonisation of public and international life by a discourse of human rights, prompted in large measure by two great World Wars and developments in absolutist states. King would situate the more recent discourse of children's rights in another context, that of the many changes, unprecedentedly rapid, which threw into focus the distinction between childhood and adulthood. He identifies the following as possible factors in creating these tensions around childhood:

> [T]he extended period of education; the global standardisation of the age of 18 as denoting the age of adulthood; earlier physical maturity; a major reduction in infantile death and a substantial increase in adult life-expectancy; the increased spending-power of young people, the emergence of 'youth cultures'; the growth in air travel; the global movement of workers, theories and research on the role parents play in their children's psychological development; greater opportunities for women to compete with men for in the labour market; the consumerist targeting of ever-younger children for advertising. (King 2007: 867)

Within this context, the global development of children's rights 'may be seen as a device within law and politics for resolving this tension by imposing some universal order, some principled values as to what children should expect from adults and the ways that adults should treat children'. King cites the United Nations Convention on the Rights of the Child (UNCRC) as one tool in this process of introducing global norms but at the same time transferring the tensions to law and politics (ibid).

There has been a discourse of children's rights since the 19th century when the focus was on the right of the child to be protected from want, neglect and cruelty, and the UNCRC contains rights in this protectionist tradition – to life, country and name, for example. It also contains articles influenced by the 'child liberationist' approach, with its focus on the child's right to autonomy. That more radical wing of the rights movement, with its roots in the civil rights movement in USA, perceived children as another minority group being exploited. Liberationists would argue that children's capacity for autonomy is greater than adults think, and so children should be able to make their own decisions and, if necessary, make their own mistakes. Those different conceptions of children and their rights continue to be played out in the implementation of international conventions, with implications for the level of respect and attention we accord children and young people.

The UNCRC was preceded by the UN Declaration of the Rights of the Child in 1924 and 1959 and the UN Standard Minimum Rules for the Administration of Juvenile Justice (Beijing Rules) in 1985. In

1979, the United Nations' Year of the Child, the decision was made to produce the UNCRC, which was adopted by the UN General Assembly in 1989. It has 54 articles, 40 of which are substantive rights applying to all children under 18. Individual children are unable to seek any redress if a right is not enforced in relation to their circumstances: the UNCRC is a political document which operates though the regular 'inspections' – and subsequent public reports – of those states which are parties to the Convention. The mechanism for implementation is, in effect, the pressure on a government resulting from a public shaming of defaulting states.

In 1991 the UK ratified the Convention, and some of its articles have had a clear influence on legislation in the UK. A good example of both the influence of the UNCRC on UK legislation and its limitations is in relation to Article 12 which states that:

1 States Parties shall assure to the child who is capable of forming his or her own views the right to express those views freely in all matters affecting the child, the views of the child being given due weight in accordance with the age and maturity of the child.

2 For this purpose, the child shall in particular be provided the opportunity to be heard in any judicial and administrative proceedings affecting the child, either directly, or through a representative or an appropriate body, in a manner consistent with the procedural rules of national law.

The clearest response for England and Wales is to be found in the welfare checklist in the Children Act 1989 whereby courts must have particular regard to the 'wishes and feelings of the child' considered 'in the light of his age and understanding'. However, this is a requirement limited by its applicability and in its ability to affect the child's life (see Chapter 6).

The European Union has also developed rights conventions, and the European Court has produced a jurisprudence of rights since its establishment in 1959. The Human Rights Act (HRA) 1998 made rights contained in the European Convention on Human Rights and Fundamental Freedoms part of the UK's domestic law and individuals, including children, can now apply to the domestic courts, rather than to the European Court in Strasbourg, if they believe that the government or any public body has infringed their Convention rights. Under section 4(2) of the HRA 1998, courts can declare legislative provisions to be incompatible with Convention rights;

they must also, as a public authority, ensure that their decisions and existing case law are compatible with Convention rights (see Fortin 1999: 350–1). However, as Fortin pointed out when the HRA 1998 was passed, 'Although these fundamental rights are theoretically available to children, there is only a relatively small body of Convention case law illustrating an appreciation that [the rights] are as valuable to children as to adults' (ibid: 353).

Similar critical comments have been made about the effectiveness of the European Convention on the Exercise of Children's Rights (ECECR). This Convention was adopted by the Council of Europe in 1995, came into force in July 2000 when the required minimum of ratification by three member states had been achieved and, by August 2006, had been signed by 24 member states and ratified by 10.[16] Its aim, 'in the best interests of children', is 'to promote their rights, to grant them procedural rights and to facilitate the exercise of these rights by ensuring that children are, themselves or through other persons or bodies, informed and allowed to participate in proceedings affecting them before a judicial authority' (Article 1(2)). Sawyer has commented that 'the content of the ECECR redescribes the procedural rights apparently granted by the UN Convention in terms so limited that the rights become entirely different' (Sawyer 1991: 153). She acknowledges the difficulty of drafting a Convention which gives children rights yet protects them from the potential damage to relationships with their parents which an exercise of rights might cause, but argues that 'the ECECR does not appear to make the attempt': instead it allows states 'sufficient latitude … to avoid those difficulties by effectively shutting the door on children's rights' (ibid; see also Kilkelly 2000).

Rights could, however, operate more positively as a tool for investment and inclusion in two particular ways: by encouraging policy consultation with children so that the services provided are more likely to be relevant and used, and by providing a means by which access to services can be ensured. Morrow has pointed out that, whilst 'a large amount of participation work with children' has occurred in the UK, and research has shown that 'young children can engage with notions of rights, decision making, and being listened to; that children would like to have a say in decisions and to be heard; and that children can see decision-making from others' points of view', children's participation is in practice limited (Morrow 2008: 122). However, she argues that the concept of participation itself needs more discussion and, in particular, attention needs to be focused on adult responses to the views of children. 'The challenge now is not only to get adults to listen, but to act upon what they hear': research suggests that children are not being 'heard' if their views do not support adults' policy and practice approaches (ibid: 129). If that happens, 'consultation' is only paying lip service to rights. Similarly, the government can reconstruct as rights-based a policy that may undermine rights for children: an example would be the justifications given for abolishing the *doli incapax* presumption for children aged 10–13. Furthermore, an important issue is the potential clash of parental and children's rights, and also the potential use of the European Convention by parents to secure services for their children. These are all issues which will be dealt with in later chapters, in particular Chapters 6 and 8.

The investment theme

As the Preface points out, the thread which runs throughout this book is that of investment in the lives of children and young people. There has been a significant change in the rationale for child-focused policy in England, and also to varying extents in other parts of the UK and other jurisdictions, in the last decade (Parton 2006: 1–2). Not only does investment for the future – in children as future citizens – provide one of the major motivations for policies of child protection, education and health, but it also provides the explicit rationale and justification for public expenditure. As Parton points out, the death of Victoria Climbié may have provided a politically acceptable momentum for change to 'safeguard' children, but the aim of policy is now much broader than a focus on prevention of abuse and harm.

In his influential book, *Safeguarding Childhood: early intervention and surveillance in modern society*, Parton seeks to find the key elements of the new strategy and to explain why 'safeguarding' has become a totemic concept. His focus on the developments in child protection and family support over the last century leads him to suggest that 'what we are witnessing is the emergence of the "preventative state", where previous conceptions of prevention are fundamentally recast and are placed at the centre of public policy rather than at its periphery' (2006: 6). *Investing in Children* is also what Parton refers to as 'A history of the present' (ibid: 2), but this book seeks to explain, not so much why an investment strategy and a preventative state have emerged, but what changes in conceptions of children, families and risk have made that policy option one that it is politically possible to pursue at the start of the 21st century. *Investing in Children* must focus, as does Parton's book, on the role of science, in particular the science underpinning the early intervention agenda, but it also seeks to make problematic the role of science in the delivering of 'successful' investment. Further, this book will go on to examine the role of the other source of authority in (late) modern society – law – in implementing policy change.

To start this exploration, the next chapter will focus on the children – or, rather, ideas about children and childhood – before reviewing, historically and in the present, the notion of investing in those children whose 'image' is the most compelling. Chapters 3 and 4 will focus on parents and notions of family – how and why ideas about parental autonomy and responsibility have been reconstructed – and the crucial ideologies which either constrain or encourage the state to invest in children. Part I of the book therefore looks at all the components that have gone through processes of remodelling so that they 'fit' together in a way that can be used to promote – and not block – a policy of investing in children. Part II will then examine the mechanisms by which this is being done, notably the 'science' of prevention and the construction and assessment of risk, and the role of law and rights. It will also provide an overview of the success of early intervention projects and an assessment of those factors which might militate against the success of those policies which aim to provide investment in childhood until at least 2020 (DCSF 2007). In doing so, it will suggest that the very constructions of children and parents that have made the new investment agenda politically possible at this point in time are ones that carry significant risks for parents and children. Further, that harnessing the authority of science may not be a viable longer-term strategy: law might need to be given more scope for securing the well-being of children – as children and as adults.

Notes

1 http://www.nortonfinance.co.uk/news/Christmas_spending_set_to_go_up (accessed 7.8.07); Deloitte was forecasting an average spend of £744 in the run-up to Christmas 2007.
2 http://www.privateschools.co.uk/school_fees.htm (accessed 29.3.08).
3 A survey by YouGov for Petplan Ltd, an insurance company (http://www.petplan.co.uk/about/press/southwest2005.asp at 27.9.06).
4 See http://media.shelter.org.uk/Content/Detail.asp?ReleaseID=50&NewsAreaID=2 (accessed 7.8.07).

5 Dawn Primarolo, *Hansard* HC (9 March 2007).
6 See for example the excellent reviews by Diduck and Kaganas (2006: 1–30, 301–32) and Herring (2007: 1–10, 393–8).
7 See also 'Ann Widdecombe Versus the Benefits Culture', ITV 1, 22 August 2007.
8 This is a sociological term denoting a stage in the construction of social knowledge: see Berger and Luckman 1966.
9 Although it actually removed taxes on tea exported to the colonies, it led to the 'Boston Tea Party' demonstration because of the issue of taxation without representation.
10 See: http://www.vam.ac.uk/moc/what_on/past/children_trouble/index.html (accessed 27.6.07).
11 See http://www.childrenshearingsscotland.gov.uk/ (accessed 7.12.07).
12 See PsychNet.UK website: this is a mental health information site.
13 Education (Administrative Provisions) Act 1907.
14 See for example Mary Carpenter's 1851 text, *Reformatory Schools for the Children of the Perishing and Dangerous Classes*. For a detailed contextual discussion, see Leon Radzinowitz and Roger Hood, *A History of Criminal Law and its Administration from 1750*, vol. 5, 'The Emergence of Penal Policy in Victorian and Edwardian England' (Clarendon Press edition, 1990).
15 http://www.everychildmatters.gov.uk/aims/ (accessed 30.10.07).
16 http://conventions.coe.int/Treaty/Commun/ChercheSig.asp?NT=160&CM=8&DF=8/9/2006&CL=ENG

Chapter 2

Transforming Parliament's children

Children are precious. The world they must learn to inhabit is one in which they will face hazards and obstacles alongside real and growing opportunities. They are entitled not just to the sentiment of adults but a strategy that safeguards them as children and realises their potential to the very best of our ability. (Paul Boateng, then Chief Secretary to the Treasury, in DfES 2003)

The 'child'

The quotation above, from the preface to the government Green Paper, *Every Child Matters*, not only presents a very complicated view of children but also reflects adult concerns about the future. Further, this one short passage incorporates several ideas about the nature of childhood and our attitudes to children: our children are 'precious', need 'safeguarding' and are worthy of our 'sentiment'; they live in a risky world with 'hazards' in the future which can be surmounted – and opportunities which can be grasped – through 'our' efforts in the present. The child which this passage imagines is also a child which 'fits' current policy with its focus on risk management, the encouragement of personal responsibility for maximising opportunities and, most recently, investment to reduce social exclusion. The child that Parliament currently imagines is not the child that previous governments and members of both Houses have imagined – though there are certainly continuities: how children are conceptualised is clearly not a process that can be separated from historically contingent adult anxieties and state needs. How, then, did our current imaginings of children – the concepts and subjectivities that we select and which become taken-for-granted – come about and why? And what is it about the currently available images of children which make them so useful for 'selling' government policy? These questions are the focus of this chapter.

The 'truth' about children

It might be assumed that our notion of the child depends on what we 'know' about children at any point in time and that our images will change as our knowledge becomes 'better' and more 'accurate'. That approach, based within a liberal interpretation of history, would look to science, our current producer of 'facts' and 'truth', to give us a clear and consensual image of the child. Yet, even within one branch of science – the medical sciences – it is difficult to gain a clear idea of what the child 'is'. 'Child' may signify a particular biological stage in life, but that could be infancy, the period between birth and puberty or between birth and the 'coming of age', or it may refer to offspring or descendants. In more archaic language, it refers to a foetus when a woman is said to be 'with child' whilst in the developmental sciences what a child 'needs' has been subject to changing interpretations of research knowledge about children. Expert advice about the feeding and sleep patterns of babies would be a prime example of ever-changing understandings about what the baby needs from its parents. In the social sciences there have also been changing and conflicting notions about the nature of the child and social meaning of childhood (see below), and it has become clear that the production of truth through scientific procedures is not itself immune to influences external to science (Berger and Luckman 1966; Day Sclater and Piper 2001; Kaganas 1999). Even, then, within this one 'truth'-producing system – science – the 'child' cannot be found without difficulty, and there are also other systems to complicate the picture further.

In past centuries, religion provided the truths and the certainties about life and behaviour, and continues to do so for some individuals and communities. Here the situation is even more complex: even within one religion, Christianity, the nature of the unborn and newborn child is still contested. When does the fertilised egg become a person? Is the child innately evil or innocent? If, within the context of the major world religions, the 'coming of age' or entry into the faith ceremonies is viewed as the end of childhood, there is still little consensus. In Judaism, there are the Bar and Bat Mitzvah at age 13; in Islam and Hinduism, puberty marks the beginning of adulthood in relation to particular duties although there are some differences in the status of young men and women. Christianity generally does not have such ceremonies, though in some Christian denominations the confirmation and baptism services fulfil that role, and Christian theology has addressed the issue of when a child should be held accountable as an adult.

Law is a third major truth-producing system: it is authoritative because in modern western societies it is allocated the function of giving finality to disputed issues and the delineation of the criminal. Because children are not adults, and the law is based on the 'the reasonable man' who is able to give consent and be held accountable, special duties, powers and rights are attached to children by law and certain activities are forbidden them by law. Yet law does not operate with one clear definition of the child. The UN Convention on the Rights of the Child – essentially a political rather than legal document – defines the child as a person under 18 years of age, unless the age of majority is earlier. Law cannot easily manage what is not binary – legal/illegal, and so in applicable/not applicable – law children are also usually defined in terms of age limits and those limits depend at least partly on the function of the legislation and whether it is to operate within civil or criminal contexts. Law – and the legal/political 'hybrid' of legislation – operates in a very compartmentalised way: 18 is not, then, always the upper limit. For example, legislation reduced the age of majority (giving, for example, voting rights) from 21 to 18 years throughout the UK in 1969 (Family Law Reform Act 1969, Age of Majority (Scotland) Act 1969 and Age of Majority (Northern Ireland) 1969) and in the Republic of Ireland in 1972 (Fourth Amendment of the Constitution Act 1972). The Children Act 1989, section 105(1), also defined a 'child' as a person under the age of 18. In the Isle of Man, however, 16-year-olds were allowed to vote for the first time in 2006, whilst in Scotland anyone of 16 or over has the legal capacity to enter into any transaction, with children of 12 or over presumed to have such capacity (Age of Legal Capacity (Scotland) Act 1991).

In some other areas of the law, the upper age limit is also now often lower than 18, notably where, in practice, a sliding scale operates when the rights of those under 18 depend 'on age and maturity'. The best known example is in relation to consent to medical treatment and the line of English cases beginning with Mrs Gillick's application to court.[1] In Scotland, subsequent legislation has produced a similar legal situation: section 2 of the Age of Legal Capacity (Scotland) Act 1991 empowers a person under the age of 16 years to consent where 'in the opinion of a qualified medical practitioner attending him [or her], he [or she] is capable of understanding the nature and possible consequences of the procedure or treatment'. This new flexible approach to the child/adult distinction is a significant development. It has resulted from law's need to retain authority in making decisions about adolescents and to do so by taking on board 'external' evidence about the maturity and lifestyles of children towards the end of the 20th century (King and Piper 1995: Chapter 3).

Within the criminal justice system, children who offend are usually treated as 'children' until their 18th birthday, the upper age limit for, *inter alia*, the jurisdiction of the Youth Court having been raised from 17 to 18 years by the Criminal Justice Act 1991, section 68. However, the term 'child' is generally used only for those under 14 years of age, the 14–17s being 'young persons', and, in relation to criminal responsibility, the child is an adult at 10 years of age in England, Wales and Northern Ireland. Children above that age are held to be culpable and can be subject to processes and punishment within the youth and criminal justice systems for crimes committed. In Scotland, the age remains at eight, but children who offend are dealt with through child protection procedures whilst the Republic of Ireland raised its minimum age from seven to 12 in 2006.

There are further anomalies and exceptions within family law, education and social security law. The Children Act 1989, Schedule 1, paras 2 and 6 and the Family Proceedings Rules 1991, Part IV, para. 4.1(1)(b), for example, allow orders for financial support to be made in favour of young people over 18 years old in certain circumstances. In education law, the child is defined as 'under 16' unless the young person has a statement as having Special Educational Needs and is a registered school pupil, in which case the cut-off point is 19 years (Education Act 1996, sections 579(1) and 312(5), respectively). In social security law, several allowances are paid up to the day before a dependent child's 20th birthday (DWP 2006).

The 'child', then, always needs context or qualification to give it meaning. Yet, despite the range of definitions reviewed above, this book is predicated on the notion that we *are* able to talk about 'children' as a category. The title *Investing in Children* makes the assumption that children are a category separate from any other, notably that of adults, and that policy and practice may be targeted at and for children. It might also suggest that the 'child' of that childhood is a generic and 'generalisable' one. Yet that notion of a specific and separate stage called 'childhood' is one that is problematic and whose genesis, life and possible death are all issues that have been contested over at least the last four decades by academics in a wide range of disciplines. It can never be assumed that Parliament always has to hand a 'useful' idea of the child or notion of childhood to encourage the passage of legislation and the spending of public money and yet, without a popular conception of childhood which is worth investing in, investment in children will not happen.

The 'birth' and 'death' of childhood

Since the publication of *Centuries of Childhood* by Aries (1962), childhood has been 'popularised, politicized, scrutinized and analyzed', as James, Jenks and Prout have noted, 'with an intensity perhaps unprecedented' (1998: 3). What was widely accepted by the end of the 20th century was that 'the modern conception of the child' (Jenks 1996: 65) traced by Aries had become the most influential image or 'vision' of what a child 'is' (ibid: 51), and notions of appropriate treatment of children – including treatment through law – flow from it.[2]

However, as Archard points out:

> Aries understands by the concept of 'childhood' a peculiarly modern awareness of what distinguishes children from adults … Previous societies, on Aries' account, lacked this concept of childhood … In reply it can be argued that the evidence fails to show that previous societies lacked a concept of childhood. At most it shows that they lacked our concept. (Archard 1993: 20)

Archard borrows Rawls' distinction between 'concept' and 'conception', using 'concept of childhood' to delineate the basic idea that children can be 'distinguishable from adults in respect of some unspecified set of attributes', and 'conception' for the specification of those attributes (ibid: 22). The idea that 'childhood' as a concept is simply an invention of the 'modern' age – with a '"big bang" theory of the initiation of childhood' at a particular point in history (James *et al.* 1998: 5) – is no longer acceptable (see, for example, McFarlane 1979; Pollock 1983; Wilson 1980). On the other hand, the idea of post-modern childhoods, that particular conceptions of childhood are socially constructed and historically contingent, 'is now commonplace' (Buckingham 2000: 6).

What that means is that – although in popular discourse we still have an allegiance to a 'modern' concept of childhood as 'innately' different from adulthood – we cannot document a single dominant conception of childhood or image of the child over the last few decades or even centuries. Many conceptions of children are available, then and now, and new images of children are being constructed as I write. In that context, Aries simply 'began the archaeology of childhood images' (James *et al.* 1998: 4). The process of 'digging' has also made clear something else: 'That a state of being, such as childhood, should be formulated through the "analytic gaze" within a particular epoch must tell us as much about the condition of our society as it does about our children' (Jenks 1996: 60). 'Childhood has always been iconic of broader social anxieties' (Wilson 2003: 424) and such anxieties have been an impetus to rethinking about children and families. These anxieties have been analysed from various perspectives: Parton, for example, reviews work on what have been referred to as the first and second 'crises of modernity' at the end of the 19th century and from the 1960s onwards, respectively (2006: Chapter 1). Qvortrup has documented how processes of industrialisation and urbanisation have, over several centuries, separated production from reproduction, with a consequent privatisation of the family (Qvortrup 2001, 2005: 2–10). Others have focused specifically on fears around childhood itself and there has been an extensive literature on what has been referred to as the 'death' of childhood.

The rise and fall of boundaries

Talk of the 'death' of childhood has been misleading: what has been argued is that the particular concept of childhood set out by Aries and those taking his approach is no longer important. For example, Cox argued that 'The story of the bourgeois child is now also the story of the fall of the bourgeois child' (Cox 1996: 204), and Postman (1982), in a sociological book entitled *The Disappearance of Childhood*, argued that the sudden flurry of interest in a particular idea of childhood was evidence of its deconstruction and pending obsolescence.[3] As Jenks summarises Postman's argument:

> These new forms of media are systematically undermining that distinction between child and adult due to an indifference to difference generated through economies in production and uniform categories of consumer. ... A child subject to a diet of violence, sexuality, exploitation and a persistent invitation to

consume cannot sustain an autonomous realm of being. (Jenks 1996: 117)

Chapter 1 reproduced the list of global factors that King believed contributed to the problematisation and blurring of the adult/child boundary. Others have argued that it has occurred to achieve outcomes which suit adult needs, outcomes which 'may be about developing new markets and commercial opportunities, or simply to permit and facilitate adult sexual fantasy' (Wilson 2003: 423).

Yet the demise of a 'unitary' conception of childhood with a clear adult/child boundary can be viewed in part as a return to earlier conceptions of the 'stages' of life which also downplayed any clear binary distinction between adult and child. Classical and medieval conceptions involved 'mystical numbers' from three to 12, notably seven, which were used to categorise not only the world but also people's lives. For example, physiologists constructed a scheme of four stages to harmonise with the seasons and the 'humours' of the body, whilst astrologers settled for seven, ruled by the seven stars (see Burrow 1986). So the 'seven ages of man' referred to by Shakespeare in the much-quoted passage below has, as its first three stages, the infant, the schoolboy and 'the lover' in a categorisation based on dominant activities or physical attributes in a particular part of life.

> All the world's a stage,
> And all the men and women merely players,
> They have their exits and entrances,
> And one man in his time plays many parts,
> His acts being seven ages.
> (William Shakespeare, *As You Like It*, Act II, Scene VII)[4]

Moss and Petrie categorise current images into three main groups: the child as incomplete adult or futurity, the child as innocent and vulnerable, and the child as 'redemptive vehicle' which takes on some of the characteristics of the other two categories (2005: 86–9). Whether or not we subscribe to this particular analysis, there is no question that not only is there now a fluid adult/child boundary but there are also several changing constructs of children and young people, some related to one another and others in conflict. The issue, then, is why particular ideas about children become so influential in social and political life at particular points in time.

An effective image: the child as 'victim'

The quotation at the beginning of this chapter referred to 'precious' children who needed 'safeguarding'. This conception of children as special and in need of adult protection has a long parliamentary history and one which is intertwined with the 'choice' of issues demanding the attention of government. We are now well aware from social scientific research that some 'problems' are successfully constructed as social problems whilst others never gain the attention of the media or politicians, that some of these issues are taken up in Parliament and that some, but not all, are successfully transformed into legislation (R. and W. Stainton Rogers 1992). A recent article has, for example, analysed why conditions and suicides in youth prisons have not led to a national 'scandal' with subsequent legislative change, whereas the death of Victoria Climbié did (Drakeford and Butler 2007). Victoria was portrayed as a victim, Gareth Mynott was not (ibid). Particular images of children have been instrumental in both the construction of social problems concerning children and the acceptability of proposed governmental solutions. This begs the question as to why this should be so.

Government Consultation and White Papers, together with debates in committee and both Houses of Parliament, reveal a variety of conceptions of children and their needs, and a resulting range – over the decades – of pronouncements about the links between child welfare, criminality, morality, national efficiency and the UK's position in the world. It is possible both to distinguish specific ideas about childhood underpinning particular pieces of legislation or case law and to generalise across time. Over the last two centuries, the range of such images has been relatively narrow, falling largely into the two main categories of the vulnerable/deprived child or the anti-social/depraved child. Drakeford and Butler argue that, in the production of a 'scandal', a morally indefensible situation or moral panic, 'morality tales and soap opera meet' and 'the actors are capable of being divided into heroes and villains' (2007: 226). The child as innocent, deprived and vulnerable can play the 'hero' and receive the sympathy, while the child as villain – the young offender – cannot. Useful and dominant images of children are historically contingent: they are the product of an interplay of economic, social and political factors which can be seen more clearly by looking at the past.

The child of the 19th century: a case study

For those campaigning for child-focused reform in the 19th century, the conception of the 'visible Victorian child' had very particular characteristics. Of most importance were ideas of innocence and malleability which at least in part replaced ideas about 'original sin' and the innate evil of children (Hendrick 1994: 8). What resulted was a very sentimental image of a child and one which is perhaps best personified by the characters in the novels of Charles Dickens: a child who was often conceptualised as vulnerable and a victim, and an image which evidenced a clear separation from conceptualisations of adulthood. The result was that 'the mid-Victorian generation gave unprecedented attention to children and the problems facing them', and the speeches of politicians evidenced a 'politics of pathos' which drew on these distinct images (Behlmer 1982: 3). Even popular pictures of children who had not been neglected portrayed them as particularly sensitive and often physically weak (Piper 1999b: 36).

One of the strengths of such images lies in the fact that weak and vulnerable children cannot speak for themselves: adults must articulate their needs and the 'voicelessness' and powerlessness of the victim-child adds weight to whatever the adult promotes on their behalf. So, when Michael Sadler was speaking in the House of Commons in 1832 in support of the Ten Hours Bill to restrict the employment of women and children, he could add to maximum effect, 'I wish I could bring a group of these little ones [here] ... I am sure their silent appearance would plead more forcibly in their behalf than the loudest eloquence' (Ward 1970: 102). This is not to say that all reformers were motivated purely by concern for the children. Working class leaders urging for factory reform in the 1830s, for example, wanted a 10-hour day for all workers, but such legislation would not have been passed by those in Parliament at that time, and so they focused on a reduction of hours for women and children with the hope that it would eventually lead to acceptance of reduced working days for adult men.[5]

The 19th century therefore produced a wealth of leaflets and books that evoked images of children who silently 'cry'. An early example in 1843 is Elizabeth Barrett Browning's poem 'The Cry of the Children', the last two lines of which read, 'They are weeping in the playtime of the others, In the Country of the free' (see Cunningham 1995: 143). Other well-publicised texts followed over the course of the next 60 years, including 'The Bitter Cry of Outcast London' by Andrew Mearn, in 1883, and 'The Bitter Cry of the Children', published in the USA in 1906 (Spargo 1969; see also Piper 1999b: 37).

One important and effective tactic in advocating state intervention and expenditure was to emphasise the stark contrast between images of a 'proper' childhood and the circumstances of 'real' children. The victims were 'children without a childhood', the phrase used by Douglas Jerrold, one of the founders of *Punch*, in 1840 to describe factory children (see Cunningham 1995: 144). However, one corollary of this image was that the child *with* a childhood should be invisible: he or she should be in his or her home or school. If 'outside' the family – and so visible – that child needed rescuing. Industrialisation had led to the employment of large numbers of children in factories and mines, and the numbers in towns had increased comparatively quickly. For example, the population of Manchester and Salford rose from 95,000 in 1801 to 238,000 in 1831 (Pinchbeck and Hewitt 1973: 389). These changes represented new and very visible 'evils' which people feared would destroy family-centred life (see Chapter 4).

The importance of these images in promoting legislation cannot be overemphasised: they pointed to new 'horrors' inflicted on innocent children, and yet in one sense they were not new horrors. Cruelty to children by employers was not new: there had been considerable cruelty to children in the 'old' workplaces – the fields and farms. In particular, the development of the gang labour system in agriculture in the second quarter of the 19th century had severely deleterious effects on children (see Pinchbeck and Hewitt 1973: 391–5). Neither was the 'sending away' of children to work outside the immediate family uncommon in earlier centuries. Many children were sent to work in the households of relatives or strangers, especially in the 16th and 17th centuries, whether they were upper-class girls (see Pinchbeck and Hewitt 1969: 25–30) or the children of the destitute placed on Poor Law apprenticeships (ibid: 223–59.) Furthermore, at the time of the 1851 census, the numbers of people living in towns were still lower than those living in rural areas (see Kitson-Clarke 1962: 117–8). The availability of images of 'poor things' in need of rescue gave campaigns the urgency they needed to be successful, but that also could not have occurred without social anxiety arising in the context of more concentrated spaces, rapid social change and economic uncertainty (Piper 1999b: 46–8).[6]

Parliament's children at this time, then, were children who, above all, needed to be removed from places where they might be harmed but also where they might be inappropriately independent. The particular conception of the Victorian child meant that protection and control were linked. On the one hand, Jane Addams, an American philanthropist born in 1859, could write: 'let us know the modern city in its weakness and wickedness, and then seek to rectify and purify it' (see Platt 1969: 96). On the other hand, Mary Carpenter's much-quoted exhortation that the child 'must be brought to a sense of dependence' (see Hendrick 1994: 29; Vaughan 2000: 352) reflected an adult desire to keep children under adult control.

The continuing victim-child

Such motivations and imagery lasted into and through the 20th century (see Piper 1999b). For example, a booklet published in the USA in 1906 by John Spargo, a Cornishman, used the phrase 'this great nation in its commercial madness devours its babes' when referring to children and young people under 16 in employment (1969: xii), whilst debates in 1932 on what became the Children and Young Persons Act 1933 included the following contributions:

> There is not an Hon. Member who knows children of the ranges of ages to be dealt with in this Bill but who will agree with me that he looks upon them as miniature and unformed, and that he would not for a moment be prepared to have to apply to them the same standard which he applies to adults. (Oliver Stanley, The Under-Secretary of State for the Home Department)[7]

> The Bill may be regarded as the Children's Charter and a shield for the young offender against being forced out of decent society. (Rhys Davies MP)[8]

A more recent example can be found in the 1990s when the family law reform agenda was dominated by the issue of divorce. The image of the child which underpinned the parliamentary and popular debates was that of the child as a victim of parental separation and the conflict between her parents (Piper 1996). Children were presented as vulnerable to short-term distress and decreased long-term life chances because of parental divorce. The White Paper preceding the Bill included, for example, the following statement: 'it is conflict between the parents which has been linked to greater social and behavioural problems among children … A reduction in bitterness and hostility was seen by consultees [responding to the Green Paper] as a central objective in reducing the harm that might be done to children of the marriage' (Lord Chancellor's Department 1995: para. 3.10). An important aim of the legislation appeared to be that of slowing down the separation process to encourage a re-think about divorce itself and certainly to endorse the need for parents to make arrangements such that children kept contact with both parents, and that such contact – and the making of arrangements for such contact – was as harmonious and consensual as possible. It was a powerful image, used to publicise several agendas, only one of which was child protection. It was also an image which was instrumental in the passage of legislation that, if it had been implemented, would have transformed divorce law.

A recent judgment – that of Munby J in *R (Howard League for Penal Reform) v Secretary of State for the Home Department*[9] – also provides what is now a rare example of the child offender and prisoner as victim. Mr Justice Munby's decision, whilst argued on the basis of rights and duties, makes frequent reference to children as victims in need of protection as in the following statement: 'For these are things being done to children by the State – by all of us – in circumstances where the State appears to be failing, and in some instances failing very badly, in its duties to vulnerable and damaged children' (at para. 172).

The status of the child as a victim has, therefore, been very important – and often still is – in helping to persuade Parliament, courts and the populace to accept change, but it has drawbacks. First, the child or young person is conceptualised as dependent with no autonomy rights: an image which can be used to the detriment of children. Secondly, it is an image which can only be generated and used in relation to specific and generally high-profile campaigns or cases. It is an emotive image and, as with images of starving children in the global South, over-use decreases its impact. It could not provide longer-term motivation for a sustained programme of investment in children. The victim-child has consequently became a problematic as well as a useful concept for reformers, in particular in relation to the 'innocence' of the victim-child.

The 'innocent' child

Innocence is a term reflective of centuries of theological, philosophical and academic debate about the nature of evil and innocence and the nature of the newborn baby in relation to those universalities. One 'side' can be characterised by Rousseau's essentially good 'noble savage', the other by Hobbes' view of life as 'nasty, brutish and short' unless the innate evil in child and adult is controlled (see, for example, Montgomery 2003). In the 18th and 19th centuries what developed was a set of images of 'uncorrupted' children – close to the purity of nature – what Cox refers to as a 'line of beautiful children' (1996: 136). Rex and Wendy Stainton Rogers reviewed the continuance of this imagery of children into the 20th century 'in such works as Barrie's *Peter Pan* and Ransome's *Swallows and Amazons'* and argued that it 'finds its natural home today in Disney Studios' (1992: 27).

Sexuality as problematic

Understandings of what was and was not 'child-like' became – and still are – a particular issue in relation to sexuality (see Piper 2000a, 2007), with innocence and ignorance about sex often conflated. This conflation of innocence with lack of knowledge or experience and, specifically, with lack of knowledge about sex has a long history. For example, the myth of the Garden of Eden links sin and sex: after they ate from the forbidden Tree of Knowledge, Adam and Eve 'knew' that they were naked[10] and that particular activities done by certain parts of their bodies were 'wrong'. However, if innocence is constructed in this way and if innocence remains a powerful concept in relation to children, the engagement of children in sexual activity – whether voluntarily or enforced through abuse – is constituted as another 'evil'. That view continued through the 20th century with the result that, as Rex and Wendy Stainton Rogers (1999) argue, 'Child + Sex = Abuse' became the only alternative to 'Child + Sex = Adult'. Further, whilst views about what is 'natural' and 'normal' in relation to the behaviour of children change over time and place – and so what is perceived as 'healthy' or 'unhealthy' sexual activity in children – the dominant strand in child protection has been, and still is, that concerning sexual predators. There is, in other words, a double danger: the fear that children will be sexually abused and also that they may choose to engage in sex.

This has created an ambivalence which has continued. For the Victorians, those 'immoral' places of the street and factory were consequently particularly dangerous for children because of the danger of the twin evils of sexual assault on them or their engaging in prostitution. The street is still seen as dangerous for children, but to make this statement specifically applicable to the early 21st century one need only substitute 'computer' for 'factory' (Piper 2007). Indeed, debates in Parliament on legislation aimed to combat on-line exploitation of children evidence an almost Victorian fear of the unknown perils facing 'our' children. For example, Baroness Masham of Ilton made this somewhat strange contribution in October

2000: 'The subject is horrifying. There are groups of paedophiles who network on the Internet. It is organised from Russia. It is beyond Europe. The police are concerned about that. The whole matter needs to be looked at.'[11]

Suzanne Ost, writing in 2002, was in no doubt that the dominant image of the child in relation to legal responses to child pornography was the old image of the innocent vulnerable child. Government ministers have used such images: 'We cannot be complacent. Protecting children from sexual abuse and the theft of their childhood and their innocence, and breaking what can become a cycle of abuse as the abused become abusers, must be a clear priority for Government, and it is' (Paul Boateng MP).[12] *Children and Families: Safer from Sexual Crime: The Sexual Offences Act 2003*, a Home Office publication, also relies on this image: 'Sexual offences against children are terrible crimes, with a profound, damaging and long-term impact on the lives of victims and their families. The public, rightly, wants to ensure that children have the best possible protection from sexual abuse' (Home Office 2004c: 2). In line with this imagery, the Internet is perceived as a threatening and depraving public space. To quote Ann Widdecombe MP: 'Internet chat rooms allow the predatory paedophile invisible access to impressionable younger teenagers from a safe distance, allowing contact to be made while the child is using the internet in the secure surroundings of its own home, or even possibly its own bedroom'.[13]

Competing images of the adolescent

The 13th birthday is an important dividing line in recent legislation. For those under 13 there is no competitor for this legal and political image of the child as sexually innocent victim, with a corresponding imperative to further protect that child. These images and ideas most certainly still pertain to the under-13s in the passage of legislation in this area. For example, the Sexual Offences Act 2003 introduces new offences which ensure that the desire to protect the innocent child keeps pace with technology. In effect, the provisions legitimate new constructions of child abuse, and a further concern about the 're-victimisation' of children through the persistence of on-line images (see IWF Annual Report 2006, 2007: 5). The Act also raises the upper age limit from 16 to 18 years for some offences,[14] so that the 'child' needing protection from sex is now also an older one. Lastly, the increased seriousness allocated to abuse of children is indicated by increased penalties.

41

There is also some indication that the victim status is no longer obviated if a child initiates sex, that sex is not necessarily in all circumstances an evil, but, at one level, this has occurred by constructing the child initiator as the victim. The equation then is perhaps that Child (victim) + Abuse (by child) = 2 victim children. The teenage Internet abuser who needs help now counts as a victim in some circumstances, whilst it is now acknowledged that the abuser may be a child:

> We should not ignore the estimate that about a quarter of all rape victims are children, and that about a quarter of the offences against them are committed by other children. We need to address the issue thoroughly, and to deal with it therapeutically rather than by criminalising the disturbed behaviour of children who commit such offences. ... Until we treat those people and deal with their extremely aberrant, dangerous and horrific behaviour, we cannot say that we are protecting children. (Hilton Dawson MP)[15]

The imagery is different for the 13–18 year-old: an image of the adolescent responsible for his or her own sexual activity has developed so that, for some children, sex with other children is acceptable:

> It is nonsense that we criminalise young people between 13 and 16 for what may be minimal sexual activity that is not of a predatory nature – when it is effectively consensual – and is part of the natural process of an adolescent growing up. ... Let us not be prudish and old fashioned. Throughout the history of the world, teenagers have explored themselves and each other, and that will continue. There is all the difference in the world between that and ensuring that activity with under-13s is unacceptable. ... There is no defence or excuse for interfering with under-13s. (Simon Hughes MP)[16]

However, there is a very fine line between the image of the child as victim and child as offender underpinning the law here. Between 1989 and 1995 around 4,000 young people under the age of 18 were convicted or cautioned for offences relating to soliciting: 'The fact that the criminal act involves sex offered by a minor appears to negate ideas of child protection and welfare: we seem to find it difficult to sustain an image of a child who is both sexualised AND deserving of rights to protection' (Piper 2000a: 4). Reviewing recent research on children involved in prostitution, Barrett and Melrose suggest that 'a more fundamental realignment of our attitude and approach is required if we hope substantially and permanently to reduce the number of children and young people being sexually exploited in our cities' (2003: 371).

Within the context of children's sexuality, the issue of sex education is also a contested terrain and one which reflects societal fears at a point in time. Stainton Rogers describes, for example, the (to our mind) extraordinary lengths to which 19th century parents went in order to prevent their children from masturbating (R. Stainton Rogers 1989: 24–5) whilst Monk has drawn attention to ambivalent messages contained in legislation and guidance about sex education for children at the end of the 20th century (Monk 2001). Further, several commentators have pointed out, for example, that 'Purity, it turns out, provided just the opening a sexualising tendency requires: it is the necessary condition for the erotic operations our cultures have made central' (Kincaid 1992: 13; see also Cox 1996: 136; Kahily and Montgomery 2003: 236–46). The usefulness of such imagery of childhood innocence for marketing has not gone unnoticed, although here too there are ambiguities (Cross 2002).

At the same time, medical knowledge about the potential long-term emotional harm caused by sexual abuse has constructed such harm as so serious that it can justify the most draconian measures of control and punishment. For example, the statement in the 1925 Report of the Committee on Sexual Offences Against Children that 'We consider that special action is called for in cases of repeated sexual offences [against children]' is one that was made in the context of a report which was otherwise opposed to special powers of detention for 'the dangerous' (1925: 61; see also Pratt 2000: 42). More recently, moral panics about sexual 'predators' have led to additional restrictions on sex offenders (Cobley 1997; Home Office 2007b; Shute 2004).

There is another issue. There are discourses and images other than those around children and youth which are legitimating some of these changes in the law, notably adult rights and the 'war' on Internet crime more generally. As the focus on the child becomes intermittent – like the disappearing Cheshire cat in *Alice in Wonderland* – so the influence of specific ideas about the needs and views of children is reduced. Further, the above review shows how easily conceptions of 'worthy' children slide into quite different images of children who commit criminal offences.

This focus on the development of images and policies relating to children and sex also illustrates how easy it is for images to be

harnessed for often quite conflicting agendas, not all focused on the welfare or rights of children. The less positive images of children revealed are influential and are not irrelevant to the investment agenda.

The child as offender

In the first edition of *Child Welfare*, Hendrick (1994) categorised material into the two dualisms of mind/body and victim/threat, but in his 2003 book he added a third, that of normal/abnormal. He described the images underpinning these dualisms as 'informing identities, used by contemporaries; although in different ways at different times' (Hendrick 2003: 14). When reviewing the moral panics of the 1990s in relation to juvenile delinquency, it is the identity of threat which is salient (ibid: 225).

The child as (dangerous) threat

Discussion of the murder of James Bulger by Jon Venables and Robert Thompson, when Jon and Robert were 10 years old, also focused on 'abnormality' as a willed state of action: they were described almost universally as 'evil' children and the focus was on the evil they had done. Jenks quotes from the press at the time the use of 'evil freaks', 'little devils' and 'the spawn of Satan' to describe them (Jenks 1996: 128): 'the implicit suggestion is that the heinousness of their offence renders them undeserving of the status of childhood' (Fionda 1998: 80). The abolition of the presumption that children of 10–13 years are *doli incapax* – not capable of being criminally liable – also 'sought to eradicate notions of the child as immature and vulnerable' (ibid; see also Fionda 2005). A version of the child as threat – a danger who must be incapacitated for the protection of society – has also legitimated legislation to deal with dangerous offenders: the Criminal Justice Act 2003 contains provisions which allow the imposition by the Crown Court of new indeterminate sentences on young offenders who have committed a listed offence.

The re-emergence of a strong image of the child as threat has been strengthened further by an image of the child or young person as 'a youth'. This development – and accompanying policy – is particularly clear in the changes to the Crown Prosecution Service guidance about prosecuting minors where, in successive versions, minors were transformed from 'juveniles' and 'young offenders' through 'youth offenders' to, simply, 'youths' (see Piper 2001). This is significant because, at present, the cultural meanings constructed around 'youth' are generally negative. The image is of an older (male) person, and, arguably, 'youths hanging about' has become 'the universal symbol of disorder and, increasingly, menace' (Burney 2002: 473). Such images have underpinned the successful passage of anti-social behaviour legislation over the past decade.

The child as reformable threat

A persistent image of the young criminal as threat has also been influenced by ideas about 'treatment' – as opposed to punishment – albeit that treatment has been reconfigured over time. For example, the optimistic image held by Matthew Davenport Hill in 1855 of the delinquent, 'a little stunted man', who could 'be turned again into a child' (1855, quoted in Worral 1997: 128) legitimated preventative action on the basis that children were 'reformable'. So the aim of those responsible for the Children Act 1908 was that children who offend should be reformed and dealt with in ways that did not put them in contact with adult offenders. Therefore that Act set up a juvenile court and abolished imprisonment as such for children under 14. Twenty years later, the Maloney Report in 1927 found that the practice of diversionary police cautioning was 'objectionable' because it usurped the diagnostic role of the court which could then put in place a programme of treatment (1927: 22). A few years after that, as noted above, Oliver Stanley assumed his fellow MPs shared his belief that children were 'immature and unformed' and so needed treating differently from adults.[17]

At the end of the 20th century these same conceptions of children underpinned the preventative interventions set up by the Crime and Disorder Act 1998. At the same time, however, there are also strong 'threats' to back up these initiatives with more possibilities for punishment. The context was New Labour's 'Third Way' ideology with its focus on the 'conditionality' of help and support in overcoming social exclusion – 'a carrot is rarely offered without mention of the possible stick'.[18] Consequently, there emerged a conceptualisation of 'tough love' (Jordan 2000) and of 'tough justice' (Goldson and Peters 2000) to theorise the application of such an approach to children as well as adults: accountability and personal responsibility are integral concepts of communitarian philosophies (see, for example, Etzioni 1993 and also Chapter 1 above) and even children must be held accountable for their responses to opportunities and for their choice of behaviours. The child was presented as one who can accept and deploy responsibility: 'This new discursive context for "juvenile justice" at the end of the 20th century is also the product of a revision of the "governmental image of ordinary individuals" such that "Everyone now is to make an enterprise of their lives" (O'Malley 2000: 26) and children who offend are no exception' (Piper 2001: 36).

The responsible offender

The two images of threat and reformable child are, therefore, joined by two more which are utilised to gain support for a radical alteration of the approach of policy and practice towards the behaviour of children. These are that the child is, and must be, capable of being held to account, and that the child must act as a citizen by contributing to the 'community'. The White Paper preceding the 1998 Act was therefore entitled *No More Excuses* (Home Office 1997), and government policy put priority on a process of 'responsibilisation' (see, for example, Rose 2000: 327 *et seq*). Morality and 'common-sense' are deployed as authority for such an image of the child and the policy approach it supports:

> Children above the age of criminal responsibility are generally mature enough to be accountable for their actions and the law should recognise this. (Home Office 1997: Introduction)

> The Government believes that in presuming that children of this age generally do not know the difference between naughtiness and serious wrongdoing, the notion of *doli incapax* is contrary to common sense. (ibid: para 4.3)

The new image of a child capable of coping with the responsibility the reforms demanded was a prerequisite for their implementation: it legitimated a system of reprimands and warnings, reparation orders and action plan orders introduced by the Crime and Disorder Act 1998 and referral orders by the Criminal Evidence and Youth Justice Act 1999. The new system restricted the 'chances' given to a child: reprimands and warnings are normally limited in their application to one 'go' at each, with the threat of prosecution and punishment for those children and young people who 'waste' these chances. Another chance is given with the referral order which is normally imposed by the Youth Court for a first (non-serious) conviction and which entails referral to a youth offender panel for a package of preventative interventions, but that too entails a return to the court for failure to agree preventative interventions or non-completion of what has been agreed (now contained in sections 25–26 of the Powers of Criminal Courts (Sentencing) Act 2000).[19]

Recent policy developments in Scotland evidence the same approach and the same crucial new image of a child capable of taking such responsibility. For example, the aims of a pilot Youth Court for 16–17 year-olds, introduced at Airdrie Sheriff Court in June 2004, include to 'promote the social inclusion, citizenship and personal responsibility of these young offenders while maximising their potential' (Barnsley *et al.* 2006: Executive summary, para. 1). Knowledge about the maturity and agency of children has legitimated policies that require such maturity in all children.

Yet these developments and, in particular, the abolition of the presumption of *doli incapax* by section 34 of the Crime and Disorder Act 1998 are out of line with traditional and continuing notions of the responsibility of children within the family justice system (Keating 2007; see also Piper 2000b). Quite divergent images of children may operate alongside one another. The consultation paper *Youth Matters* included the following statement which reflects a new duality: 'It is wrong that young people who do not respect the opportunities they are given, by committing crimes or behaving anti-socially, should benefit from the same opportunities as the law-abiding majority. So we will put appropriate measures in place to ensure they do not' (DfES 2005: Preface).

What this section has shown, therefore, is that wildly divergent constructs of children, influenced by developments in science, politics, religion and economics, can coexist and can wax and wane in importance over time. Those pushing for changes in policy and practice will utilise whatever construct is the most useful in that time and place.

The responsible citizen-child

Some theorists and campaigners, notably child 'liberationists', have welcomed the possible demise of the long-standing 'traditional' conceptions of children as 'simply' victims or threats. They see the former as unhelpful to a proper development of autonomy in the young and have welcomed the neo-conservative and Third Way ideologies which have reflected and encouraged the construction of children as capable of responsibility and active citizenship. These ideas around the 'agency' of children can endorse increasingly important rights-based initiatives to give children more autonomy and, together with constructs of minors as products, citizens, and dangerous nearly-adults, have lessened the impact of longer-standing constructions of the child as vulnerable and dependent.

The focus on the agency of children also points up the fact that children themselves can influence changes in constructs of childhood, but such work also shows that children can be affected in their daily lives by dominant ideas about them (James and James 2004). Indeed, recent research in the hospital setting has shown how children have incorporated into their thinking adult ideas about protecting them from risks such that children constrain their own actions (James, Curtis and Birch 2008). Whether children are seen as actual or potential victims of harm or as responsible neo-adults has implications for their daily lives as well as for policy. Further, ideologies, notably discourses around responsibility and moralisation, have impacted on children.

Remoralisation

These developments in relation to young offenders can also be viewed as part of a 'remoralisation' project, a project to 'responsibilise' both adults and children into being active responsible citizens, which brings together family and youth justice policies (see Chapter 3; see also Day Sclater and Piper 2001; Koffman 2008: 120–1; Vaughan 2000). *No More Excuses*, the White Paper about youth justice policy in 1997, gives the message that young people who offend are to be treated as responsible for their actions: the argument, as we have seen, is that it is not commonsense to do otherwise.[20] Kaganas and Diduck have identified a comparable new image in law of the responsible child underpinning developments in the family justice system, notably in relation to contact arrangements. Focusing on the 'good' child of separated parents, they point to the fact that children as well as adults now appear to be the target for 'education' so that they make the right decision in relation to contact with their non-residential parent. This, they note, is a blending of paradigms of children as both dependent and independent (2004: 961).

The community child

The context for this new image of the responsible child, the citizen who is able to make the choices required, is different from that of a century ago, however. What no longer operates is the thinking behind the opening words of the hymn written by Sir Cecil Spring-Rice in 1918, and still inexplicably popular for weddings, 'I vow to thee, my country, … the service of my love'. Instead, 'The location for this brand of citizenship is "the community", a concept with a special place in the lexicon of New Labour' (Hendrick 2003: 207). This is evident in the headings for Chapters 3 and 5 in *Youth Matters* which are, respectively, 'Empowering Young People' and 'Young People as Citizens: Making a Contribution'. Three of the four key challenges set out in this document relate to children as current citizens, whilst the stated aims of the government are to engage and empower young people in the provision of services, encourage volunteering within the community, and provide better information and advice so young people can make informed choices (DfES 2005: para. 12; see also para. 16 and Chapter 2). This builds on the duty imposed on children's services by the Children Act 2004 to improve the well-being of children in relation to 'the contribution made by them to society' (section 10(2)(d)). The child envisaged is one whose welfare 'needs' him or her to contribute to 'society'.

The 'good' young person envisaged in this document works hard and then gets a job, has a good relationship with his or her parents, and has strong commitments to friends and the local community. The community, not society or country, is the discursive context (Vaughan 2000: 348), and 'community' signifies volunteering (see Buckingham 2000: 187) and also not being anti-social, engaging fully in school and out-of-school activities and staying within the family home. This imagined good child – which chimes perfectly with policy initiatives – is a far cry from the 'wet' and weepy Victorian victim but is very similar to the adult envisioned by policy over the last decade. For adults, 'To refuse a position of work is to cast oneself out of the moral community in which one had been enmeshed and invoke upon oneself harsh measures' (Vaughan 2000: 348–9); for children and young people, the opportunities to be presented to them must similarly be accepted, and the new image of the responsible citizen-child gives 'proof' that this is not an unreasonable expectation.

This image is not simply 'the child as product' which has underpinned educational policy for a long time. The image of the 'trainable child', which legitimated the Victorian policy of 'payment by results', instituted in 1862, continued and underpinned the more recent trend to educational managerialism which began in the 1970s and is epitomised by the White Paper, *Choice and Diversity* (Department for Education 1992). Some have referred to this and related consumer marketing developments as the 'commodification' of children (Crew and Collins 2006). However, the new citizen-child does not need the prescriptive training endorsed by policies in the early 20th century but, rather, will benefit from help and support to fulfil his or her potential (Vaughan 2000: 357). The ability to make his or her own choices is, therefore, a crucial aspect of the new child and, within our so-called consumer society, that skill extends to the ability to choose consumer goods as well as service and support goods. Here again the image contrasts with the image of the child as victim: instead of the 19th century view of children 'as encapsulating precious and unworldly qualities which may be corrupted by commerce', children had been 'progressively *included* as consumers' by the end of the 20th century (Holland 1996: 159).

The child in current policy

To what extent can we talk about the child as rights holder or as present or future citizen? There is the 'more active subjectivity' of the child who must be responsible for his or her own life (Vaughan 2000: 348), but citizen status is ambiguous. Hendrick argues that New Labour 'wrestles with how to provide a compelling notion of citizenship for young people without giving them meaningful rights' when, essentially, 'it does not *trust* its child subjects' (Hendrick 2003: 253–4). 'Children cannot be left alone since they are apprentice adults who, for the sake of the "project", have to enter civil society fully "trained"' (ibid: 254).

Policy developments over the last two decades have not, it would appear, depended on, or led to, the development of a strong image of the child with rights. The conceptions of children which legitimated the Children Act 1989 included the child as victim in need of protection and the child with sufficient maturity to be able to provide for his or her wishes and feelings, but the focus was on parents and their partnership with the state (see Chapters 1 and 4). The rights accorded children were those to be consulted, to tender complaints, to have their best interests as the determinant in decision-making and to be represented when the state was involved in their upbringing. The debates on what became the Children Act 2004 were also largely conducted with reference to a rights-less child. The exception was with regard to the provisions which became sections 10 and 12 about the new database and the recording of 'concerns' when issues of children's rights were raised, though the critical arguments failed to secure amendments (see Penna 2005: 145, 147; and see Hier and Greenberg 2007 for a wider discussion of these issues).

It is also difficult to find the child as victim in most of the recent political documents relating to children who offend or behave anti-socially, or, indeed, in documents about 'youth' generally. In *Youth Matters* (DfES 2005b) the child as threat – on different levels – can be seen, as can the child as current citizen, but the image which predominates is that of the future productive citizen (Piper 2007b), the 'citizen-worker-in becoming' (Lister 2005: 455). The current well-being of children is the focus, but the aim is that they will have sufficient well-being to be good future citizens. So the children underpinning current policy are both citizens of today – with responsibilities which accrue from being given access to opportunities and being asked to take part in consultations and make choices – and citizens of tomorrow with the responsibility to take up all opportunities which will fit them for a productive and responsible future. An image of children and young people as citizens with defendable rights to take part in public life and family decision-making is not yet sufficiently clear to influence policy and its implementation.

There is another important corollary. Where 'real' children cannot measure up to the 'innocent victim' or the 'responsible active young person' then the child is no longer treated as a child. The modified construct of the 'good' child – the intended recipient of adult respect, protection and services – is one which excludes from that category any 'real' child who is seen as evil or dangerous, but also excludes one who is perceived as 'irresponsible', who does not take up opportunities offered. The 'worthy' child, then, is one who is sufficiently responsible to be seen as worthy of investment, is sufficiently dependent and innocent to garner support, and becomes the focus of investment for the future in a risk-based society. This image is based on significant continuities of imaginings as well as significant recent changes. These new ideas about our minors are now taken for granted, but they are amazingly strange. Children can no longer be counted as children unless they behave responsibly like adults! This image does, however, justify and encourage investment in such children to an extent not possible before.

Yet, ideas about children cannot be divorced from ideas about the family and the notion of investment itself. Conceptions of 'family' – and in particular a resurgence in the perceived importance of its moral role – will be dealt with in Chapter 4. The next chapter will examine the idea of investment in children and how the changing notions of the child – together with new discourses of risk – have enabled and prompted new notions of investment. Issues of children's rights will be pursued further in Chapter 6, whilst Chapter 8 will ask whether the continuing and enhanced negative images of children – and their parents – are undermining the investment agenda.

Notes

1 See *Gillick v West Norfolk and Wisbech Area Health Authority and Another* [1986] 1 FLR 224, HL and subsequent cases in relation to giving or withholding consent to medical treatment.

2 'Modernism' – and 'post-modernism' – have different meanings depending on context. Here 'modern' refers simply to the period beginning after the end of the medieval period and during which a universal idea about childhood emerged. The terms 'post-modern' or 'new modern' have been used to designate new ways of thinking which have undermined a liberal, consensualist view of society and art and which function with pluralities and fragmentation.

3 See also the anxieties expressed in the 'popular psychology' of the media and discussed by child psychologists (Winn 1984), historians (Cox 1996; Cunningham 1995) and educationalists (Buckingham 2000).

4 A study has drawn on these categories: see Stewart, I. and Vaitilingham, R. (eds) (2004) *Seven Ages of Man and Woman, A look at life in Britain in the Second Elizabethan Era* (Swindon: Economic and Social Research Council).

5 Frederick Engels wrote two articles on this issue, 'The Ten Hours Question' for *The Democratic Review*, a Chartist publication, and then 'The English Ten Hours Bill' for a German journal in 1850. For a translation of the latter article, see http://www.marxists.org/archive/marx/works/1850/03/10hours.htm.

6 See also, for a discussion of similar developments in the USA, Gordon 1988.

7 *Hansard* (Commons) 1931–1932, col. 1167 (12 February 1932).

8 ibid, col. 1185.

9 [2002] EWHC 2497 (Admin), [2003] 1 FLR 484.

10 *The Bible*, Authorised King James Version, Genesis Chapter 3, Verse 7.

11 *Hansard* HL col. 1559 (4 October 2000).

12 *Hansard* HC col. 1274 (30 March 2001). American research gives the same message about the dominant discourse: see de Young 2007.

13 *Hansard* HC col. 1079 (14 March 2001).

14 For example section 45: indecent images of children.

15 *Hansard* HC coll. 215–6 (15 July 2003).

16 ibid, col. 202.

17 *Hansard* HC col. 1167 (12 February 1932).

18 See an article by C. Peveritt on the HERO website – the Higher Education and Research gateway – at: http://www.hero.ac.uk/uk/inside_he/archives/2004/the_ethics_of_if6906.cfm.
19 The Criminal Justice and Immigration Act 2008 section 48 provides for a conditional caution for young offenders.
20 It should be pointed out, however, that the Welsh Assembly has located its youth justice services in Health and Social Services rather than in Crime Prevention (see Muncie 2004: 275–6), and, therefore, the images of children are more ambiguous.

Chapter 3

Upgrading risk-based investment in children

Indisputably, over the last two, or at most three, decades childhood has moved to the forefront of personal, political and academic agendas and not solely in the West. The moving spirit of this process is extremely complex and can be seen in an entanglement of factors: a structural readjustment to time and mortality in the face of quickening social change; a re-evaluation and positioning of parenthood ...; a search for a moral centre ... and *an age-old desire to invest in futures now rendered increasingly urgent*. (James, Jenks and Prout 1998: 5; emphasis added)

Policies for children have been at the heart of the New Labour project to refashion the welfare state ... Children and childhood become a prime site for state intervention of a pre-emptive kind. (Parton 2008: 175)

The importance of economics and science

Parents look after their children because they are precious: they love and cherish them. At a personal level, that statement needs no supporting academic evidence, albeit that 'love' may take many forms and that other motivations may coexist. At a national level, too, love may prompt action. As the last chapter showed, images of children as victims – as destitute, abused or starving – 'tugged at the heart strings' of Victorians and proved effective in eliciting responses of compassion and concern. Yet emotions of love and concern may not be evoked by some of the other images of children examined in that chapter. Other more pragmatic and 'hard headed' motivations and justifications then become necessary if public money is to be expended on children. At this point the 'age-old desire' to spend money on children with a view to future benefits becomes important. Investment in the young is a long-standing motif of law and policy: it is a corollary of the notion of the 'modern' childhood conceptualised as a period of preparation and 'training' for adulthood. The objective is to produce healthier, more productive and non-criminal future members of the economy and civic life that save the state from expenditure in the future.

In practice, particular pieces of legislation have often required more specific justifications, usually linked to current national needs or social anxieties. What will become apparent is yet another paradox: as more complex notions of the interests and rights of the child have developed over time – and the images of children and young people have become more varied and diverse – the justifications for spending the nation's money on children have, arguably, become narrower in that they are almost exclusively related to future gains. Further, as Parton (2006) argues, investment in children has been harnessed as a crucial component of a much wider political agenda of transformation of the welfare state. The development of actuarial approaches, using quantitative research data, to understanding the causes and correlates of, for example, criminality, ill health and unemployment, have aided this focus on investment for the future by appearing to give the certainty of science.

It is education – a process intrinsically linked to notions of preparation and training and so expenditure and effort for future gains – which has, unsurprisingly, been the focus of the greatest investment expenditure on children in the past and present. The current funding of university students via a system of loans repayable when income after graduation exceeds a certain amount is the latest evidence of a financial gain approach to education at the level of the personal and the social. Perhaps more surprisingly, Education Acts have, historically, sometimes been motivated by reasons other than economic ones.

Investing in democracy: the education of children

Education has always been an issue which has prompted conflict, not only around religious and moral ideas about the roles of parents but also about the aims and effects of education in a democracy. As a report to the 56th Commission on Human Rights noted, 'A legislative proposal placed before the House of Commons in 1807 to provide two years of free primary education in parochial schools was rejected on two grounds: unwillingness to bear the anticipated costs and fears that education might make "the lower orders" discontented' (Tomaševski 1999: para. 10). The ever-present concern about expenditure was at that time, two centuries ago, joined by the anxiety that an educated working class would not wish to stay in their 'rightful place' in society and would, instead, resort to riots or worse. However, the United Kingdom survived the disturbances at the end of the Napoleonic Wars and, instead of the revolutions that occurred in many European states in 1848, experienced only relatively small Chartist demonstrations, including one at Kennington Common (now the Oval cricket ground). This social stability encouraged the passage of the Reform Acts in 1832 and 1867, giving the vote to middle class and 'respectable' working class men respectively.[1]

At that point, the nature of the political anxiety about mass education changed. The 1867 Act, which had almost doubled the electorate, led to a desire on the part of the government to 'educate our masters'[2] – the total of approximately 1,500,000 men then enfranchised – such that they were able to exercise their vote responsibly (Shipman and Shipman 2006: 6).[3] The anticipated investment gain from the 1870 Education Act was, therefore, that of the continuance of a liberal democracy and a stable government. And, at the end of the 19th century, the same argument was advanced with regard to post-elementary education by the Royal Commission on Secondary Education when it stated that 'Elementary education is among the first needs of a people and especially of a free people'. However, the report continued, 'it is by those who have received a superior kind of education that the intellectual progress of a nation is maintained' and argued that reform of secondary education was essential 'not merely in the interests of the material prosperity and intellectual activity of the nation but no less in that of its happiness and moral strength' (1895 Part I: V). Whilst this statement reveals a particular view of a liberal secondary education, it also points to non-economic benefits of education for citizens: that they become happier and more moral, democratically engaged, adults.

These ideas are very long-lasting: recent policy developments, as noted in Chapter 2, have used an image of the 'responsible citizen child' who can and should engage in 'civic duties', an image which has been part of a particular Third Way construction of active citizens. For example, *Youth Matters* specified three key challenges which related to the role of children as citizens in a democracy: engaging and empowering young people in the provision of services, encouraging volunteering within the community, and providing better information and advice so young people can make informed choices (DfES 2005: para. 12). Some of this was in response to the grave concern at the democratic disengagement within the UK, most evident in the fact that the percentage of the population voting in elections has been declining. Only 39 per cent of 18–24 year-olds voted in the 2001 General Election, compared with 70 per cent of those aged 65 or over, a concern which led the Electoral Commission to run their 'Votes are Power' campaign in 2002. This 'sought to mend the broken link between having an opinion and voting' by reframing voting 'from merely choosing a political party to taking affirmative action',[4] a stance in line with current political notions of active citizenship.

Concerns about the weakening of active involvement in democracy have also led to the policy trend to encourage and then mandate citizenship education in schools. Citizenship is now part of the National Curriculum, being a statutory 'entitlement' at Key Stages 3 and 4 since 2002 and part of the Guidelines at Key Stages 1 and 2 since 2000. There is an Institute for Citizenship, a charity set up in 1992 by the then Speaker of the House of Commons, the Rt Hon. Bernard Weatherill MP, which helps produce teaching materials for schools and young offender institutions, whilst the Department for Children, Schools and Families had, until recently, a 'citizenship' section on its website dedicated to providing guidance and teaching materials for all levels of school children. Now to be found on the 'Youth Information' website, the information for young people about citizenship reflects, with some additions, the idea of the citizen-child underpinning *Youth Matters*:

The things you will learn in Citizenship will help you to:

- become informed;
- express your views;
- find out how your community is organised and what you can do to influence how it works;
- recognise there are different communities at local, regional, national and international levels; and
- appreciate the importance of looking after the environment.[5]

All these developments represent a continuing investment of political time and public money in education for democracy.

Investing in defence and commerce: health and nutrition

Two more specific rationales for investment have been national security and international trade: again an earlier example was a spin-off from education reform. Universal elementary education – albeit not always a full-time education until well into the 20th century[6] – made children 'visible' to the authorities and led to increased concerns about the health of the population. This concern was heightened by the poor physical condition of recruits to the Second Boer War of 1899–1902. In 1899, 32.9 per cent of the recruits who were medically inspected were rejected as unfit (Hendley 1995: 263) and 'the prevalence of notions of social Darwinism in this period meant that the health of a nation's citizens began to be directly linked to ideas of national strength' (ibid). Consequently, with a growing threat in particular from Germany, investment in boys as future soldiers and sailors as well as skilled workers in commerce and shipbuilding, and in girls as efficient, thrifty mothers and wives, was seen as crucial. Investment could be justified in terms of the needs of national defence, the maintenance of the Empire and its trading concerns. Two key planks of that investment were reforms that could be implemented via the school: the provision of dinners by the state and the introduction of, and referrals from, school medical inspections.

These may seem to be very minor investments in children's health but, in terms of the modifications of ideas around parenting and investment, they were absolutely crucial steps towards current concepts. The publication of the Education (Provision of Meals) Bill caused considerable controversy despite over two decades of pressure by campaigners because of its implications for notions of parental responsibility (see Chapter 4). It was eventually passed in 1906, successfully presented as a measure to ensure more effective learning by better nourished children and drew on 'pathetic' images of children for this purpose. For example, General Booth of the Salvation Army argued that, 'There are few more grotesque pictures in the history of civilisation than that of compulsory attendance of children at school, faint with hunger because they had not breakfast' (Booth 1890: Chapter VIII 'The Children of the Lost'), and a London County Council (LCC) Report of 1907 reported 50–60 per cent of children as still coming under the category of 'indifferent nutrition' (see Alden 1908). The Act consequently gave local authorities the power to spend money on the provision of free school meals.

Despite the strong investment arguments, expenditure on school meals has been limited, then and now. In 1914 the Government announced that it would provide grants to cover half the cost of meals – but these were cut back because of military expenditure in World War I. By the outbreak of World War II, when only 50 per cent of local authorities were providing free meals, the Government announced it would fund 70 per cent of the cost of providing meals and in 1947 took responsibility for full funding, a responsibility transferred back to Local Education Authorities in 1967. As part of a drive to reduce the cost of school meals, the 1980 Education Act removed the requirement that all school meals should have certain minimal nutritional standards. School meals have always had a set cost to be paid by the parent unless a child is entitled to free school dinners (although entitlements have been narrowed since 1980 (Brannen and Storey 1998: 74)).[7]

More recently, the Government's response to the pressure triggered by chef Jamie Oliver's campaign for healthy school dinners was to approve extra money for the school meals service over a number of years. Government guidelines now suggest that the minimum spend per meal should be at least 50p for primary schools and 60p for secondary schools. There is now another issue which is becoming even more important, that of nutritional standards. 'Sustain' had been campaigning for over a decade for the catering industry to impose voluntary controls on advertising 'junk food' to children and supported both the 2004 and 2005 Food Bills. Both were, however, private – not government – bills, introduced by MPs Debra Shipley and Mary Creagh respectively. The Children's Food Bill 2005 was, almost a century after the 1906 Act (1908 in Scotland), designed to ensure school meals are 'of benefit to their health and wellbeing' (clause 1(2)) and would have placed duties on the Food Standards Agency. However, the Government set new national nutritional standards for school lunches in 2006 (School Food Trust 2006), all parts to be phased in by September 2009. The desired investment is now not just to ensure more cost-effective learning, but also to improve the health of children in order to save future expenditure in the health services. Getting children on board a healthy eating policy is, of course, another matter (see Ofsted 2007).

Yet 'old' arguments continue. The debates on the 2005 Food Bill were reminiscent of those in 1906–08. Annette Brooke MP quoted a teacher as saying: 'What is the point of spending a fortune on key stage 3 secondary strategies when so many kids are just not capable of learning as their brains are not functioning? It is like trying to fine tune the engine of a car that has got the wrong fuel in it.'[8] One hundred and twenty-five organisations supported the Bill but, as with many private members' bills, insufficient parliamentary time was allocated.[9]

The current anxieties about the armed forces are also reminiscent of older motivations. A report from the National Audit Office shows that defence needs – notably stemming from the 'war on terror' – as well as health service costs and school efficiency are again driving the child health agenda. The report notes that increasing levels of obesity and resulting health problems have reduced the number of young people able to join the services. It refers to research done by the Army in 2005 which showed that only a third of 16-year-old boys would pass the body mass index set for all recruits and that, in response, the Army reduced the index target (National Audit Office 2006: 53) because of a general 2 per cent shortfall in staffing and severe personnel shortages in certain areas (ibid: 1). In the Royal Navy, ships currently sail with crews on average 12 per cent below strength (Norton-Taylor 2006).

Investing in law-abiding adults

The state has always been concerned to ensure children grow up as good law-abiding citizens. Referring to the 'criminal classes' in Great Britain in 1890, Booth noted that, 'To the loss caused by the actual picking and stealing must be added that of the unproductive labour of nearly 65,000 adults' (Booth 1890: Chapter VII 'The Criminals'). Investment policies with that aim have perhaps attracted legitimacy more easily than most child-focused expenditure. As noted in Chapter 2, the differences have been in the way the children who offend or who are deemed to be at risk of offending are conceptualised, with consequent differences in legislative responses. At the beginning of the 20th century, it was early criminological work on the links between criminality and social conditions that was harnessed by those campaigning for the 'depraved' child to be treated differently, and images of the young offender which drew on existing notions of the 'deprived' child were effective in leading to the setting up of a juvenile court by the 1908 Children Act. With similar objectives of reform rather than (or in addition to) punishment, the Children and Young Persons Act 1933 established the principle that still imposes a duty on 'every court' (including criminal courts) in England and Wales to 'have regard to' the welfare of the child 'who is brought before it'. That principle also applies to Northern Ireland where it must be implemented 'with a view to furthering [children's] personal, social and educational development'.[10]

By the end of the 20th century, with the electoral success of New Labour, new approaches to managing the risk of future offending via investment in preventative services as well as penal measures were implemented. The Crime and Disorder Act 1998 and the Criminal Evidence and Youth Justice Act 1999 led to the introduction of the civil 'remedies' of child safety, anti-social behaviour and parenting orders (see Chapters 4 and 8), as well as to the reprimands and warnings to be used by the police and the referral orders and action plan orders for the (criminal) Youth Courts. Whilst the civil orders are problematic (see Chapter 4), parenting orders, final warnings and referral orders in particular were intended to, and often do, provide preventative and supportive services for parents and children with a rationale of investing resources early in the criminal 'career' of an young offender and his family (see Chapter 7).

Some of these new processes and legal criteria have facilitated involvement in rehabilitative programmes – in the 'reformative' tradition of the 19th century – or restorative justice processes – in the 'responsibilising' and 'making good' ideologies of the later 20th century. Others have stemmed from the new, negative perceptions of young people, notably the 'incivilities' being displayed by 'anti-social' youths, and have led to investment in policing and the imposition of anti-social behaviour orders. The policy aim is to produce future 'civil' and 'civic-minded' citizens, and the focus is on the 'moral' duties of (young) citizens. This amalgam of ideas was set out by the then Home Secretary Jack Straw in a talk to police officers when New Labour first came to power:

> The essence of 'zero tolerance' is that anti-social activity, acts of vandalism and rowdy, loutish behaviour should not be tolerated because they severely damage the quality of people's lives and lead on, if unchecked, to much more serious criminal behaviour. … Disorder and incivility can have a knock-on effect on more serious crime. The risks of being a victim of violent crime are four times greater in a disorderly neighbourhood than an orderly one. … This evidence powerfully reinforces the case for a zero tolerance approach to disorder. (Straw 1997)

The investment agenda is not, then, simply an issue of children's services but also of youth justice processes and outcomes. The links made between incivility and crime, and the perception that society is becoming decivilised, justify, on the one hand, civil orders to constrain the freedom of young people who are not behaving responsibly and, on the other, the provision of opportunities to be and become responsible citizens. So, selective use of the currently available images of children has also legitimated major investment in the present in the form of prison accommodation for greater numbers of children and young people, stemming at least in part from the introduction in recent legislation of more legal routes to custody. In particular, the CJA 2003 has introduced in section 226 a new sentence of detention for public protection by which 'dangerous' young offenders can be given an indeterminate custodial sentence for a very wide range of sexual and violent offences in circumstances where previous legislation would not have allowed or mandated custody. This has been criticised (see, for example, NSPCC 2006) and may not be a wise investment: there is little evidence of its effectiveness in terms of deterrence or rehabilitation and, as an incapacitative measure, its impact on future levels of criminality cannot be great.

Investing in inclusion

What this book is about, however, is the new and seemingly all-encompassing imperative to invest which developed in the late 20th century. Its origins are in a set of discourses around inclusion and exclusion that have been politically very important for New Labour. Social exclusion 'became a keynote of New Labour's repositioning for election in 1997' (Fergusson 2002: 175), and the introductory paragraphs to the UK's first National Action Plan on Social Inclusion include the statement that 'The UK Government's commitment to overcoming social exclusion lies at the core of its political programme'. Member states of the EU were encouraged to produce a plan, and common objectives were agreed at the Nice European Council, the UK submitting its first plan in 2001 (see Atkinson 2003: 262 and the website of the Department of Work and Pensions).

Fifteen cross-departmental reviews were established as an integral part of the 2000 Spending Review, entitled *Prudent for a Purpose,* and included reviews entitled 'Sure Start and services for the Under Fives' and 'Young People at Risk' (HM Treasury 2000: Chapters 24 and 25). The latter review 'sought to identify cost effective policies for helping young people between the ages of 5 and 19 to make the transition safely and successfully from childhood to adulthood'. The following year the Government also set up the Local Network Fund for Children and Young People based, with the new Children's Fund, at the then DfES, with the objective of enabling communities, 'with limited opportunities or access to services that many young people take for granted, to develop projects and activities for children and young people'.[11] The same year the Government set up seven cross-cutting reviews: those relevant to the public services concerned the public sector labour market, children at risk, tackling health inequalities, the role of the voluntary sector in public services, and improving public space. The Treasury statement announcing the review included the following comment on children 'at risk':

Children at Risk do not form a self contained, defined group. Many children and young people can be vulnerable to risk factors at some point in their development which, without the support of preventative and effective services, can lead to crisis and in some cases lasting effects which perpetuate the cycle of deprivation and poverty. As well as the human cost the long term costs to society can be enormous.[12]

The terms of reference for the Children at Risk review required the review 'to establish the key outcome targets for children's services', and the work was split into five working groups for this purpose: health and well-being; achievement, enjoyment and participation; protection and responsibility; identification, referral and tracking; and planning.

In 2002 the then Chancellor Gordon Brown announced spending decisions based on these reviews which promoted the engagement of non-governmental groups in reaching the outcome targets:

And at the heart of the next stage of children's services are voluntary and community partnerships that are increasingly a vital link between the needs children have, and the help they receive. ... So ... the Chief Secretary to the Treasury is today announcing details of a new three-year fund of £125 million that voluntary organisations can draw upon for their public service work.

And I can also confirm that the budget for the Children's Fund – helping volunteers and charities assist vulnerable children – will be £200 million a year to 2006.[13]

Three years later, the 2005 Budget revealed the scope of the new agenda: 'The Government's aim is to promote a fair and inclusive society where everyone shares in rising national prosperity and no one is held back from achieving their potential through disadvantage or lack of opportunity. ... Education and skills are central to this ambition' (HM Treasury 2005: para. 5.1). The following statement from that Budget is also to be found in policy documents and speeches before and after 2005 and is reproduced verbatim at the beginning of the same chapter, entitled 'Building a Fairer Society', in the budgets of 2006 and 2007.

> The Government is committed to promoting fairness alongside flexibility and enterprise to ensure that everyone can take advantage of opportunities to fulfil their potential. The Government's reforms of the welfare state reflect its aims of eradicating child poverty and supporting families to balance their work and family life, promoting saving and ensuring security for all in old age. (ibid: 101)

Specifically, as noted in Chapter 1, the Government set an aim of halving the child poverty rate by 2011 (HM Treasury 2005: para. 5.14; see also DCFS 2007: 7) through a threefold strategy of financial support for families together with measures to address unemployment, by 'tackling material deprivation' and by 'improving poor children's life chances' (HM Treasury 2005: para. 5.15). As part of the third strategy, 524 Sure Start programmes had been put in place by 2005 (ibid: para. 5.16). Multiple risks are to be managed in this new approach, and early intervention in the lives of children is to be primarily for the purpose of investment. 'Teenagers are our future leaders, entrepreneurs and parents and their experience of youth is hugely significant in shaping the direction they take in their lives' (Chancellor Gordon Brown quoted in DfES, 2006b).

In this policy agenda, exclusion and child poverty are closely correlated with high levels of 'worklessness': the main investment is in prevention of worklessness and of offending. The 'evil' to be prevented is exclusion from an economically productive and civic adult life. What we have here is not just a reason for investment by the state but, to use the phrase coined by Anthony Giddens (1998), a 'social investment state' in which the government's policy priorities are now *explicitly* explained as investment. It denotes investment in human capital, and its origins might be seen in the Commission on Social Justice's report of 1994 and earlier writings by Tony Blair (see

Lister 2005: 451). The social investment state has also been seen as a means of reconstructing society morally as well as socially, with an important emphasis on 'civic renewal' (ibid: 452) through, for example, physical regeneration, as in the 1998 New Deal for Communities, and the co-opting of youth into volunteering.

It is argued that the social exclusion discourse is simply a new policy word: 'The inclusion terminology is new but not the intention. Rescuing "at-risk" youth was the prime aim when the uniformed youth movements were created a century and more ago' (Roberts 2005: 124). Welshman (2007) has traced the link specifically between the theories of 'transmitted deprivation' in the 1970s and current social exclusion policies. Others see the term 'social exclusion' as a more acceptable replacement for the previous 'underclass' terminology which had faced severe criticism, notably in its overtones of criminality and, in the USA, race (Knepper 2007: 37–9). Popularised by Dahrendorf (1987) and Field (1989) in the 1980s in order to draw attention to the difficulties facing those left behind by economic change, it was quickly taken over and used pejoratively by writers on the New Right (see, for example, Murray and Phillips 2001) and by the media. Knepper quotes, for example, the *Sunday Times* headline of 1999: 'A violent underclass is a threat to us all' (Knepper 2007: 38). More recently, a *Daily Telegraph* article included the following statement: 'This Government is not solely to blame for all Britain's ills. The development of a state-supported, amoral underclass stretches back a long way' (Randall 2007).

According to David Miliband, however, 'It was not just a change in terminology, or governmental plumbing, but a policy departure that aimed to address the moral vacuum at the heart of Conservative policy, but also the policy limitations in inherited assumptions on the Left' (Miliband 2005). The new phrase 'social exclusion' was, then, 'meant to signify a moral commitment to helping the poor with a comprehensive programme, consistent with the idea of being tough on crime' (Knepper 2007: 39). Its official definition, first used by the then Prime Minister Blair and then reproduced in policy documents, is that is it 'a short-hand label for what can happen when individuals or areas suffer from a combination of linked problems such as unemployment, poor skills, low incomes, poor housing, high crime environments, bad health and family break-down'.[14]

The creation of social capital is also linked to the social inclusion agenda amid concerns that 'across the political spectrum … levels of social capital are being eroded in contemporary society' (Edwards 2003: 305). Social capital is a term used by Putnam to prioritise the value of social networks, 'who people know, the information channels and norms of reciprocity' (Roberts and Devine 2003: 309–10; see also Putnam 1993). Surprisingly, there is a convergence here with thinking on remoralisation and the importance of family. For some commentators, the focus on social capital represents a more conservative approach in the fostering of 'traditional' family relationships to increase that capital (Edwards 2003: 305)[15] and so supports a political reluctance to challenge familial ideology.

The linked policy agendas of social inclusion, social exclusion and investment in children and social capital arguably constitute an ambivalent discourse.[16] The provenance of the concept of social inclusion 'lies in some of the more radical political philosophies of the European (and particularly French) tradition. Those roots lie in commitments to social rights, to social citizenship, to social solidarity and to mutuality and the collectivisation of risk' (Fergusson 2002: 175). Yet the 'New Deal' aspects of inclusion policies which focus on getting people back to work[17] have their roots in US workfare schemes.[18] Current policy could therefore be viewed as representing a narrow concept of social inclusion and exclusion with a focus on measurable outputs (Muncie 2004; Williams 2004: 81). It does not exhibit the positive values of the inclusion agenda on mainland Europe but instead has a narrow focus on risk (Fergusson 2002: 175) and on future employment needs. Gray has gone further to argue that 'Beyond the discursive rhetoric, the eradication of social exclusion is not articulated via any vision of social justice which seeks to remove the structural constraints arising from the unequal distribution of socio-economic resources' (Gray 2005: 940).The recent opening statement by Graham Allen MP in a parliamentary debate on the Comprehensive Spending Review might also suggest a narrow focus on the risk of future financial outlay: 'The public expenditure consequences of failure to invest early are immense. Further expenditure will be needed to fund disrupted classes, missed opportunities to get qualifications or work, antisocial behaviour, expensive interaction with the criminal justice system, drug rehabilitation, or a lifetime dependency on benefits'.[19] Critics of this narrower perspective would argue that the production of social capital may not act as an alternative to social justice (Baron *et al.*; Edwards 2003: 306).

However, given the difficulties of successfully arguing for an increase of public expenditure on children, and given strong familial ideologies that have historically acted as a strong barrier to investment (see Chapter 4), the Government's policy to 'invest in the potential of every single child in our country' (Brown 2002) may 'represent a politically astute discourse for politicians to use in a culture unsympathetic to children and alongside a rhetoric hostile to cash benefits' in the context of little public concern about child poverty (Lister 2005: 455). Even research currently undertaken for the Department for Work and Pensions suggests that 'there are significant public misconceptions about child poverty, and that many people don't think child poverty exists in Britain' (Ed Balls, Secretary of State for Children, Schools and Families, 2007).[20]

Change for Children

Whatever the criticisms of, and motivations underpinning, these socio-economic policy developments, they have created a very clear investment justification for a new agenda for state action on children. The policy papers preceding the Children Act 2004, *Every Child Matters* and *Youth Matters*, explicitly put forward risk management as investment. The message is that children need to be protected from a variety of negative outcomes that might ensue if appropriate action is not taken (James and James 2008). *Every Child Matters*, a Green Paper published by the DfES in 2003, ostensibly as a result of the death of Victoria Climbié and the Laming Report, had, as Parton argues, 'a much longer and more complex genealogy' than one child death scandal (Parton 2008: 167). The document stated that:

> The Government's aim is for every child, whatever their background or their circumstances, to have the support they need to:
> • Be healthy
> • Stay safe
> • Enjoy and achieve
> • Make a positive contribution
> • Achieve economic well-being.

There is currently a government website headed 'Every Child Matters, Change for Children', and there are links from it to numerous documents with one or both parts of this heading in the title.

The website for the *Every Child Matters* programme explains this outcome-based approach and the specific risks it aims to reduce:

> The five outcomes are universal ambitions for every child and young person, whatever their background or circumstances.

67

Improving outcomes for all children and young people underpins all of the development and work within children's trusts.

The outcomes are mutually reinforcing. For example, children and young people learn and thrive when they are healthy, safe and engaged; and the evidence shows clearly that educational achievement is the most effective route out of poverty.

Improving outcomes also involves narrowing the gap between disadvantaged children and their peers. The Government is focusing particularly on improving outcomes for looked-after children and children with special educational needs and disabilities, and on reducing the incidence of teenage pregnancy and the number of young people not in education, employment or training.[21]

All sectors of government whose remit impacts on children and young people have targets related to these outcomes. In *Change for Children in the Criminal Justice System* (Home Office 2005) the 'key focus' of the criminal justice system is on the second and fourth of the five outcomes specified in *Every Child Matters* (DfES 2003): making positive contributions by being law-abiding and staying safe by ensuring children are not victims of crime.

In line with the outcomes, the policy aim of the Children Act 2004 is to increase the possibilities of directing resources at children over a wide range of services. Its main – and much contested – contention is that inter-agency co-operation, more flexible funding possibilities and increased communication and data sharing will make all the difference. The outcomes were incorporated in section 10(2) of the Children Act 2004 in the duty on children's services to improve 'well-being':

The arrangements are to be made with a view to improving the well-being of children in the authority's area so far as relating to—
(a) physical and mental health and emotional well-being;
(b) protection from harm and neglect;
(c) education, training and recreation;
(d) the contribution made by them to society;
(e) social and economic well-being.

Section 10(4) lists the seven partner agencies of children's services, and section 11(2)(a) extends to a wider range of bodies the specific duty to ensure that 'their functions are discharged having regard to the need to safeguard and promote the welfare of children'. The list of 13 bodies includes youth offending teams, governors of prisons or secure training centres, the police and NHS trusts. Local Safeguarding Children's Boards established under section 13 (to replace, *inter alia*, Area Child Protection Committees) will include representatives of most of the bodies listed in section 11, together with a representative from the Children and Family Court Advisory Support Services (CAFCASS). The policy aim of these Boards is better communication, a higher priority given to safeguarding children's welfare and more effective delivery of services.

The regulations for producing the Children and Young People's Plan (CYPP), which replaced the mandatory Children's Services Plan, require the local authority to relate the plan specifically to the five outcomes, to outline its 'key actions' and to detail the allocation of its budget (Children and Young People's Plan (England) Regulations 2005 (SI 2005 No. 2149), regulation 4). However, regulation 4(2) has already been amended to put more emphasis on early intervention. Instead of a 'vision' statement, the CYPP must include the following:

> (a) a statement as to how the authority intend to achieve the improvements referred to in regulation 4(1), with specific reference to the following—
> (i) the integration of services provided by the authority and its relevant partners to improve the well-being of children and relevant young persons;
> (ii) arrangements made by the authority under section 11(2) of the Children Act 2004 (arrangements to safeguard and promote welfare); and
> (iii) *arrangements for early intervention and preventative action*
> (SI 2007 No 57, regulation 4, in force 1 October 2007, emphasis added)

Early intervention is also a target in relation to young offenders. The Government's response, at the end of 2005, to the Audit Commission's 2004 Report on youth justice refers to its policy aim as to 'shift services towards prevention and early intervention in an integrated way, across services, before children reach crisis point' (YJB 2004: para. 6.2).

Legislation since 2004 has also furthered the *Every Child Matters* outcomes. *Youth Matters: Next Steps* proposed a duty on local authorities 'to ensure that young people have access to a wide range of positive activities' (2006a: Summary, p. 3) which has been legislated in the Education and Inspection Act 2006. Section 6 imposes duties on local education authorities (LEAs) in England whereby the LEA must secure for the under-13s 'adequate facilities for recreation and social and physical training', and, for persons aged 13 to 19, must, 'so far as reasonably practicable', secure access to 'sufficient' educational and recreational leisure-time activities. These must be aimed at 'the improvement of their well-being', defined by reference to the five outcomes as incorporated in the Children Act 2004.

Finally, to take an example from 'change for children' reforms related to child health, the *National Service Framework for Children, Young People and Maternity Services* sets out a 10-year programme regarding health and social care and making links to education services (DH and DfES 2004). Standard 1, 'Promoting Health and Well-being, Identifying Needs and Intervening Early', applying to all children and young people, states the following target: 'The health and well-being of all children and young people is promoted and delivered through a co-ordinated programme of action, including prevention and early intervention wherever possible, to ensure long term gain, led by the NHS in partnership with local authorities' (ibid: Executive Summary, 6).

Risk and early intervention

The Children Act 2004 represents a policy agenda now permeated with concepts of risk. It is motivated by concern to reduce the risk of bad futures for children, the choice of target and preferred outcome is based on risk, the basis of assessment of children is risk, the targets of interventions must manage their own risk by responding to opportunities given, and risk removal or reduction is the outcome monitored. Actuarial calculations of risks of bad outcomes in adulthood justify early intervention in the lives of children to reduce the likelihood of these poor outcomes. An early example of new expenditure arising from the social investment approach to identifying and targeting children at risk arose from the cross-cutting review process noted above. The Children's Fund, whose remit taken over by Children's Trusts in April 2008, was set up in 2000 to promote a £380 million programme of preventative work with children primarily in the 5–13 age group (HM Treasury 2000: para. 25.4) and with 25 per cent of the Fund ring-fenced for crime prevention work. The three underlying principles of the Children's Fund were stated as:

- Prevention
  To address the gap in preventative services for children and young people at risk of social exclusion, by providing increased and better coordinated preventative services for 5–13 year-olds and their families
- Partnership
  To take responsibility at local level for the delivery of the Children's Fund plan, involving partners from the statutory and voluntary sectors, community and faith groups ...
- Participation
  The voices of children and young people are at the heart of the Children's Fund, with children and young people being involved in the design, operation and evaluation of the programme.[22]

Children's Fund partnerships will have received over £780 million over the period 2003–08.

Research about the onset or persistence of offending by children and young people is, as already noted, vital to the legitimacy and ultimate success of these high profile inclusion strategies 'to break cycles of poverty and criminality' (Edwards 2003; HM Treasury 2004; HM Treasury *et al.* 2004). The Action Plan setting out the Government's 'next steps' in tackling social exclusion states very clearly that 'through early identification, support and preventative action positive change is possible' (Cabinet Office 2006: 8) and sets out an agenda for 'a lifetime approach' with tables of risk factors for the early years stage (ibid: 45–8). This new technicalised form of investment in children, borrowing from developments in youth justice, relies on research findings about correlates and statistically significant factors to decide on geographical areas and on individual children to be targeted.[23] Chapter 5 will examine in more detail this shift to a conception of risk as developed in the youth justice system and yet one that has set the agenda for wider preventative schemes: the 'at risk' now include those at risk not only of offending but of a range of undesirable outcomes. Conversely, the *Every Child Matters* reforms of the Justice Board (YJB) aim to 'shift services towards prevention and early intervention in an integrated way, across services, before children reach crisis point' (YJB 2004: para. 6.2) and are seen as essential 'to prevent the poor outcomes that blight children and young people's lives and have negative effects into adulthood' (ibid). This also takes on board the investment approach of the Audit Commission's report on youth justice: 'If effective early intervention had been provided for just one-in-ten of these young people, annual savings in excess of £100 million could have been made' (Audit Commission 2004: 10).

That youth justice initiatives have been a 'push' for early intervention more generally is not, in retrospect, surprising. Such programmes – which attract the support of public opinion in a society which gives priority to law and order – have enabled the provision of uncontentious 'new' money for the focus on children at risk. An example is the development of junior and senior YISPs (Youth Inclusion Support Panels) and the programmes, for 8–12 year-olds and 13–18 year-olds respectively, for which they are responsible. These are now high-profile developments which gained their early funding from the Children's Fund and are now promoted by the YJB and often run by youth offending teams (YOTs). They involve multi-agency planning, and by 2004 there were 90 senior and 60 junior YISPs (YJB 2004: para 6.3). The YJB website stated in 2006 that:

> YISPs have been designed to help the Youth Justice Board achieve its corporate target of setting up evidence-based programmes that reduce the likelihood of targeted young people committing offences or anti-social behaviour. ... Support and monitoring is provided to YOTs through the YJB's Prevention Programme Support team to ensure that a YISP, or other means of identifying young people at risk of offending, is established in every YOT area in England and Wales.[24]

Another source of new money for children at risk has been via the Crime and Disorder Reduction Partnerships, notably the Prevent and Deter initiative which is linked to youth offending teams (YJB 2004: para 6.4).

The role of this ever-enlarging youth justice system is problematic[25] in that areas of social policy are in effect being 'criminalised' (Drakeford and Vanstone 2000), and some of the discourse prevalent in these new policy areas jars. One example is the reference to 'basic command units' – the highest crime police areas where the establishment of a YISP is given priority (see NACRO 2004).[26] There is a paradox that, whilst punitive 'fall-back' positions have been developed to deal with social policy deficits, the YJB has developed inclusive strategies for 'at risk' children, some of which were taken over by the then DfES for use in a non-criminal system (Williamson 2005: 15–16; see also Smith 2005b).

Limiting investment expenditure

This extensive set of initiatives and policies – all prompted and justified by a focus on reducing risks of poor outcomes for children – does not ensure that greater investment in children will happen. The rationing of public resources persists as a fact of political life, but a different kind of rationing is provided by the social inclusion agenda. First, investment which is strategic and targeted is now explicit Government policy. *Youth Matters* refers to this with regard to investment in youth facilities/support services (paras 18, 31, 63; for fuller details see Chapters 3 and 6). Expenditure must comply with criteria for targeting and effectiveness. The new Children's Trusts have a crucial role: they 'are engaged at the forefront of a reconfiguration of both targeted and universal services for children' (DfES 2005e: 2).[27]

Secondly, investment and its rationing can be done on an *area basis* where expenditure can be closely controlled and outputs can be monitored. Research would suggest the nature of the community in which children live is a very important correlate of offending (see Chapter 5). Such an approach fits into the wider social policy context which gives priority to the fostering of values of community responsibility and involvement, and to the channelling of resources through initiatives designed to utilise and encourage participatory area-based regeneration. The choice of geographical area and desired outputs is politically or administratively, not legally, determined, and the dominant discourse is of inclusion and explicitly one of investment.

Thirdly, the approach of social inclusion policies – as made clear in the quotations above from the 2005 Budget Report but most evident in *Youth Matters* – is that it is *opportunity based*. The approach is contextualised within the citizenship agenda and legitimated by the new image of the citizen-child who is mature enough to take the responsibility required. Throughout *Youth Matters* there is a notion of balance: between challenge and support (para. 68); between rights and responsibilities (para. 8). The discourse is of opportunities, increased choice, positive activities, respect and support. Opportunities to 'escape' from poor outcomes are offered to those excluded or at risk of exclusion, and it is the responsibility of the young to accept the challenges offered. Opportunities and so investment are not offered to those who have 'made themselves' undeserving.

This approach has already been put into operation in previous initiatives via contracts which have no legal status but can have detrimental effects if broken. Earlier examples of this form of 'contractual governance' to control individual conduct (Crawford 2003: 481–2) can be found in the referral order for young offenders, the New Deal, and home-school agreements introduced by the School Standards and Framework Act 1998. Since then, other contracts have been piloted and promoted. For example, in its response to *Youth Matters: The Next Steps*, the Government proposed to encourage greater use of 'acceptable behaviour contracts', made between the local authority, police, youth offending team and others and the child or young person (Home Office 2004: para. 11), and later issued guidance (Home Office 2007). Such a policy has been successful in the sense that 7,500 such contracts or agreements were signed in 2005/6 compared with 3,948 in 2003/4 (Respect Task Force 2007: 1–2).

New youth measures are sold as both an investment in the future and a saving now. For example, the Audit Commission used 'James' Story' to argue that the provision of family support and services to prevent James' offending would have been a much cheaper alternative: 'The costs of these support services would have been £42,000 up to the time he was 16, compared with the actual costs of £184,000 for the services he did receive, including court appearances and custody' (2004: 93 at 195; see also Appendix 6). In order to ensure such earlier cost-effective services are provided, the Audit Commission proposed that incentives should be provided to encourage local authorities to do so or money should be ring-fenced: 'This is essential if investment in long-term prevention programmes is to compete with the pressures to deliver improved outcomes in the short term' (ibid: 94 at 198).

Further, the prevalent discourse of managerialism ensures that investment will be concentrated on that which is measurable, and its focus is the five outcomes specified in *Every Child Matters*. The following is the Government's explanation of the 'The Outcomes Framework':

Keeping the outcomes in mind at all times helps us all to focus on how services can better be brought together around the child, young person and family. But if the outcomes are to be really effective in driving change, it is important to be clear what they mean in practice and how progress towards them will be measured.

We have developed an outcomes framework to act as a basis for agreeing local priorities and planning local change. The framework shows the relationships between outcomes, aims, targets, indicators and inspection criteria.[28]

However, whilst outcomes are the aim, what is actually measured is outputs – those targets that can be measured. The four-page grid from *Every Child Matters Outcomes Framework* gives, for example, the following as 'Priority national targets and indicators' for the 'Children and Young People live healthy lifestyles' aim of the 'Be healthy' outcome: 'Average alcohol consumption (DH); % Children who are regular smokers (DH); % Children consuming 5 portions of fruit & veg a day (DH)' (2005: 1). This relates to one of five aims for the 'Be healthy' outcome. In the section specifying how the inspectorate will judge the contribution of services to improving outcomes, the following judgements have to be made across the five aims of the 'Be healthy' section:

1.1 Parents and carers receive support to keep their children healthy
1.2 Healthy lifestyles are promoted for children & young people
1.3 Action is taken to promote children & young people's physical health
1.4 Action is taken to promote children & young people's mental health
1.5 Looked after children's health needs are addressed
1.6 The health needs of children & young people with learning difficulties and/or disabilities are addressed. (ibid)

The same approach is taken to the 'be safe', 'enjoy and achieve', 'make a positive contribution', and 'achieve economic well-being' outcomes.

Investment as problematic in practice

Despite concerns around specific issues such as smacking and data storage, the passage of the Children Act 2004 provoked very little popular concern. The mix of universal and targeted services appeared to offer no threat to family; the policy was presented as a sensible reorganisation to maximise resources for safeguarding children and there was no specificity about extra resources. The Act in effect reverses the incorporation – at the end of the 1960s – of children's services into generic social work departments by the Local Authority and Social Services Act 1970, resulting from the Seebohm Report (1968). So the family and its autonomous importance is not seemingly an issue. Further, as noted, the Green and White Papers which preceded the 2004 Act and the subsequent *Youth Matters* Green Paper used a discourse of increasing opportunities and were permeated with strong arguments for investing in preventative services, whilst the proposals for new means to reduce drug use, teenage pregnancy, youth offending and 'worklessness' fed easily into popular anxieties.

However, investment as a justifying concept has its drawbacks. The child becomes a risk-managed investment and, in this economic discourse, the fear is of a bad investment, that the investment may not prevent offending, unemployment, obesity, teenage pregnancy or any other of the national priority targets. So the investment agenda requires a 'pay-off': if the benefits do not accrue or are not likely to materialise, then investment will cease (Lister 2005: 455–6).[29] In this context, the Preface to *Youth Matters* shows the potential punitive face of investment: 'It is wrong that young people who do not respect the opportunities they are given, by committing crimes or behaving anti-socially, should benefit from the same opportunities as the law-abiding majority. So we will put appropriate measures in place to ensure they do not' (DfES 2005b: 1). The result is that, 'Active, responsible citizenship is encouraged, indeed mandated, but children must take the consequences if they do not 'play ball'' (Piper 2001) and, as Horwarth notes, 'we could end up making a distinction between those deserving help and support and those who need punishing' (Horwarth 2006: 7). This focus justifies the 'this is your one chance' approach of much of current Government child and youth policy, indeed all domestic policy. The citizen is a person who is seen as 'a customer in whom choices must be cultivated as he or she seeks to fulfil him- or herself and maximize his or her quality of life' (Vaughan 2000: 354).

What is also of concern is that new projects of social investment in children are often given a very short period of funding in which to prove their worth in the same way that individual children must use their opportunities – or their opportunity cards – responsibly to good effect. For both projects and children, poor returns justify either closure or diversion to more punitive methods of regulation. In 2000 Vaughan wrote that 'Just as social policy is becoming more conditional, so is juvenile justice' (2000: 349). We might say that just as juvenile justice has become conditional, so have children's services. This approach could have severe practical implications as Goldson warns: to 'adulterize' and 'responsibilize' those minors who used to be referred to as 'children in trouble' amounts, he argues, to 'the abrogation of professional responsibilities toward "children in need"' (2000: 262). 'In need' was supposed to be an inclusive concept and not one that stigmatised, but the lack of resources has, in practice, done just that. A conditional investment in children could make matters worse. Access to services that children might not otherwise have had – if funded in the context of risk of offending – may stigmatise the child as a criminal, even if eight years old.

Investment policies to enable children to become productive and healthy future citizens has prompted, not surprisingly, the criticism that 'the emphasis seems to be more about supporting the process of *becoming an adult* than fostering the active enjoyment of childhood' (Williams 2004: 80). Only to an extent has this criticism been addressed by the third of the five stated principles underpinning *The Children's Plan*: 'Children and young people need to enjoy their childhood as well as grow up prepared for adult life' (DCSF 2007: 5). Whether this principle will be taken seriously and act as a counterweight to notions of investment gains remains to be seen, as does the extent to which the new Safeguarding Boards, Children's Trusts and the work of the YJB can more effectively tackle the reasons for poor outcomes. Experience from past practice cannot fail to raise doubts as to the effectiveness of the components of this new investment venture. Will more weight be placed on the duty to 'have regard to' the promotion of the child's best interests? Will information be more effectively gathered and shared? Will risk assessments and predictions be sufficiently accurate? Section 15 of the Children Act 2004, which deals with the funding of Safeguarding Boards, is permeated with discretion: the bodies specified 'may make payment' and they 'may provide' goods and services and, as Chapter 6 will argue, the courts have not generally interfered with this discretion even if that means children do not receive services. Further, as Eileen Munro has noted,

'Improving the way professionals share information and dovetail their services has been the holy grail of child welfare reform for decades' (Munro 2003), a seemingly unattainable objective which diverts from more pressing solutions.

The relatively easy passage of the Children Act 2004 and the somewhat bland and optimistic statements in *The Children's Plan* mask, however, other issues, notably how parents are to be co-opted and coerced into the investment venture. The ideology which has helped to mould the image of the child into that of the responsible future citizen, yet someone who is still – at times – innocent and dependent, is associated with a remoralisation agenda which itself has strengthened ideas about parental responsibility. How does this square with investment in the child and intervention in the child's family? This is what the next chapter will consider.

Notes

1 For a recent new analysis of the 1867 Act, see Hall *et al.* (2000).
2 The phrase coined by Robert Lowe, who was to become the Chancellor of the Exchequer.
3 Accessed at http://www.imprint.co.uk/books/Shipman_Ch1.pdf.
4 See http://www.electoralcommission.org.uk/media-centre/votesare power.cfm.
5 http://www.dfes.gov.uk/citizenship/section.cfm?sectionId=16&hierarchy =16 (accessed 11.10.07); now http://www.youthinformation.com (accessed 12.5.08).
6 The 1893 'Half-Time' Act allowed 10 and 11-year-olds to work half the week and attend school the other half: the provision was abolished by an Act of 1918.
7 See also http://www.channel4.com/life/microsites/J/jamies_school_ dinners/porridge/index.html (accessed 9.10.06). However, an extra category was added in 2003 in relation to Child Tax Credit.
8 *Hansard* HC col. 593 (28 October 2005).
9 See, for example, http://www.womens-institute.co.uk/campaigns/ childdiet-c.shtml (accessed 9.10.06). The second Reading was resumed in July 2006.
10 However, the Criminal Justice and Immigration (CJI) Bill of 2007 proposes an amendment to section 44 of the Children and Young Persons Act 1933 such that new subsections 1A and 1B will be inserted to make it clear that the 'principal aim' of the youth justice system, to prevent offending by persons under 18, must take precedence: see Chapter 8.
11 See http://www.everychildmatters.gov.uk/strategy/localnetworkfund/ (accessed 25.9.07).

12 See http://www.hm-treasury.gov.uk/spending_review/spend_ccr/
spend_ccr_child.cfm (posted in 2001; accessed 7.11.06).

13 Statement to House of Commons, 15 July 2002; see http://www.hm-
treasury.gov.uk/spending_review/spend_ccr/spend_ccr_voluntary/
spend_ccr_fromSR2002speech.cfm.

14 Tony Blair's statement was reproduced in the House of Lords the
following day by The Lord Privy Seal (Lord Richard): *Hansard* HL col.
WA 20 (9 December 1997); now see: http://www.crimereduction.gov.
uk/websites/websites18.htm (accessed 25.9.07).

15 For other analysts, poor school attainment is a crucial aspect of the
'missing link', that is, deficient social capital, in the perpetuation of
deprivation (see Bruegal and Warren 2003: 319). See, for current research
on social exclusion, the ESCR funded Families and Social Capital Project
which is based at South Bank University.

16 'At its simplest, a discourse is a social process in which, through language
(used in its broadest sense to include all semiotic systems) we make sense
of the world around us, but also the process by which the world makes
sense to us' (Cox, 1996: 6, referring to O'Sullivan *et al.* 1994).

17 See http://www.newdeal.gov.uk/.

18 The origins of community initiatives to tackle multiple deprivation are
less clear: see http://www.neighbourhood.gov.uk/page.asp?id=617.

19 *Hansard*, Westminster Hall, 17 April 2007.

20 'Eradicating Child Poverty', speech given at the *End Child Poverty*
conference on 10 December 2007.

21 http://www.everychildmatters.gov.uk/aims/outcomes/
(accessed 11.10.07).

22 See http://www.everychildmatters.gov.uk/strategy/childrensfund/
(accessed 25.9.07).

23 See, for example, Beinhart *et al.* 2002 for the results of the Communities
that Care survey of factors associated with greater or lower risk of
'problem behaviour' in a sample of children in years 7–11 in 2001/2.

24 http://www.yjb.gov.uk (accessed 26.10.06); the website at 7.12.2007 states
that YISPs 'have been designed to help the YJB achieve its corporate
target of reducing the number of first-time entrants into the criminal
justice system by 5 per cent by 2008'.

25 See the policy aim to give 'prevention of offending' a wider remit – see
Responses to YJ, *Next Steps* (paras 8 and 30).

26 See also see DfES 2004: para. 4.22.

27 Whilst there is no requirement to call the new administrative bodies
Children's Trusts, the aim must be to secure 'integrated working at all
levels'. See http://www.everychildmatters.gov.uk/aims/childrenstrusts/.

28 http://www.everychildmatters.gov.uk/aims/outcomes/
(accessed 11.10.07).

29 Note also that it is seen as part of the 'hollowing out' of the welfare
state' (Roberts and Devine 2003: 312) and as 'governing at a distance'
(Crawford 2003: 487, 490).

Chapter 4

Reconstructing parental responsibility

The family is a fundamental building block of society, and the success of families is, first and foremost, down to the commitments and behaviour of the individuals within them. … It is right to be wary of state interference in family life. However, it would be far too simplistic to demand that the state withdraw altogether. The role that families play within society requires a legal framework to function effectively. (*Building on Progress: Families*, PMSU 2007: 10)

Traditionally, parenting has been a 'no-go' area for governments – but now it is an essential area for us to focus on. (Alan Johnson, then Education Secretary, February 2007, cited in Lubcock 2008: 20)

A modern family policy starts from what helps family life to flourish. Our vision is of all families being confident in their ability to achieve the best for their child. (*The Children's Plan*, DCFS 2007: 19)

The parent: problem or partner?

The development and implementation of child-focused policy requires, as we saw in Chapter 2, particular ideas about the child, childhood and a child's best interests. But the role of parents is also crucial in any investment agenda for two reasons. First, there is an interplay of ideas about the child's best interests, historically contingent political and economic factors, and notions about morality and the role and remit of 'the family'. Without complementary ideas about the family, policies to benefit children will face difficulties. Secondly, when children live with 'their' family, the state cannot invest in a particular child without intervening in that family. To do that, one or both of the following still contentious ideas must be seen as acceptable by parliament and public:

- The state can (and should) intervene in the family against the wishes of the child's parents when parents are 'the problem'.
- The state can 'share' responsibility with parents for the upbringing of their children: parents ought, or wish, to be partners with the state in this enterprise.

Whether these notions are generally acceptable again depends on a complex mix of factors, including perceptions of children, what are deemed to be the 'pressing needs' of the state and ideas about how far and in what ways parents should be responsible and autonomous or held accountable. Further, the extent to which intervention and sharing are countenanced has a direct bearing on how risk-based services can be delivered and, in particular, whether those services should be universal or targeted and whether any 'enforcement' will be deemed legitimate.

Historically, religious and social ideas about how parents 'should' behave and bring up their children, and norms about how much privacy and authority they should be accorded in so doing, have been crucial in encouraging or blocking child-focused provisions. Even during the 'long reign' of the previous Conservative governments, 'The more intimate features of family life were seen as a distinct private sphere lying beyond the boundaries of legitimate state intervention' (Gillies 2008: 96). Provisions to regulate the behaviour of parents, employers and others (with or without cost implications for those people or those 'policing' them) or to explicitly authorise state expenditure (local or national) on children do not see the light of day if the strong social norm, backed up by specific religious or moral precepts, is that the family is sacrosanct and all aspects of a child's upbringing must be left entirely to one or both parents.

This norm of non-intervention is one end of a continuum of degrees of intervention into family life by the state and one which largely describes the approach before the 19th century. The exceptions – where the state did intervene – can be found in those medieval, feudal courts which dealt with the wardship of minors, and in the Poor Law established in Tudor England. Both institutions dealt mainly with children without parents. Wardship courts dealt originally only with rich children, the Poor Law mainly with those made orphans through death or abandonment: the autonomy of the family was not an issue. The problem arose when the child *did* have a family but that family was not financially independent.

The difficulty of giving assistance to such families is evidenced by the various categorisations of adult (parents) over the centuries into the 'impotent' and 'idle' poor, and the development of the principle of 'less eligibility' by the Poor Law Amendment Act 1834 (see Cretney 2003: 635–42). If the state felt forced to look after children, parents were in effect punished by labelling, by the receipt of minimal relief under deterrent conditions and, during the decades when outdoor relief was not given, by separation from their children in the workhouse. This strand continues. The Children Act 1989 mandates the local authority to provide accommodation under section 20 to children – but not the children's family – who come within its provisions. Further, the courts have upheld in *R (W) v Lambeth LBC*[1] what is a essentially a deterrent policy of placing homeless children in foster care so that applications for accommodation are discouraged (see Chapter 6).

But parental responsibility is not a 'dead' historical or purely theoretical issue. As Collier notes, 'For some, indeed, no less than the very future of the "family" is what is at stake in the contestations around the legal status of fatherhood' (Collier 2001: 510). In particular, in the UK there is current debate as to the extent to which the status of parental responsibility should be accorded to unmarried fathers because sections 2–4 of the Children Act 1989 provide no automatic status for them (see the discussion below). There is also academic critique of any extensions of state power into the family (see, for example, Guggenheim 2005) and frequent comment in the popular press about the 'nanny state'.[2] The state cannot intervene directly in the family – however compelling the science to justify a particular early intervention might or might not be – unless there is clear legislative approval and there are also clear legal criteria to do so. Section 31 of the Children Act 1989 in relation to children at risk of significant harm within their family is one of the few examples of legislation which allows compulsory intervention (see Chapter 6). Unless parental behaviour can be brought within this or any other child protection or criminal law provision then the issue moves to that of how parents can be 'persuaded' to take up services for their children.

The history of child-focused legislation over the last two centuries is consequently reflective of a gradual process by which the norm of family autonomy has been remodelled and the responsibility of parents recast. The arguments of reformers have their place in this remodelling but their strength and influence has depended on what we might refer to as social anxiety. Because of social, political and economic changes – and the angst which results – particular social issues become more acute, provoking more urgent calls for finding a solution and a greater readiness to rethink political, social and moral assumptions. What this recurrent process has not produced in the UK, however, is a gradual move to the logical end of the continuum where the state takes nearly all responsibility for children. As Cretney has noted, the Curtis Committee (1946) – a major influence on the Children Act 1948 – had been fully aware of the strength of public opinion critical of any incursion into parental rights (Cretney 1998: 226) and the *Review of Child Care Law* in the 1980s had also made very clear the importance of upholding the autonomy of the family (DHSS 1985: 6).

There are still limits to incursions into parental autonomy. The Children Act 2004 ultimately included a compromise provision relating to the defence of reasonable chastisement for anyone hitting a child (see Chapter 6): the amendment to the then clause 49[3] meant that 'smacking' was not fully outlawed. This was criticised by the Parliamentary Joint Committee on Human Rights but accepted as upholding 'traditional' parental responsibility to discipline children. Policy documents continue to uphold parental authority but they also do something else:

> So, the aim is to support families in all their variety. But this is not an area of policy that government can simply pursue on its own. Family policy necessarily reaches into the private domain where the state can only act in conjunction with individuals and families. Some families need a modicum of support. The role of government is to provide them with a platform, to enable them to take responsibility for themselves. (Prime Minister Tony Blair in PMSU 2007: 4)

What has occurred has been a significant reconfiguration of parental responsibility alongside the new images of children and young people that were examined in Chapter 2. New Labour governments have evidenced 'a preoccupation with the governance of parenting' (Henricson 2008: 150) and what Lubcock has termed a new phase of 'performance managed parenting' (2008: 15). The result has been that parents have been accorded more, not less, responsibility for their children's development, but that responsibility has been recast as accountability (Reece 2005). Parents can now be held responsible for a whole range of behaviours exhibited by their children: a situation in marked contrast to that in the early 19th century when parents were rarely held accountable even for their abuse of their children. Responsibility is now a concept, however, which reinforces and reflects government investment policies. Without it, the investment agenda would be more costly and less acceptable, although there are disadvantages to this concept which may well, in the long run, have a deleterious impact on families (see Chapter 8).

To summarise: the last two centuries have seen two strands in relation to parental responsibility. First, parents have lost responsibility in that they have been forced to share aspects of their child's upbringing with the state and, secondly, parents have been made responsible for an ever-widening range of harms to their children. Both strands have depended on the development of the idea that parents *can* harm their children and can be held to account, and both strands have evidenced differential impacts on mothers and fathers. How did this happen? I will try to answer this by examining particular aspects of children's lives where state intervention and expenditure has been a social and parliamentary issue in the past and the present: their employment, their offending, their sexual activity, their education and nutrition, and their treatment by their parents.

Keeping children (and their mothers) at home

Employment of children

From the early 19th century, those campaigners concerned about the very poor conditions in which children were employed were increasingly motivated by a vision of 'children without a childhood' (see Chapter 2). Their response was to argue for regulation of those new and harmful 'spaces' that had been created by a rapid process of industrialisation and urbanisation. The hurdle that they faced, personally in their own thinking as well as in the social response, was a strong moral norm about the role of the family as well as strong fears about the ability of the working class family to fulfil that role. What emerged as very important during this period was the idea of the family as essentially a moral, autonomous and paternalistic unit, in which the 'moralisation' of children was even more important than their physical protection. The basis for such thinking was a Victorian interpretation of tenets of the Christian religion that placed the father as the 'natural' head of the family and that accorded him whatever moral, religious and practical authority he needed to ensure the moral values of society were adequately inculcated in the dependent members of the family. Consequently, the socialisation of the young was, and in some world religions still is, perceived as a divinely ordered system. To interfere with a father's power and responsibility to carry out this task was (and in some cultures and jurisdictions still is) seen as too dangerous a risk.

The first piece of legislation to protect children in employment – the Parish Apprentices Act of 1802 – was one where parental responsibility was not an issue, the (orphan) children having been sent to northern mills by Poor Law Boards (see Cretney 2003: 628–9). The successful extension of this Act to all children, by the Cotton Mills Act 1819, reflected the argument that factories and mines were places where parents could not be expected to be able to protect and guide their children. Consequently, intervention to help such children would be no interference with the authority of the family and, in particular, of the father. This was important because the moral agendas being pursued by reformers depended on particular historical perceptions of how children were being 'wronged'. What reformers constructed as most 'seriously wrong' in relation to the treatment of children also flowed from their moral codes about how social and private life should be organised.

The great fear – linked to that of the great 'danger' of sexualised children (see Chapter 2) – was, then, that children (and their mothers) would be out of the reach of the 'moralising' influence of the home and the father (and husband).

> The saving of the industrial child reflects a moral concern: the presence of women and children in industry was repeatedly linked to *their* depravity. The picture of vice and indecency in factories and mines was drawn as much to point to the dangers of a demoralised working class ... as to protest on behalf of child victims. (Cannan 1992: 53)

Those moral fears are clearly evident in the speech made in Parliament by Lord Shaftesbury (then Lord Ashley) in 1844 in the debate on the Factories Bill dealing with hours of labour. After outlining the poor working conditions of children, he focused on the women who 'not only perform the labour but occupy the places of men'. He was particularly concerned that they were 'forming various clubs and associations', and to illustrate his point he related the following eye-witness account:

> A man came into one of these clubrooms, with a child in his arms; 'Come lass,' said he addressing one of the single women, 'come home for I cannot keep this bairn quiet, and the other one I have left crying at home.' 'I won't go home, idle devil', she replied, 'I have thee to keep and the bairns too, and if I can't get a pint of ale quietly, it is tiresome … I won't go home yet'.

His point was that these changes in employment were 'a perversion … of nature' and were having 'the inevitable effect of introducing into families disorder, insubordination and conflict' with a resultant deleterious effect on 'the health of the females; the care of their families; their conjugal and parental duties; the comfort of their homes; the decency of their lives; the rights of their husbands; the peace of society; and the laws of God' (see Piper 1999b: 41).

In this complex interrelationship of religion, ideologies of the family and socio-economic changes, the home was accorded an almost mystical power. To quote the comment of R.W. Cooke Taylor (a reformer and Factory Inspector) in 1874: 'That unit, the family, is the unit upon which a constitutional Government has been raised which is the admiration and envy of mankind. Hitherto, whatever the laws have touched, they have not invaded *this sacred precinct* …' (quoted in Pinchbeck and Hewitt 1973: 359, emphasis added); 'I would far rather see even a higher rate of infant mortality prevailing … than intrude one iota on the sanctity of the domestic hearth' (quoted in Bilston: undated). Given such views, early employment legislation was legitimated by the construction of government intervention in the workplace, not as an interference in the family, but as an endorsement of a strong sense of paternal responsibility. So Michael Sadler, speaking in favour of an amendment to the Ten Hours Bill in 1932, urged punishment for the factory master 'who knowingly tolerates the infliction of this cruelty on abused infancy, *this insult upon parental feeling*' (quoted in Ward 1970: 101, emphasis added).

The result of this recasting was the protection of children but also the protection of their mothers in a way which restricted their economic and social autonomy whilst emphasising paternal authority. New differentiated notions of parental responsibility emerged.

Keeping children 'moral'

Though parents were indeed 'sending' their children to factories and mines, the above reasoning meant that the family continued to be seen as a protective and inviolable unit. This notion of family was contingent on particular ideas about the overriding moral function of patriarchal family life, still evident in the statement of the Maloney Report in 1927 that 'The neglect that is being talked about, however, is not a want of physical care but an attention to the control and moral education of children' (Dingwall *et al.* 1984: 216). That priority, however, meant that state intervention could be justified if parents themselves were constructed as 'wicked' on the ground that *they* were the source of wickedness in their children. If the 'evil' child is constructed as a victim of irresponsible parents who have deprived him of proper paternal moral control then the child can legitimately be protected by the state from the possibility of becoming permanently 'evil'. The state can intervene to remedy the deficit and substitute the moral guidance provided by state institutions for that which should have been provided by the family.

Whilst this idea surfaced in the 18th century and led to the setting up by charitable bodies of 'preventative' schemes and voluntary industrial schools to respond to juvenile criminality (see Pinchbeck and Hewitt 1973: 530–2), that was not yet sufficient to justify state action and expenditure. Parliamentary Bills for wider provision failed in the 1820s (see Dingwall *et al.* 1982: 214 *et seq*). The social insecurity occasioned by rapid industrialisation, apparent particularly in the 1840s, facilitated a reconfiguration of aspects of the dominant moral code (see Piper 1999b: 43–4). It became more widely acceptable to send children 'at risk' of criminality to industrial schools for training and convicted young offenders to reformatories. Several Industrial School Acts were passed in the period 1857–80, and the Youthful Offenders Act 1854 made reformatory schools an alternative to adult prisons and houses of correction for juvenile offenders. In a further twist, the new thinking was justified as 'good' for the parents: 'The evil was as much the spiritual harm which befell the abusers as the physical or moral damage sustained by their victims' (Dingwall *et al.* 1984: 218).

This idea of an overriding parental duty to keep children 'moral' has never gone away and, as we shall see, has been recast in relation to the five outcomes of *Every Child Matters*.

Safeguarding children from sex

A major reason why, in the 19th century, the city street became constituted as a space which was a danger to children was because it was a place where parents could neither protect their children from sexual assaults nor control their children's sexuality. In that space, the child's innocence would be destroyed by contact with sexuality, morals would be corrupted and she (and it was usually a she) would become 'depraved' (see Chapter 2). This conflation of dominant fears can be seen, for example, in the evidence given to the 1882 Select Committee about girl street sellers in Liverpool. That included the statement that 'though she may carry a basket, there is very little difference between her and a prostitute' (quoted in Behlmer 1982: 89). Similarly, Gordon's research in North America found, 'The Victorian conviction that children should be domestic and unseen, and the fear of [sexual] "precocity" in children, were part of the characteristic anti-urban bias of so many reformers of the time' (Gordon 1988: 40). The fears about sexual knowledge continued into the early 20th century: Pryke notes, for example, in relation to the early Boy Scouts movement, that the prevalent approach was that the boy's parents 'were best placed to plant the "sacred knowledge"' (Pryke 2005).

Again, the focus on children often hid much wider anxieties. The campaign to amend the law on the age of consent was, arguably, not essentially child-focused: the aim was to control females – whether children or adults. The Criminal Law Amendment Act 1885 raised the age of consent for girls to 16 but for boys only to 14: '[E]ach unprincipled, impure girl left to grow up, and become a mother, is likely to increase her kind three to five fold', wrote a Mrs Wardner in 1879 (see Platt 1969: 27). When Jane Tyrell was (unsuccessfully) prosecuted under section 5 of the new Act, Lord Coleridge CJ pointed out that the Act 'was passed for the purpose of protecting women and girls against themselves',[4] (see Piper 2000: 26).

Class and gender, then, played a role in constructing particular images of innocent children and good parents. Middle class fears that 'their' ideas about appropriate behaviour for women were not being upheld within the 'unrespectable poor' sections of society became focused on prostitution and the age of consent. The Social Purity Movement (see Cox 1996: 149) was in effect a symbolic moral crusade to impose a particular form of morality and also a particular idea about what the good parent 'should' do. Evidence of the horror with which this issue was met can be found in the title of a book written by William Logan – *The Great Social Evil: Its Causes, Extent,*

Results and Remedies, published in 1871, and in the phrase 'fear that starts at shadows' used by William Acton in the preface to his book, *Prostitution Considered in its Moral, Social and Sanitary Aspects* (2nd edn, 1870, reprinted 1972 at p. viii).

Such state intervention in the lives of women and children upset no moral code: it occurred only when the state was supporting a paternal role or itself taking on the paternal role: 'The state gradually became a sort of moral husband through the development of forms of "protective legislation" (Smart 1992: 25; see also Piper 2000: 31). So, regulating employment and prostitution equated to enforcing particular segregated gender roles as well as safeguarding children and 'good' parents had to uphold such roles. Again, the family's inability to provide successful moral training legitimated state intervention and, in this case, the expense of regulation and prosecution. Again, it differentiated maternal and paternal responsibility.

Protecting children from harm at home: the beginnings of accountability

The Prevention of Cruelty and Better Protection of Children Act 1889 (the 'Prevention of Cruelty Act') was a very significant marker of a change in attitudes to parental responsibility. Its success probably did not flow from any radical change in popular attitudes to parental cruelty at that time because Pollock's research, using newspapers in the period 1784–1860, shows there had already been prosecutions of parents for assault (Pollock 1983). One Justice of the Peace had explicitly denied that 'the father had a right to do as he pleased' (ibid: 62–4; see also Dingwall *et al.* 1984: 219); the idea that assault on wife or child was simply 'excessive' discipline was being contested by the mid-19th century.

Neither had notions of the sanctity of the home changed radically. For example, the following sentiments were published in 1883:

> Estimate the healing, comforting, purifying, elevating influence which is ever flowing from the fountain, and you will understand the sacred ministry of the home to the higher culture of mankind. It is a mighty restraint of the selfish passions. It is the centrifugal force which continually widens the orbit of life, and bears us into the light of distant suns. (Brown 1883:[5] 47, quoted in Behlmer 1982: 46)

Cooke Taylor (see above) 'chose' child poverty above intrusions into the 'sacred' family because he believed the greater 'evil' was interference with family life. The following comment by Lord Shaftesbury, made as late as 1871, is often quoted to illuminate this point: '[T]he evils you state are enormous and indisputable, but they are of so private, internal and domestic a character as to be beyond the reach of legislation, and the subject, indeed, would not, I think, be entertained by either House of Parliament' (see Pinchbeck and Hewitt 1973: 622).

What had changed was that physical evidence of child cruelty had become more visible once the Education Act of 1870 had ensured more children attended school (see Hendrick 1994: 29–33, 50) and, moreover, this greater knowledge occurred in the context of another decade of social and economic unrest (Piper 1999b: 46–7). This generated fears about the political stability of the country and specific fears about the 'health' of England and the British Empire. For example, General William Booth (1890) of the Salvation Army wrote *In Darkest England and the Way Out*, a report entitled with reference to the then perception of 'Darkest' Africa. He, and others, notably Charles Booth in his 17-volume *Life and Labour of the People in London* (Booth 1902–3), provided detailed evidence about the lives of the very poor, what William Booth referred to as 'the submerged tenth'. At the same time as both William and Charles Booth began publishing, Beatrice Webb was writing about the East End of London in her diary in 1886: 'There are times when one loses all faith in laisser-faire and would suppress the poison at all regards for it eats the life of the nation' (Webb 1926: Chapter 6). Non-intervention in the family was losing its stranglehold.

It was these factors, together with images of the parentally abused child as one with 'no refuge at home', which led to change in notions of the family and which, in turn, enabled the state to justify intervention to punish parental cruelty. What resulted was a 'rebalancing' of perceived evils. Nevertheless, the first 'Prevention of Cruelty Bill', introduced in 1888, failed and the successful Bill of 1889 incorporated amendments (see Piper 1999b: 47). The resulting Prevention of Cruelty Act created the offence of ill-treating or neglecting a girl under 16 or boy under 14 years of age, as well as other specific offences, and gave the courts civil powers to remove a child to the care of a 'fit person' who could retain the child even if the parent objected. As Cretney notes, there was a precedent in the Infant Felons Act 1840 which had been passed against vigorous opposition (Cretney 2003: 634, n. 44), but that Act, largely inoperative, gave the

Court of Chancery powers only to transfer the care of the child of a convicted serious offender: a parent who had in any case forfeited moral authority. The 1891 Custody of Children Act, which empowered courts to refuse to uphold a parent's right to custody, should also be seen in the context in which it was passed. It was a response to the use of *habeas corpus* proceedings by parents who wanted to 'get back' the children in Dr Barnardo's homes. The assumption was that these parents had abandoned their children and were not fit to have them back.

The debate on further legislation to strengthen the provisions of the 1889 Act in 1894 prompted Lord Herschell to say that the powers that the 1889 Act had conferred had led to fears being expressed that 'it might involve so much interference with parental control as to lead to dangerous results' (*Hansard* xxiv, col. 1609 (1894), quoted in Pinchbeck and Hewitt 1973: 629).

Yet it *was* very 'dangerous' – though not in the way Lord Herschell envisaged. What it did do was provide an implicit public endorsement of the idea that parents could be the source of harm to their children, and not just moral harm. This strand – the idea that what parents do or do not do is important and worthy of state control – is an essential component of the current concept of parental responsibility. However, what the 1889 legislation did not do was dent the idea that parents were still totally and solely responsible for the upbringing of their children. That idea was breached by the issues of state-mandated education and state expenditure on the feeding of school children, which led to the acceptability of a limited idea of partnership between parents and state.

Parental partnership with the state

Teaching children

Decades of disagreement about the role of religious bodies in providing education postponed adoption of the first Education Act (Forster's Act) until 1870 (see Tomaševski 1999: para. 10). When it was passed, its significance was not that the state for the first time financed education or that it provided free primary education: it did not. The 1870 Act empowered School Boards to provide free schooling if they so wished, but the abolition of (parental) fees in state schools was not legislated until 1891. Further, in 1833 the Government had started to direct grants to provide schools and had set up an Education

Department in 1856. The 1870 Act's importance in actually providing universal education is also contested in that there is evidence that immediately before the Act was passed 'most people were literate, most children had some schooling; and parents were paying fees for it' (West 1970). In 1861 the Newcastle Commission on education had proposed further state aid only to existing schools, arguing that 'almost everyone received some amount of school education at some period or other' (ibid). Forster himself said the aim was to fill the gaps left by voluntary provision and thought that School Boards would only be needed in areas where there was a serious deficiency (ibid).

Even if there had been a clear deficiency of places, this might not have been sufficient: the Taunton Commission enquiring into the provision of secondary education in the 1860s did find that the provision was inadequate, but nothing was done until the 1902 (Balfour's) Education Act. The idea of parental responsibility for education of children was still strong. The significance of the 1870 Act is, therefore, that the state legislated its right to educate children and control their attendance against the wishes of parents. After 1870, as West argues, once the machinery had been set up by the Act, 'Even Forster … could not stop this administrative horse from galloping' (West 1970).

Feeding children

Universal education made more visible not only the effect of cruelty to children by parents but also the fact that some parents could not feed their children. As noted in Chapter 3, visibly starving children posed a dilemma for the new School Boards set up after 1870: starving children cannot learn properly and so were wasting the public money spent on their education. Yet to feed those children was seen as undermining the duty of the family to do so and might further erode the sense of responsibility it was felt parents should hold.

Those bodies organising the feeding of children through charitable effort were also opposed to the state taking on that role. Their concern was still that responsibility and 'moralisation' might be undermined. The Charity Organisation Society (COS), a very powerful umbrella organisation, summed up its approach to family services in its 1889 Annual Report, when it argued that 'everything should be done to help distress in such a way that it does not become a matter rather of public than of private concern' (quoted in Mowat 1961: 27). The COS consequently denounced the proposal for state-funded school meals in its report, 'The Better Way of Assisting School Children':

> It is better, in the interests of the community, to allow ... the
> sins of the parents to be visited on the children, than to impair
> the principle of the solidarity of the family and run the risk of
> permanently demoralising large numbers of the population by
> the offer of free meals to their children. (quoted by Pinchbeck
> and Hewitt 1973: 358)

Similarly, the Scottish evidence to the Select Committee considering
the 1906 Education (Provision of School Meals) Bill was opposed
to the Bill. Witnesses not only believed that charitable action was
proving adequate but that any government intervention 'would
undermine parental responsibility without improving the overall
situation'. Indeed, when the scope of the 1906 Act was confined to
England and Wales, the *Charity Organisation Review*, the journal of the
COS, noted how Scotland had been fortunate to escape 'this injurious
measure' (Stewart 2001: 185).

However, the passage of a more comprehensive measure for
Scotland, the Education (Scotland) Act, in 1908 revealed another factor:
the Scottish Liberals, in the face of increasing evidence of exceptional
need, wished to 'subvert the socialist "threat" by gaining the social
policy high ground' (Stewart 2001: 190). The fear of 'collectivism' was
a very real fear that helped to push thinking over the line dividing
'interference' with parental responsibility from responding justifiably
to malnourished school children. It was also a fear persisting into the
20th century: as Cretney notes, the Conservative Party campaign in the
General Election of 1924 warned that, if the Labour Party were elected,
'the home will be destroyed ... Children will be taken away from their
mothers and made the property of the State' (Lyman 1957, quoted in
Cretney 2003: 573, n. 44). The argument in response, from socialist and
some other political groups, was that the causes of starvation were
structural ones that parents could not address. It was not the fault
of parents, and so, some argued further, it did not undermine the
responsibility of parents to feed their children.

There was another factor, evident in Beatrice Webb's diary (see
above). Liberals and philanthropists started to accept the limits of what
they could achieve in the face of what were perceived to be serious
threats to the nation: state intervention and investment in families
might then be the lesser of two evils (see Chapter 3).

What this historical survey suggests is that policy change in relation
to teaching and feeding children was crucial, not only in developing

notions of investment in children but also in significantly reconstructing notions of parental responsibility. Indeed, the publication of *The Children's Plan* (DCSF 2007) emphasises once again the vital importance of the fact that parents and government came to accept the school as a site of partnership between parent and state, and as a space within which support and services – and surveillance – can be provided. It is the school which is to be the hub of a large proportion of the policies which the Plan outlines for children and families to build 'brighter futures'. The 21st century school is to 'play a central role' in relation to children, families and communities (ibid: 145, Box 7.1).

Intervention in parental partnerships

At the time of the above debates about school meals, the general rule was still that a married father could exercise exclusive authority over his child and that the married mother had no legal rights in relation to either care or control of her children. As Cretney notes, 'the law does not necessarily reflect everyday life' (Cretney 2003: 566–7), and parents then may have been as unaware of the legal situation as parents at the end of the 20th century were in relation to a cohabitant father's lack of rights (Pickford 1999; Sheldon 2001). Be that as it may, 19th century legislation had made few inroads into the father's common law rights (Cretney 2003: 566–9). State intervention was consequently less a question of intervening in 'the family' and more an issue of acting against the authority and wishes of the father. The Guardianship of Infants Act 1925 was significant in paving the way for later changes in thinking about the family, whereby the privileged legal position of the father became unjustifiable. It did not, however, address the demands of the women's lobby, notably the aim of NUSEC (National Union of Societies for Equal Citizenship) that men and women should have equal rights as parents. Not until the Guardianship of Infants Act 1973 did that actually happen. In the 1920s the view that prevailed was that children needed one source of authority in the family: duality of control would lead to harmful conflict and the courts were not a suitable place to resolve this.

What the 1925 Act did concede was that women could obtain custody by applying for a court order and that when the court had to determine such application, section 1 of the Act would apply. Section 1 of the Act read:

Where in any proceedings before any court ... the custody or upbringing of an infant ... is in question, the court, in deciding that question, shall regard the welfare of the infant as the first and paramount consideration, and shall not take into consideration whether from any other point of view the claim of the father, or any right at common law possessed by the father, in respect of such custody, upbringing, administration or application is superior to that of the mother, or the claim of the mother is superior to that of the father.

Eventually, a case in 1970 established that this welfare principle was paramount.[6]

Subsequently, courts reflected and confirmed constructions of the child's best interests which gave priority to care by the primary caretaker, the mother, and, whilst such an assumption no longer applies, its existence helped to rebalance earlier constructions of the overriding importance of the father. Further, potential or actual 'duality of control' meant that, for the sake of the child, the state might legitimately supervise arrangements when the parental partnership broke down. The 1925 Act therefore led to the acceptance of the idea that it was legitimate for the courts to oversee and to adjudicate the decisions made about children on marriage breakdown (Cretney 2003: 573).

Further developments in thinking around parental responsibility eventually led to the introduction of a new legal concept of parental responsibility by the Children Act 1989 (see Piper 1995: 35–7). This established the principle that each parent who has or acquires parental responsibility can separately exercise that responsibility and that the state needs the co-operation or consent of both parents when it is acting in partnership with parents. The implementation of the Act caused initial difficulties, for example, in relation to decisions such as the choice of school for a child and the release of school reports (Piper 1994, 1995). The other side of the coin is that partnership with the state may be imposed on one or both parents (as in effect it was in relation to school meals and medical inspections) and that a lack of cooperation in partnership can itself be grounds for triggering compulsory intervention. The threat of a local authority application to the court for a care order under section 31 of the Children Act 1989 is the obvious example. Social work guidance enjoins the professional to work in partnership with parents, but parents may feel they are not equal partners when the failure to co-operate might lead to a court order which allows their child to be taken away (Eekelaar 1991: 41;

King 1995; Masson 2005). Partnership between parents and between parents and state may have become the new 'messages' of legislation by the end of the 20th century, but in practice that ideology might not reflect the lives of families (Piper 1993: 161–9) or the realities of parent social worker relationships (see Kaganas *et al.* 1995).

Parenting responsibly: a widening remit

The new legal concept of parental responsibility (PR) was intended to be very important in the legal structure of the new framework for private and public family law, but its function was more than that. The policy intention was that it would encourage a rethinking about the responsibilities of the family and a downgrading of any idea of parents having rights over their children. The *Gillick* case had established parental rights as existing for the child's benefit, and the new concept of parental responsibility was crucial. As one of the Law Commissioners, then Professor Hoggett, now Baroness Hale of Richmond, said, 'its aim was to emphasise the practical reality that bringing up children is a serious responsibility rather than a matter of legal rights' (Hoggett 1989: 217). Earlier, the Law Commission had noted that 'it might well be more appropriate to talk of parental *powers*, parental *authority*, or even parental *responsibilities*, rather than of rights' (Law Commission 1982: para. 4.19), a position it endorsed in 1985 (see Eekelaar 1991: 37), although it believed it was not practicable to provide a list of factors relating to parental responsibility (Law Commission 1988: para. 2.6).

Law 'on message'

The ideological and legal significance of parental responsibility as a concept is hard to overestimate. It was 'the conceptual building block used throughout the [Act]' (Hoggett 1989: 217). But it was also sending a message that fitted into both New Right ideology and communitarian or 'Third Way' ideas about the family as a source of 'responsibilisation' (Day Sclater and Piper 2000; Eekelaar 2001). Parental responsibility was also constructed to include responsibility for continuing to parent 'jointly' after divorce and for reducing any parental conflict over arrangements for children. As the *Report of the Matrimonial Causes Procedure Committee* had argued: 'we think it important that divorcing couples should be encouraged and advised to maintain their joint responsibility for their children and cooperate in this respect' (1985: para. 2.24), and the notion of the good parent constructed in these documents was one who gave priority to private ordering and to the maintenance of contact with both parents.

This overtly normative use of law and the crucial policy importance of a particular conception of the good parent was something which confused even practising lawyers. A sample of family law solicitors said they found it very difficult to explain PR to clients, as a question on the then Legal Aid Board's checklist for franchised firms required them to do. Their confusion stemmed from the fact that they were indeed trying 'to convey a message that went beyond legal concepts' (Piper 1999a: 103). In the context of divorce and separation, one said, 'I try to define parental responsibility ... *it being a recognition of being a parent* ... it's not open to one parent to make decisions unilaterally. But basically *to convey the impression that they are both still involved*' (ibid: 106, emphases added). Parental responsibility has become an attitude (Reece 2005: 470), a shifting construct which imposes responsibility. The growing importance in policy of the use of divorce mediation was another site where parental responsibility was both constructed and used as a technique to persuade parents to agree (Piper 1993).

The new informal dispute resolution processes and the concept of PR meant that legal as well as political discourse came to support the increasingly strong idea that parental powers are for the benefit only of the child, not the parent (Reece 2005: 460). For some solicitors interviewed in the mid-1990s, 'that meant conveying a particular idea about the parental responsibility of separating parents: "I would ... try to emphasise to the clients that it is their responsibility to do what is in the interests of children"' (Piper 1999a: 104).

Developments in the 1980s, in particular the high profile enquiries into child deaths on the one hand and large-scale investigation of sexual abuse on the other, had also brought into focus the issue of the power of the state – in this case local authority social services departments – and parental autonomy (Eekelaar 1991). More than one conception of parental responsibility underpinned debates on what became the Children Act 1989 with, arguably, the idea of responsibility for parenting belonging to parents, not the state, gaining dominance (ibid). The new legal concept of parental responsibility can be seen, then, as part of a wider shift to notions of parental responsibility and the role of the state (see also: Reece 2005: 460; Edwards and Halpern 1992: 118) and one that is mirrored in images of children as responsible citizens and as citizens of the future who take up all opportunities the state offers.

The responsibility of fathers

The state of the law in relation to the 'allocation' of parental responsibility to unmarried fathers is reflective of tensions between encouraging individual parental responsibility and of not undermining the family as an autonomous unit. Only married fathers gain parental responsibility automatically (Children Act 1989, section 2(1)): unmarried fathers are not yet automatically accorded parental responsibility, notwithstanding the amendment relating to registration on the birth certificate by the Adoption and Children Act 2002 and the fact that a father without parental responsibility can still be subject to the enforcement of his financial responsibility. Law here has been used to encapsulate long-held policy aims to encourage marriage, paternal responsibility and a stable family unit. An unmarried father can acquire parental responsibility if, with the mother's consent, he is registered as the father on the child's birth certificate, he makes a parental responsibility agreement with the mother, or the court makes an order (section 4, as amended). It is the latter option which, in practice, reveals the tensions because, whilst unmarried fathers are denied automatic parental responsibility, the case law arising from section 4 suggests that unmarried fathers who apply to the courts for an order are rarely refused parental responsibility. The three fold test of commitment, attachment, and having a legitimate reason for the application[7] has not proved a difficult hurdle to surmount and the *Re S (Parental Responsibility)*[8] case made clear that it was quite difficult to be categorised as a 'feckless' father (Kaganas 1996). Awarding parental responsibility is seen as both a reward for going to the trouble of applying – itself constructed as evidence of responsibility – and an encouragement to be responsible. This legal status awarded on minimal 'qualifications' is a far cry from the 'active parenting' model which other policy documents encourage (Collier 2001: 527).

The latest government proposal is that the default option – not the opt-in one currently operating – should be joint birth registration. The Green Paper putting forward this proposal is entitled *Joint birth registration: promoting parental responsibility* (DWP 2007b) and further remodels parental responsibility. It argues that 'Children have a right to know their parents take responsibility for them' (ibid: para 17): a 'good' parent does not undermine their children's 'rights' but the unmarried mother does not oppose the father's registration and the father does not shirk from being named. Parental responsibility has become a normative tool to encourage parental engagement and to operate as a shadow for bargaining and informal ordering. It has both resulted from and also encouraged a particular construction of parental responsibility which legitimates a focus on what the good parent 'should' do. A good example of the usefulness of this new construction can be found in relation to divorce.

Victims of separating parents: extending parental harms?

In the 1980s the idea of children as victims of divorce emerged in the social sciences, in political discourse and in the practices of mediation (Piper 1993). As noted in Chapter 2, the abortive Part II of the Family Law Act 1996, and debates on the Bill are perhaps the clearest evidence of the continuing usefulness of constructions of children as victims. 'Old' images were drawn on to promote the belief that children are harmed by parental conflict and separation and that parents are to be held responsible for that. The Act would have mandated parental attendance at a meeting to acquire relevant information and, at the very least, to consider attending mediation. The preferred outcome, the one that would constitute a separated parent as 'good', was the maintenance of contact by the child with both parents. Otherwise the child would be the 'victim' of her parents' divorce (see Piper 1996).[9] It justified changes in the process so that parents would have had to 'reflect' for a longer time than non-parents.

Other harms have been emphasised. The principle in section 1(d) of the Family Law Act 1996, 'that any risk to one of the parties to a marriage, and to any children, of violence from the other party should, so far as reasonably practicable, be removed or diminished', and the debate on Part IV (domestic violence remedies) constructed the child as harmed by domestic violence. More recently, the Government White Paper on parental separation confirms an intention to 'strongly promote' the use of mediation and to 'strongly encourage' parents to attend (DCA, DfES and DTI 2005: 11). The aim is not simply to divert parents from (expensive) court procedures but also to provide 'high quality accessible and child-focused information' which could assist 'even parents who would not have come to court in … focusing on their ongoing parental responsibilities and roles' (ibid: 20).

Notions of potential harm parents can cause to children have, consequently, been extended to cover two new 'harms' – harm caused by parental conflict and by experiencing inter-parental violence. The symbolic message to parents is that their separations and their arguments harm children, whilst their 'choice' not to acquire information such that they can responsibly make their own choices means they are not acting as good parents. This is not to say that parents do not welcome advice and information. In 2004 the Home Office published a research report based on the *2001 Citizenship Survey* (Home Office 2003b) in which 89 per cent of parents answering the relevant question stated that they were satisfied with the quantity and amount of parenting advice available. However, the research found 'key subgroups' of parents who had unmet needs for information (Creasey and Trikha 2004: iii). 'Fathers were less likely than mothers to be aware of, or have used, at least one formal source of advice … and were also less likely to have asked for advice' (ibid). Young parents, parents with higher levels of education, and able-bodied parents were more likely to have used sources of advice (ibid). The sub-text of the report was that all parents should be accessing advice. They cannot make proper choices or parent satisfactorily without it if they are to be seen as good 'citizen parents'.

Ensuring children behave responsibly and achieve the five outcomes

Increasingly, parents are being held to account for all aspects of a child's behaviour and development. They are to be the preventers of harm. It is the mothers who are to blame for 'bad' boys: they should have stopped them becoming anti-social or criminal (Campbell 2006)[10]; and it is fathers who are responsible for the illiteracy of their sons: they should have read to them more often (see, for example, DfES 2007d: 5, and the publication, now available on the 'teachernet' 'Engaging Fathers' website). What this evidences is a movement from parental responsibility to parenting responsibly, a transition from authority to accountability which has been rendered unproblematic, argues Reece, by the 'cataclysmic shift in meaning in the course of the 1990s' (Reece 2005: 463).

From authority to accountability

Parental authority has not been taken away but undermined by the need voluntarily to seek help and act in partnership with all relevant agencies. The clear message is that the help offered to parents to improve their parenting *should* be accepted: 'responsibility *for* their children has been undermined by their responsibility *to* external agencies' (ibid: 468). Reece points out the strange inversions of meaning that have resulted from this: 'It is interesting that "responsibility" is able to mean its opposite. "Authority" is the reverse of "accountability". While authority embodies independence and freedom, answerability implies dependence and loss of control' (ibid: 467–8).

The *Every Child Matters Outcomes Framework* (DfES 2005c), to be used by children's services in implementing the Children Act 2004, provides evidence to support Reece's arguments that parental partnership with the state, by all parents, is underpinned by new strong norms. For each of the five outcomes, there are five or more points as to what this entails or means and then a final point in italics which states the role of 'parents, carers and families'. The first four are that parents should 'promote healthy choices' (in relation to the child's exercise, lifestyle etc), 'provide safe homes and stability' (keeping children safe from abuse, crime, bullying etc), 'support learning' (at school and in recreation), and 'promote positive behaviour' (by engagement in community activity and law-abiding behaviour for example). All these imply normative frameworks for parenting. Only the fifth outcome, 'to achieve economic well being', is somewhat different – 'Parents, carers and families are supported to be economically active' – although even here there is the assumption that the good parent will not be unemployed.

A recent article argues that the demands on parents to improve their 'performance' as parents have intensified (Lubcock 2008: 20). The pressure on parents is for them to take advice, to seek out opportunities to improve the educational and employment prospects of all family members, to make use of fiscal opportunities, and generally to raise their aspirations. 'In this way, the responsibility for the achievement by the government of its aspirations for social mobility is firmly placed in the hands of parents' (ibid: 21).

Every Parent Matters, a recent policy document, brings together this focus on the responsibility of parents and the importance of scientific evidence in supporting policy pronouncements (see Chapter 5 below). It states that parents are 'a crucial influence' on children's development and notes that 'the evidence of the importance of parental impact is building [sic]' (DfES 2007d: 2), and then deals in detail with proposed policy relating to various aspects of parenting with an emphasis on early years and involvement in schools. There are threats of 'intensive' help where parents fail to comply with these norms:

There remain a small number of households whose behaviour causes disproportionate nuisance in their communities. ... the

Respect Action Plan announced the development of Family Intervention Projects in fifty local authority areas. Since September 2006 these projects have been using intensive tailored action with supervision and clear sanctions to improve the behaviour of persistently anti-social households. (ibid: 32)

'Encouraging' mothers and fathers

Parents are to be a 'moral and social *guarantor* for their children' (Wyness 1997: 312, emphasis added; see also Reece 2005: 460), and bad parents are still deemed to create 'moral' deficits in their children which the state wishes to address. 'Parents refusing all the government's offers to join the mainstream moral community are viewed as endangering their children's moral development, thereby threatening the well-being of the community as a whole' (Gillies 2005). A review of the increase 'in the number and scope of mechanisms used to encourage parental responsibility in the youth justice context' analyses a 'matrix of powers' to 'instil' parental responsibility: the liability of parents in relation to the new parental compensation orders, the power of the courts to bind over parents, the introduction and increasing scope of parenting orders, and the sanctions for non-compliance (Hollingsworth 2007). There has been an increased use of these court orders as well as of parenting and acceptable anti-social behaviour contracts and agreements (Respect Task Force 2007). As Rogers notes, there remains a 'contradiction between the positive image of parents as drivers of constructive change within the DfES and parents problematised within the Home Office as errant carers of youngsters who have colonised the street' (2006: 2).

There are still gender issues in parenting: one focus is on encouraging fathers to take responsibility in particular ways. *Youth Justice – The Next Steps* evidences the government's aim to encourage youth justice agencies to make more use of parenting orders and contracts, 'more actively *engaging fathers*, making sure *both parents* generally come to court and ensuring courts consider a Parenting Order when they fail to attend court' (Home Office 2003: 5, para. 9 (emphasis in the original)). Another gendered policy is that of placing sanctions on resident parents – usually mothers – who fail to promote contact with the non-resident parent (DCA, DfES and DTI 2005; see also Children Act 1989, sections 8, 11A–11O). Arguably, the increasing high profile of shared residence orders is also reflective of a gendered approach (Kaganas and Piper 2002).

Mandating responsibility

There are also very different families within which all this operates. There has been what Diduck has referred to as a 'shifting familiarity' with, in practice, a much wider variety of individuals who may count as family (Diduck 2005). The result, she argues, is that this 'familialising' of society 'may be just what the doctor ordered': 'It engages with individualism's valuing of personal choice and its focus upon the subjective quality of individual life and relationships, but succeeds in shaping those values within the contours of the traditional family' (ibid: 253). Nevertheless, these apparent contradictions 'sustain social norms through which families remain discrete, identifiable, moral and regulatable units' made up of individuals instilled with an ethic of responsibility (Diduck 2003: 43). Now, as we have seen, children are also expected to endorse such an ethic: there are 'dual responsibilities' of parent and child, notably in relation to the child's behaviour (Hollingsworth 2007), but also in relation to their part in other family decisions and activities. Parents must be responsible, but also accountable, and so must their children.

These developments have utilised research on the links between family functioning, education and criminality, as did early 20th century policies and, as with the 'remoralisation' strand of family policy strand at the end of the nineteenth century (see Day Sclater and Piper 2000), it has produced measures to 'train' parents into responsibility. The focus is on outcomes against which deficits in upbringing can be measured and risk assessed, and parents enjoined to do better. Anything which does not lead to optimum outputs in the child is available for classification as a parental shortcoming which justifies state interference. The paradox is that, while the relative 'immunity' of parents from compulsory intervention to remove a child from their care was strengthened by the criteria for a care order in section 31 of the Children Act 1989, the social and legal pressure to act in the best interests of their child was and is mounting.

The frequent reference to scientific research findings means it is now taken for granted that bad parenting is 'really' bad for children. Baroness Butler-Sloss, speaking in the House of Lords in a debate on 'Children' in March 2007 – in response to the UNICEF report on Child Poverty (UNICEF 2007) – stressed the 'duties' strand of the definition of parental responsibility in section 3 of the Children Act 1989:

> Duty is an uncomfortable word. But parenting, as we all know, involves responsibilities and duties. … it requires a commitment

– and a commitment for life. ... We have to get the message across to the entire country about the long-term adverse effect on children of bad or inadequate parenting. It will also affect people's ability to parent the next generation after the current one, so ... we need to recognise that bad parenting will continue if we do not get at the generation who are not yet parents.[11]

Science, with its 'knowledge' about long-term effects, and social fears that we are risking another generation of parents seen as 'bad' are crucial factors in linking conceptions of children, parents and investment in a risk-based programme to combat social exclusion and to enhance the well-being of children. That will be the focus of the next chapter.

Notes

1 [2004] 1 FLR 454 at para. 118.
2 There is even a website devoted to cartoons lampooning the 'nanny state': http://www.cartoonstock.com/newscartoons/directory/n/nanny_state. asp.
3 See www.publications.parliament.uk/pa/jt200304/jtselect/jtrights/161/ 16102.htm.
4 *R v Tyrell* [1894] 1 QB 710 at 712.
5 Brown, J.B. (1883) *The Home: In its Relation to Man and Society.*
6 *J v C* [1970] AC 668.
7 See *Re H (Minors) (Local Authority: Parental Rights) (No. 3)* [1991] 2 WLR 763, affirmed in *Re G (A Minor) (Parental Responsibility Order)* [1994] 1 FLR 504.
8 *Re S (Parental Responsibility)* [1995] 2 FLR 648.
9 For a different perspective on this 'civilising' of separating parents, see von Krieken 2005.
10 Interestingly, recent research has suggested that boys not living with their mothers were more likely to become persistent offenders (Haas *et al.* 2004).
11 *Hansard* HL col. 1831 (29 March 2007).

Part 11

The mechanisms for, and success of, investment policies

Chapter 5

The science of prevention: constructing and assessing risk

Risk assessment and prevention is not just a political debating point, it has become a major organisational vested interest. (Rod Morgan 2006: 3)

It is always better to prevent failure than tackle a crisis later. (*The Children's Plan*, DCFS 2007: 6)

The science of effective parenting

The last chapter focused on the crucial role of parents in the success of any child investment policy: the way in which their autonomy and responsibility are conceptualised means that parents are seen either as a hurdle to change or a partner in it. The focus on what exactly parents 'do', rather than who or what they are, has sharpened throughout the last decade (Lubcock 2008: 14), and 'good' parenting is now seen as one of the most important factors in ensuring good outcomes for children. Good parents have responsibilities 'to be active citizens on behalf of themselves and their children' (ibid: 23), and so 'poor' parenting is constructed as a risk factor in relation to poor outcomes and social exclusion. What is of note is that it is now taken for granted that these links are 'facts'. Scientific research from medical and social sciences has proved these links because, in the 21st century, only science can produce 'facts'. Scientific evidence is now more than ever the legitimation for government statements in relation to parenting and children. Indeed, it is the legitimation for all policy which is part of New Labour's 'modernisation' of public services. *Professional policy making for the twenty-first century* stated that policy should be 'soundly based on evidence of what works' (Cabinet Office 1999: para. 7.10), and the skills of policy makers should, therefore, include 'a grounding in economics, statistics and relevant scientific disciplines in order to act as "intelligent customers" for complex policy evidence' (ibid: para. 1.6).

More recently, in the Foreword to *Every Parent Matters* (DfES 2007: 1), Alan Johnson made the following statement: 'Being a parent is – and should be – an intensely personal experience and parents can be effective in very different ways. However, we also have a growing understanding, evidenced from research, about the characteristics of effective parenting' (DfES 2007: 1). The document is then littered with references to research. For example, para. 2.1 states that 'Recent research has shown the importance of parental warmth, stability, consistency and boundary setting' in helping children develop learning skills, and has eight separate footnotes referring to research to support a list of 'facts' about the importance of parental interest and involvement. Chapter 3, on 'The Early Years', states that 'We have clear evidence ... of the impact of parental engagement ... research has shown a direct link ... Evidence suggests that ...' (DfES 2007: para. 3.1) and again has references to research projects. Chapter 4 on 'Parents of School Age Children' (para. 4.1) has a similar 'research shows that' opening, and Chapter 5 refers to evidence that parents remain important during the child's teenage years (para. 5.1)

The 2006 White Paper, *Care Matters: Transforming the Lives of Children and Young People in Care*, also reveals a confidence in scientific research:

> In the past we have not been good enough at identifying problems quickly enough so that the need for care can be prevented. And yet there is *clear evidence* that early identification can help us to predict where problems will arise. ... *We know* that those who are in need ... are far more likely to enter the care system ... (DfES 2006a: para. 2.7; emphasis added)

This is not new. Science has played a role in facilitating the formulation and passage of legislation for well over a century and *Hansard*, the official transcript of parliamentary business, is littered with examples of politicians referring to science to support their case: this book contains several of them. However, it is particular versions of scientific evidence that are of crucial importance in the legitimation of policy, just as they are in relation to decisions by the courts about individual children in child protection cases. So it is significant that a medical approach has been taken to the issue of crime prevention.

> In medicine and public health, it is widely accepted that prevention is better than cure. The same is true of offending. Public health prevention is often based on identifying and tackling risk factors. For example, smoking, lack of exercise, and a fatty diet are important risk factors for heart attacks ... This book aims to summarize what is known about early risk factors for offending and about effective intervention that can be used to tackle these risk factors. (Farrington and Welsh 2007: 3)

The passage above opens a book entitled *Saving Children from a Life of Crime*. David Farrington has been responsible for the largest longitudinal research study in the UK, following up over 40 years 411 boys who attended primary school in the 1950s. This has generated data about factors associated with a young person's movement into criminality. Without scientific knowledge about correlations between poor outcomes – in this case offending – and factors in the lives of children, there can be no construction of risk and so no basis for investment in prevention. However, the generation and selection of facts for use in policy development is not unproblematic.

The construction and assessment of risk is the focus of this chapter, but there are related issues which will be dealt with in Chapters 7 and 8. One of these is the effective targeting of interventions on those most at risk of poor outcomes. Even if an intervention is something to be voluntarily accepted, it can stigmatise those who ask for the assessment and/or support, and it will inevitably exclude from services those who do not ask for them. The solutions to this might be universal services or area-based services so that individuals need not be targeted. But there are difficulties with each of these possible solutions, stemming from different constructions of the role of parents and the state, which previous chapters have reviewed. *Every Parent Matters* reminds each local authority that the *Parenting Support Guidance* (DfES 2006b) enjoins them to develop a strategy for delivering parenting support services: 'It suggests that parenting support to deliver improved outcomes for children should be seen as a continuum from information, early intervention and preventative services through to the use of enforcement measures' (DfES 2007: para. 6.2). What would be of great concern would be compulsory intervention on a wide scale, but all these options require particular notions of parental and state responsibility as well as confidence in investment, and, as we have seen, all of these have served as barriers or purse-openers in the past.

Concepts of risk in child protection and youth justice

> We recognise that other conditions than mere inherent vice may have entered into an offence; that the child's upbringing at home, the discipline he receives in the home circle or lack of it, the economic conditions under which he lives, the squalor and misery of his life, even the companions with whom he associates in school or out of it, may have much to do with turning that child into an offender than any spirit of natural evil.[1]

So argued the then Under Secretary of State for the Home Office over 70 years ago in pressing for more welfarist approaches to the treatment of young offenders. His list of factors predisposing to offending – though in somewhat outmoded terminology – is quite modern in its content. It also points up the fact that it was the offending of children, rather than their protection, that prompted quantitative research to establish statistical correlates of offending, whether family and personal factors or links to relative structural deprivation. Data on the causes and correlates of criminality – the risk factors – are used to determine which localities and which individual children should be targeted for new resources and preventative programmes. The assumption underpinning this focus – whereby other factors in the child's life may be downplayed – is that a focus on preventing future offending is in the child's best interests: after all, except for the few successful criminals, it is not the best career choice.

Risk of offending

Risk also developed as an important concept within what is now referred to as 'actuarial justice', whereby technology and statistical calculations are used to enhance the risk-management of high-risk groups. Within the 'New Penology' – coined by Feeley and Simon (1992) – reflected in actuarial justice, crime is seen as normal and something to be managed, so the focus becomes how to use technology and statistical calculations to identify which groups of people are most at risk of (re)offending and which intervention programmes or surveillance should be used in response. Risk management and the categorisation of offenders by levels of risk become key aspects (Simon 1998). In policy terms, this approach leads to (early) preventative services at one end of the spectrum of options, and tools to control or incapacitate those most likely to (continue to) be dangerous at the other end. In between, the 'ordinary' offender can be dealt with in the community, not least to counter-balance the increased cost of the provision of custody for offenders placed on longer sentences because they are deemed to be the greatest risk.

The focus on risk is reflected in the Sentencing Matrix, headed 'The Correlation of "Seriousness" and the Risk of Re-offending', to be found in the latest edition of the *Youth Court Bench Book* (Judicial Studies Board 2005: section 2.9). For each of the three levels of seriousness (low, medium and high), particular court orders are suggested for the three different levels of risk of offending (low, medium and high). Several sentencing options are suggested for all levels of risk but others are not available if the young offender is judged to have a high risk of re-offending. Assessments of risk can, therefore, lead to an increase in the 'punishment' or be the entry point for new sentences. There are also now special sentencing provisions, to be found in sections 224–229 of the Criminal Justice Act 2004, available for 'dangerous offenders' – adult or minor. They provide indeterminate custodial sentences to be mandatorily applied if the court deems – or must assume (section 229) – that there is 'a significant risk to members of the public of serious harm occasioned by the commission by him of further specified offences' (section 225(1)(b)).

The focus on offending risk factors has, in practice, precipitated wider concerns about children. The Government's response to *Every Child Matters: Next Steps* includes a set of proposals designed to help youth offending teams (YOTs) to 'work with other services to address some of the wider factors linked to tackling re-offending, such as educational non-participation and problems with drugs, alcohol or mental health' (DfES 2004: para. 4.22). This approach focuses on other risk factors simply for the purpose of determining how to reduce the risk of offending. Effective inter-agency work is, therefore, recommended because 'Many of the factors that may increase the risk of offending lie in the hands of agencies outside the criminal justice system' (National Audit Office 2004: para. 15). So YOTs may work with children's trusts but, if so, they remain linked to criminal justice and crime reduction agencies (DfES 2004: para. 4.22).

However, 'actuarial justice' has also been used to pursue objectives other than simply the prevention of offending, and has become part of the family-centred New Labour crime policy which was developed in the mid-1990s (see Giddens 2000 and also Chapter 4). Issues of family dissolution and crime are linked together in policy such that 'tackling one problem cannot be accomplished without taking on the others' (Knepper 2007: 109), but that is not new. Pearson, in reviewing the comments in the 1930s of such eminent writers as George Orwell, T.S. Eliot and F.R. Leavis about the 'terrifying disintegration', the 'irresponsible family' and the 'absence of restraint' 'since the war', asks 'which war was that?' (Pearson 2006: 6). The complaints about the young and their parents are perennial: they occur after every war – and between wars – but the contention now is that there is clear science to tackle the malaise and to do so in relation to a wider set of poor outcomes.

Risk in child protection

A scientific knowledge base has developed separately in relation to the risk of neglect and abuse to a child. The focus for social workers has been the identification of indicators of risk of harm and also, since the Children Act 1989, on the evidence required to prove that the 'significant harm' threshold in section 31 has been surmounted. The risk to be assessed is whether the harm will continue or occur in the future and, where 'likelihood' of harm is at issue, the courts have defined this as 'a real possibility, a possibility that cannot sensibly be ignored having regard to the nature and gravity of the feared harm in the particular case'.[2] Alongside this runs a lower threshold test – whether the child is 'in need' under section 17 of the same Act. The risk to be assessed is whether a child is likely or unlikely to develop properly but, as we shall see in Chapter 6, the duty to promote and safeguard the welfare of children in need is legally 'soft' – it does not ensure in practice that children's needs are met. There is no statutory duty to investigate and assess, as there is under section 47 when there is a risk of significant harm.

Messages from Research (DoH 1995) precipitated a 'refocusing' policy agenda. The report showed that, while local authorities had given priority to assessment and inquiries regarding risk of significant harm, only a quarter of such assessments led to child protection conferences and only in 13 per cent of cases was the child put on the child protection register as a result. It argued that 'Too many minor cases were rigorously investigated with the result that a large number of minnows ... got caught up in the child protection net' and stated that 'the research evidence suggests that, for the majority of cases, the need of the child and family is more important than the abuse or, put another way, the general family context is more important than the abusive event within it' (ibid: 54). The report argued that this was not only costly but also alienated the 75 per cent who were assessed to no purpose. The research review therefore supported the idea that scarce resources should be used more freely for family support services rather than assessment of risk. However, the pressure of work on social services departments, together with media attention to their shortcomings, has meant that, in practice, and notwithstanding the refocusing policy agenda, risk assessment and intervention have focused on harm within a child protection ethos.

There are ambiguities arising from parallel histories of risk-based assessment and intervention in child protection and in juvenile justice, and yet the thrust of the safeguarding agenda for children's trusts and the remit of programmes run under the direction of the Youth Justice Board are converging in the sense that they have a common knowledge base about risk factors and pathways. It is consequently sometimes quite difficult to be sure whether the focus of a writer or speaker is risk of harm or risk of offending. For example, the Portsmouth Children's Fund advertised the aim of its Youth Inclusion Support Panel as ensuring 'young people at risk … receive the support they need' but goes on to explain that 'Through research it is suggested that joined up services will prevent young people becoming involved in crime'.[3]

Risk factors, actuarial science and crime pathways

In our reviews of risk and protective factors and prevention programmes, we describe the highest quality research studies (prospective longitudinal studies and randomized experiments),[4] as well as the most rigorous literature reviews (systematic and meta-analytic) that include only high quality projects. (Farrington and Welsh 2007: 6)

Those urging for early intervention policies are anxious to stress the scientific credentials of what is 'known' after 'decades of rigorous research in the United States and across the Western world' (ibid: 159). This section will review this research, first in relation to offending, and then more generally.

Offending

Risk factors have been studied in relation to two main points in a criminal career – the first criminal action and the last. What in other words are the factors which correlate with starting offending and which correlate with desistance from it? Conversely, what factors are protective factors that work to restrain a child from engaging or continuing in criminality? Work on resistance and resilience is also relevant to both stages in terms of personal factors.[5] What is particularly pertinent to current policy developments is the relative importance of the role of structural and personal characteristics in predicting offending or desistence: whether, for example, the actions of the community or parents are more influential than personal factors or wider structural issues. The even more crucial question as to whether intervention helps or hinders will be left to Chapter 7.

The results of research studies have been analysed within a variety of theoretical frameworks. The most influential has been that of developmental criminology whereby 'pathways' to criminality and the events in it which activate or aggravate criminal activity are analysed. Those 'events' include family and parenting factors, and the results have been used as evidence of the need to focus on parents in preventing crime. Other criminologists have focused on structural disadvantage, rather than human agency, as an explanation, or on the 'cycle of violence' thesis (see Knepper 2007: 111–3).

The general conclusions of research about the correlates of offending – prior factors that statistically increase the risk that a child will start or persist in offending – are now well known, widely disseminated and frequently summarised. For example, Farrington (2007: 605–13) recently summarised the research on the following individual risk factors: low intelligence and attainment ('important predictor'), empathy ('the empirical basis is not very impressive'), impulsiveness ('the most crucial personality dimension that predicts offending'), and social cognitive skills (some of the evidence is 'not convincing'). In addition, he reviewed the research on family risk factors, and the explanation given for them, by grouping them into the following five categories: criminal and anti-social parents, large family size, child-rearing methods (poor supervision, poor discipline, coldness and rejection, low parental involvement with the child), abuse or neglect, and disrupted families. He explicitly excluded socio-economic factors such as low family income and poor neighbourhood (ibid: 613–19).

The problem, as Farrington notes, is that,

In explaining the development of offending, a major problem is that most risk factors tend to coincide and tend to be interrelated ... The concentration and co-occurrence of these kinds of adversities makes it difficult to establish their independent, interactive, and sequential influences on offending and anti-social behaviour. Hence any theory of offending is inevitably speculative in the present state of knowledge. (ibid: 619)

Criminologists have used the fact that crime is mostly committed by those aged 13–30 to argue that offending is 'one of a number of psychosocial disorders' (including problematic use of alcohol and drugs) that are characteristic of youth, in the sense that they rise in prevalence or frequency, or reach a peak in adolescence or early adulthood (Smith 2007: 641). Such an approach not only leads to a focus on the influence of events and transitions which are exclusive to children and young people but also to a focus on desistance: if crime is in a sense 'normal' for young people, why do some 'grow out of it' and others not?

Desistance

Smith summarises the six types of explanation for continuing offending which have been provided. The first may appear tautologous – that some people do not desist because they belong to the distinct group of people who engage in various forms of anti-social behaviour throughout the life course (as opposed to the normal adolescence-limited offending). The other factors relating to the strength of social bonds, the effect of being stigmatised by responses by the youth justice system, people's position in the social structure, the balance of opportunities for both legitimate and criminal activities, and the influence of peers have all been revisited by research in the last decade or so (Smith 2006: 6–7).

The Edinburgh Study of Youth Transitions and Crime included research on desistance from offending in relation to indicators of exclusion and came to the following conclusions:

There was no evidence that deprivation at the level of the individual family was associated with continuing to offend. Young people from higher social classes and intact families were no more likely than others to desist from offending.

Desistance was, however, associated with the characteristics of the neighbourhood where the young person lived. Continuing to offend was more common in deprived neighbourhoods, whereas desistance was more common in advantaged ones. Also, desistance was less likely in neighbourhoods perceived to be disorderly, and where residents were dissatisfied with the neighbourhood (Smith 2006: 4).

As Smith notes: 'These findings are interesting, because they suggest that the resources and dynamics of the neighbourhood are more important than the resources available to the individual family as an influence on behaviour change in young people' (Smith 2006: 14). The Edinburgh project included a focus on neighbourhood influences in relation to cannabis use, hard drug use and delinquency (McVie and Norris 2006), with the following dependent variables: population instability (using census data), economic deprivation, recorded street crime rates, community satisfaction, community safety, neighbourhood incivilities and collective efficiency, the latter two based on interviews with residents (ibid: 14–17). They found that a higher level of delinquency within areas was strongly associated with all seven of the neighbourhood factors: there was less association between drug use and neighbourhood variables except in relation to frequent hard drug use (ibid: 19). Nevertheless they concluded that the impact of neighbourhood characteristics 'is relatively weak in comparison to the effect of individual characteristics, such as gender and personality' (2006: 6; see also 20–1).

The role of social capital, 'social interactions, networks and network opportunities' (Boeck *et al.* 2006: 19), in young people's 'navigation' of risk pathways has been highlighted in recent research in the Midlands region of England by Boeck and colleagues. They found a complex situation where 'social capital can be a resource for resilience and the avoidance of crime, but can also be the context in which decisions about crime are made'. The young offenders interviewed had more restricted networks and opportunities than the control group of young people accessed through local schools and youth groups (ibid. 2006: 21). They conclude that their findings 'suggest that an exclusive focus on individual behaviour change and corrective programmes on thinking patterns can have only limited impact over the life course' (ibid) because of the importance of social context and of life transitions on pathways into and out of crime.

The four-year project entitled 'Pathways into and out of Crime: Risk, Resilience and Diversity', sponsored by the Economic and Social Research Council (ESRC), has generated a wealth of data and publications. One study focused on the ways in which interventions by professionals in education and youth justice impacted on the different pathways in relation to crime. The report noted several significant themes emerging from the data which included the 'importance of context in determining whether a factor is risk or protection' and 'the importance of the relationship with individuals delivering interventions' (Hine *et al.* 2006). The authors explain, 'Young people have described circumstances in which factors traditionally assumed to signify risk, for instance drug use, can in some contexts actually be protective', and 'Young people have varying experiences of professionals, with many having a range of different professionals involved in their lives at the same or different times. They describe those professionals that are most helpful to them as being the ones that treat them with respect, listen to them and consequently earn their trust' (ibid: 2006). A recent Edinburgh study has also similarly noted that 'Bonds with teachers and parents, and parents' involvement in school, were associated with desistance from offending' (Smith 2006: 4).

A research report, *Offenders of the Future? Assessing the Risk of Children and Young People Becoming Involved in Criminal or Antisocial Behaviour,* produced by very experienced researchers (McCarthy *et al.* 2004), has married science and practice: it has been published by the DfES as a manual 'to assist practitioners identify families with children aged between four and twelve who are at risk of becoming involved in criminal or antisocial behaviour and to target interventions that aim to reduce that risk'.[6] It has detailed sections on assessment of risk in different contexts and includes appendices giving information about a very wide range of assessment scales and instruments, including those to assess resilience in relation to particular situations or aspects of development (ibid: especially 79–98). The authors summarise their conclusions about resilience as follows:

The majority of children with identifiable risk factors do not engage in crime or antisocial behaviour. Despite challenging circumstances, children can develop resilience depending on the complex interplay between risk and protective factors.

There are three primary ways in which children can display resilience:

1. By achieving positive outcomes even though they are at high risk.
2. By adapting successfully to stressful situations.
3. By recovering quickly from a crisis.

Research studies have delineated the characteristics of resilient and non-resilient children. Children with a stronger sense of attachment to other people, a more positive outlook on life, more plans for the future and more control over their lives are more likely to demonstrate resilience (ibid: x).

The report also usefully summarises the different models operating in this area to explain the relationship between risk, protection, resilience and need: 'The additive model views risk and protective factors as being on a continuum, the interaction model suggests that risk and protective factors interact in a dynamic way, and the pathways model suggests that the effect of specific risk and protective factors are context-specific and depend on timing' (ibid).

Family disruption

There has been, perhaps, the most debate on the statistical correlation between offending and family 'disruption', evidenced as shown in earlier chapters by the policy focus on parental responsibility and by the remit of the 'Protection and responsibility' cross-cutting review set up by the Treasury in 2001 as part of the 'Children at Risk' review:

> This group will concentrate on reducing the involvement of children and young people in crime and supporting children and young people as the victims of crime. Parental and sibling involvement in crime and inadequate parental supervision and support are among the strongest risk factors of future criminal behaviour. (HM Treasury 2001)

Persistence

There has also been a particular focus on persistent offenders. The White Paper *No More Excuses* (Home Office 1997) referred to a 'small hard core of persistent offenders ... responsible for a disproportionate amount of crime ... research has found that about 3% of young offenders commit 26% of youth crime'. Indeed, the persistent young offender was subsequently defined in particular precise ways for different stages of the youth justice process (see NACRO 2000). More recently the Home Office stated that 'in any one year, approximately 100,000 people commit half of all crimes and just 5000 people commit about 9 per cent of all crimes – around one million in total' (Home Office 2004: 32–3). Annex B to *Criminal Justice: the Way Ahead* had also referred to the same general statistics, arguing in relation to the subgroup of persistent offenders, 'Although they represent only 10% of active offenders they accumulate at least 50% of all serious convictions' (Home Office 2001), and it is easy to find examples of government ministers using these 'facts' (see Garside 2004: 17). As Garside has noted, 'The idea that a significant proportion of all crime is committed by a relatively small number of persistent offenders is not new, but the current government has placed it at the centre of its criminal justice policy' (Garside 2004: 5). For example, in 2004, the Prolific and Other Priority Offender Strategy was launched by the Home Office and the Youth Justice Board (now YJB) issued accompanying guidance, notably on the Prevent and Deter strand of the strategy (see NACRO 2006a and 2006c; see also Chapter 7 below).

Garside, however, critiques the science underpinning this policy priority, notably the composition of the Offenders' Index, a database containing the details of all individuals convicted of standard list offences in England and Wales since 1963 (see Prime *et al.* 2001), and the government's interpretation of the statistics in it (Garside 2004: 14–15). For example, 'Those who commit new offences but are not caught, or who are cautioned, will not register' (ibid) and so, as Julian Prime and colleagues themselves noted of the data in the Index, 'we do not know how representative this subset of offenders is of all offenders' (Prime *et al.* 2001; see Garside 2004: 16). He concludes that, 'in the context of crime rates that are measured in tens of millions, it stretches credulity to breaking point to claim that is possible to achieve meaningful reductions in crime by targeting a few thousand of the usual suspects' (Garside 2004: 18).

Risk and needs as problematic

> If a child is assessed as being 'at risk', this does not necessarily mean that the child is 'in need'. Need exists where there is an identifiable, effective and available solution to a perceived problem. Risk assessment and needs assessment are different, although they often go hand-in-hand and *can sometimes be confused*. Once an assessment of risk has been made, the focus can turn to the identification of need in order to establish which children and families are in need of, and can benefit from, interventions that are available. (McCarthy *et al.* 2004: x; emphasis added)

The above statement would suggest that only confused thinking can conflate risk and need, but that assumes clear and unchanging constructions of risk and need, an assumption which is contestable. Risk, it is argued, has 'undergone significant operational and epistemological revision' (C. Smith 2000: 367), both in child protection and youth justice, and 'needs' should be viewed as a cultural rather than a scientific construct.

Woodhead, for example, argues that there are different usages of children's needs which 'become merged and confused when rendered into apparently unproblematic generalizations about children's needs' (Woodhead 1997: 75). Instead he identifies four categories of needs: as a description of children's psychological nature; as an inference from what is known about the pathological consequences of particular childhood experiences; as a judgement about which childhood experiences are most culturally adaptive; and as a prescription about which childhood experiences are most highly valued in society. 'Need', then, is as malleable a concept as 'risk', and Hannah-Moffat has argued that the distinctions made between risk and need are sufficiently 'fluid and flexible' to be merged (Hannah-Moffat 2005: 30). She argues that the relatively new concepts of 'criminogenic needs' and 'dynamic risks' allow a fusion of risk and need in 'third generation' risk assessment tools, those which developed out of the earlier clinical assessments of risk and those using 'static historical factors' to make statistical predictions of risk' (ibid: 32). The result, she says, is that earlier critiques of the growing dominance of 'actuarial justice' and the new penology within youth justice (see, for example, Kemp-Leonard and Peterson 2000) may have been misplaced: there are now 'disparate and contradictory forms of risk-based penal governance' of which we need to take account (ibid: 44).

Such an approach suggests that 'risk factor' is not an unproblematic scientific term, and Farrington and Welsh note that it is not used consistently. For example, an explanatory variable such as parental supervision may be termed a risk factor, whereas the risk would relate, say, to the category of 'poor' parental supervision, or might be used to divide the population into low and high risks (2007: 17). A major problem, they say, is determining 'which risk factors are causes and which are merely "markers" or correlated with causes' (ibid: 19). Establishing a causal risk factor would entail, amongst other things, establishing that the prediction stands after controlling for, or stands independently of, all other variables (ibid). Because establishing this commonly entails randomised trials with control groups, this is not always a feasible or ethical proposition, and so such evidence cannot exist. Further, a key issue is that of establishing precisely what the factor is a risk of and for whom, for example in terms of the age of the offender and the type and nature of offending. As Farrington and Welsh point out, 'A single risk factor may predict or cause multiple outcomes, just as a single outcome may be predicted or caused by multiple risk factors ... There may also be multiple causal pathways between risk factors and outcomes' (ibid: 21).

There may also be more than one explanation for a causal connection. There may be 'social causation' when risk factors predict outcomes, or there may be 'social selection' when certain types of people are differentially exposed to certain risk factors. For example, a recent Canadian study compared the rates of physical aggression exhibited by 2–3 year old children cared for by their own mothers (home care) with those of children cared for by workers in group day-care centres. They found that, whilst aggression was significantly more common in children looked after by their own mothers, there was strong social selection associated with family risk factors (for example, maternal education, family size). Therefore the higher risk of physical aggression in maternally cared for children was found only to be associated with high risk families (Borge *et al.* 2004).

Assessment tools

Assessment is not only a major practice tool for social workers and medical professionals but also a gatekeeper. It operates to open or close the way for intervention or treatment for a child or her family ... Further, the scope and results of the assessment influence or determine the nature and extent of the intervention ... [and] compliance with detailed guidance about assessment and the completion of the requisite questionnaires, scales and pro-forma, constitute a type of insurance for those who work in a field where certainty of outcome is impossible. It is difficult then to over-estimate the importance of assessment. (Piper 2004: 736)

Assessment is crucial to the preventative investment programme for two reasons: first, to assess whether there is a risk to an individual child, group of children or local area – of harm, offending or other poor outcomes – and whether any intervention is required (which may or may not require a legal threshold); secondly, to assess what sort of intervention is required. There is now a very wide variety of assessment tools developed by different sectors and different agencies to assess children and young people for a range of specified risk and need factors (see, for example, DfES 2006d: Appendix 3; McCarthy *et al*. 2004). Not surprisingly, therefore, *Every Child Matters*, in a chapter devoted to 'Early Intervention and Effective Practice', focused on how 'information collection' could be improved and information shared, to 'ensure professionals share concerns at an early stage' (DfES 2003: 52) and 'to ensure reliable data transfer' (ibid: 55). In addition to new national computerised recording systems, the main proposal was for a common assessment framework or CAF (ibid: para. 4.13 *et seq*). This proposal did not come out of a vacuum. In consultations prior to the issue of the *Framework* (see below), the Department of Health had been urged to issue a common assessment for the use of the inter-agency network but had not done so (for a criticism of this decision, see Calder 2003: 14).

The Common Assessment Framework

As noted in Chapter 3, all arrangements to promote co-operation between children's services and their partner agencies must now be 'with a view to improving the well-being' of children in the authority's area so far as relating to the five outcomes specified in the Children Act 2004, section 10(2). Further, all the agencies listed in section 11 must carry out their function 'having regard to the need to safeguard and promote the welfare of children'. The overall aim of assessment is therefore to acquire the information necessary to ensure that the well-being and welfare of the child are protected and promoted. However, in practice, assessment is for a specific purpose and, as *Every Child Matters* pointed out, children may be assessed many times during their childhood (DfES 2003: para. 4.13). Not only do health visitors conduct universal assessments in early childhood, there are also the baseline assessments in the first year at primary school as well as more targeted assessments done on referral to educational psychologists, social services and specialist medical services, for example.

Consequently, 'children with multiple needs may be subject to multiple assessments by different people, each collecting similar information but using different professional terms and categories' (DfES 2003: para. 4.14). Assessment can also have a damaging psychological impact on those assessed: it 'can set the tone for further contact, it is your first opportunity to engage with new or existing clients, and it can be perceived as a judgement on their character and behaviour' (Walker and Beckett 2003: 6). Referral around the system can engender feelings of frustration and stigma in children and their families seeking support or specialist referral (see Banks *et al.* 2002 for the recent report by the Scottish Executive on young carers and their families). The proposal in *Every Child Matters* for a common assessment framework for use by all professionals 'in the frontline' (2003: para. 4.15) makes sense for pragmatic reasons and as part of a response to the failure to protect Victoria Climbié.

The new CAF, it was said, would draw on the *Framework for Assessment of Children in Need and their Families* (the *Framework*, DoH *et al.* 2000, implemented April 2001, now incorporated into the 2006 guidance), Asset (the tool used in the Youth Justice System), the SEN and health visitor codes of practice and also the tool used by Connexions, the advice service for young people. However, guidance notes that the aim is 'early identification of need' (CWDC 2007: 1), not risk. With a common assessment tool, 'core information' could 'follow the child between services to reduce duplication' (DfES 2003: 51). A similar message is given in *Every Child Matters: Next Steps*: 'A common assessment framework should help identify their needs earlier and avoid duplication between agencies' (DfES 2004: para. 3.14). Therefore, if a child is already known to more than one specialist service, a 'lead professional' would act as a gatekeeper for information sharing (DfES 2003: paras 4.20 and 4.22). Two of its objectives are that responsibility for initial assessments should be 'more firmly embedded in universal services', and that children should take an active part in the process (ibid: para. 4.16) so that the concerns of and about children can be taken more seriously at an early stage. It is therefore envisaged that the child's school will in practice often be taking the initiative in assessment because that is the service with which there is day-to- day contact (ibid: para. 4.21), a policy in line with the Government's stated concern to reduce the number of (expensive) referrals to social services for initial assessments (ibid: para. 4.14).

The DfES led the development work on a common assessment. By 2004 it has already drawn together the Children's National Services Framework and other projects into the Information Sharing and Assessment Programme. The CAF was piloted in 2005/06 and its implementation over all areas should have been completed by April 2008.[7] Whilst the Youth Justice Board (YJB) is training staff to understand and interpret CAF assessments already completed on young people referred to youth offending teams (YJB 2006), the CAF will not replace the YJB assessment tools.

Child protection and well-being

The CAF is, therefore, located within the approach of children's services rather than youth justice. Within the child protection system, assessment has been subject to very detailed guidance for some time. Previous guidance on law and practice was superseded by 10 volumes on implementing the Children Act 1989 (DoH 1991) and later by new assessment guidance. The *Framework for the Assessment of Children in Need and their Families* (DoH *et al.* 2000), summarised in *Working Together to Safeguard Children* (DfES 2006d: 109 (Figure 2) and Appendix 2), used an 'ecological triangle' to focus assessment on relevant environmental, social and economic factors, as well as on the more traditional issues around the child's developmental needs and the parenting capacity of her carers (see, for example, Walker and Beckett 2003: 14–16). The triangle was developed from an earlier, more sophisticated version of the ecological approach where the child was envisaged as set within ever-widening concentric circles (see Duncan *et al.* 2003). It is seen as a valuable aid in widening assessment issues and, therefore, the range of 'solutions'.

Those parts of the CAF forms which require an assessor to make judgements mirror the Framework triangle in its three sections. There is also a Pre-Assessment Checklist in which the recorder has to tick whether the unborn baby, child or young person 'appears to be' 'healthy', 'safe from harm', 'learning and developing', 'having a positive impact on others', and 'free from the negative impact of poverty'. If any 'no' responses are recorded, the worker must decide whether any 'additional services' are needed and could be provided; if any responses are 'no' or 'not sure' then the worker must decide whether an assessment under CAF would 'help'.

A concern is that, without substantial extra resources, the initial common assessment could not adequately be located in universal services without reducing expenditure on specialist services. The National Family and Parenting Institute has noted that agencies working with children expressed reservations about the CAF:

> it was felt that unless substantively more resources were ploughed into family support provision ... local authorities would be left in a position of needing to redefine what is meant by 'in need' when setting any eligibility criteria for who should receive services. As resources become overstretched, these eligibility criteria will inevitably be set closer to child protection thresholds. (Rogers 2006: 3)

Raynes (2006) is also concerned that the CAF and other national assessment tools give a wrong impression that the thresholds for compulsory intervention or eligibility for services can be established scientifically and unproblematically.

Further, the training for implementation of CAF is another example of the developing professional and commercial 'vested interest' in 'data gathering' through assessment, flagged up by Rod Morgan in the quotation at the beginning of this chapter. For example, the website of the consultancy company 'Outcomes UK' has a section devoted to the training services available in relation to the CAF.

Assessment of young offenders

Asset will continue to be used as the primary tool for assessment of young people within the youth justice system.

- *Asset* is designed to focus on assessing risk of reconviction, risk of serious harm to others, and risk of vulnerability.

- *Asset* is more detailed than CAF, and provides the framework for thorough analysis of offending behaviour required for writing reports and intervention plans.

- Research evidence has shown the validity and reliability of *Asset*.

- *Asset* data add to our knowledge about young people who offend, and can be used to inform decisions about the need for, and allocation of, resources. (YJB 2006: 2)

The above statement about Asset is to be found in the draft guidance on the common assessment framework (CAF). Asset[8] is the assessment tool produced for use specifically with young offenders, in parallel with the developments above, by the YJB after its establishment under section 38 of the Crime and Disorder Act 1998. In line with the statutory aim of the youth justice system – that of the prevention of offending (Crime and Disorder Act 1998, section 37) – the focus of Asset is assessment of risk of offending. Such assessment is said to allow 'a degree of flexibility in both sentencing and constructing the intervention plan on a final warning' and might lead to intensive intervention to deal with family and school problems at an earlier stage (Audit Commission 1996: 69). There are particular problems with practitioner use of the YJB's assessment tools, however.[9]

Asset is essentially a score-based decision-making system. If using the Core Profile tool, the professional youth worker conducting the assessment has to rate on a scale of 1 to 4 the extent to which a particular 'dynamic risk factor' applies, and then scores are added at the end. There are 12 such ratings which have to be totalled with a maximum 'high risk' score of 48 (Asset Core Profile: 19). In addition, there are extensive sections on 'positive factors', 'indicators of vulnerability' and 'indicators of risk of serious harm to others', with tick boxes and spaces for 'evidence' or further details (ibid: 20–6). The result is a numerical level of risk and an indication of the intervention required.

Other examples of this type of assessment can be found in relation to the Final Warning Scheme (see Chapter 2). The guidance to the police and youth offending teams includes reference to the Gravity Factor System developed by the Association of Chief Police Officers to 'reflect the public interest principles in the Code for Crown Prosecutors' (Home Office/YJB 2002: paras 4.21–4.23). The police should use this system in Step 6 of the decision-making stages for deciding whether to reprimand, warn or prosecute a young offender, because here the crucial question is 'how serious is the offence?'. The resulting score is on a scale of 1 to 4, with 4 always resulting in a charge, whether or not it is the young offender's first offence (ibid: see Annex D).

Further, if the police refer the young person for a 'prior assessment' by the youth offending team (YOT) (Home Office/YJB 2002: paras 8.1–8.3), a shorter Final Warning Asset tool will normally be used. Again, the score determines the intensity and duration of the offence-based preventative programme (para. 10.13; see also, for guidance to Chief Police Officers, Home Office 2006a). The matrix provided suggests one to four hours of a suitable programme for a low risk score (0–9) and 10 or more hours where a score of 20+ leads to 'risk concern' (para. 10.14).

Whilst Asset essentially assesses risk of (re)offending, section 2 of the Core Profile tool focuses on 'family and personal relationships'. There are more obviously offence-focused questions about the 'criminality' of the young offender's family, but, given the research on correlates of offending, there are also tick boxes for 'experience of abuse' and 'witnessing other violence' in the family context. As in other sections of Asset, the assessor must rate numerically the extent to which the family relationships 'are associated with the likelihood of further offending'. A high score normally leads to an intensive programme of intervention, but that intervention might be solely focused on reducing the risk of reoffending and might be a response that ignores or downgrades the life history factors which led to the risk score. An obvious example would be the risk assessment of a child from an abusive home. Assessment in areas such as disability, discrimination and mental health has also had a lower priority in the youth justice system than in child and family services. As Walker and Beckett have noted, young offenders are three times more likely to have mental health problems than other young people and yet are often neglected (Walker and Beckett 2003: 98). This is of concern because, in 2000, of 15–20 year-olds in prison service establishments, 90 per cent had a diagnosable mental health problem (Lyon *et al.* 2000).

Neverthless, if Asset assessment reveals behaviour attributable to harm within the family, there can be referral to, and the involvement of, children's services, although this might entail the different form of assessment in the *Framework* and two sets of timescales (Calder 2003: 28), which might be problematic. Another concern is that 'it is not apparent that basic information is routinely being shared between services' (NACRO 2003b: 5) so a full picture of a child might not be built up. Further, it is argued that YOT members should attend *Framework* training about child development and welfare, because that is seen as 'vital for sharing the corporate parenting culture and associated aims and objectives' which would be necessary for 'looked after' children who offend to receive relevant services and care to help in reducing their offending (ibid). Hudson has argued that, even with the inclusion in the assessment checklists of new 'dynamic' factors, such as empathy with victims and acceptance of responsibility, the assessment might lead to inappropriate or disproportionate intervention (Hudson 2003: 49–50).

Initiatives have aimed to bridge these different professional cultures in the child protection and youth justice systems. A National Children's Bureau project running from 2005–07 researched the developments of links between children's trusts and YOTs (NCB 2007), and another focused on 'looked after' children in Young Offender Institutions (NCB 2006). This is in line with government thinking. The Quality Protects programme to provide additional children's services has, as a specific objective, the bringing down of offending rates amongst 'looked after' children to the level of the general population in the area.[10] The Public Service Agreements for 2001–04 also included this convergence as a target (see NACRO 2003b). More importantly, the policies outlined in *Every Child Matters: Next Steps* were 'designed to support further progress by Youth Offending Teams ... by helping them work with other services to address some of the wider factors linked to tackling re-offending' (DfES 2004 at para. 4.22). The Children Act 2004 now enjoins such co-operation, and there is guidance on statutory inter-agency co-operation and the governance of children's trusts, including the role of YOTs (DfES 2005d). Six areas are currently demonstration sites for increased levels of involvement between children's trusts and YOTs.[11]

There are other concerns about Asset in practice. A follow-up study for the YJB of the reliability and validity of Asset concluded that there was an 'acceptable' level of consistency between individual assessors (inter-rater reliability) but found some significant divergences. The report suggested that, in some cases, YOT staff 'may be allocating ratings on the basis of perceived problems rather than the extent to which these were associated with the likelihood of further offending' (Baker *et al.* 2005: 6; see also p. 53 and Tables 4.11 and 4.12 for deviations from the normative score as given by a panel of experts). They gave as an example 'female offenders with lots of "welfare needs"' (ibid). This points up the clear predictive role of Asset – perhaps at the expense of clearer investigation and referral on welfare needs. This research also examined the relationship between the assessment and the design of the intervention plan, the assumption being that targets would be related to items scoring 3 or 4 in the assessment of risk factors (ibid: Chapter 5). The report concluded that designs were disappointing, with poor wording and a lack of directly related and SMART ('specific, measurable, achievable, realistic and relevant, and time-limited') targets (Baker *et al.* 2005: 62).

Research for the YJB on persistent young offenders was also very critical. The authors summarised their concerns as: the lack of understanding and training of YOT and Youth Inclusion Programme staff with regard to risk factors; the dearth of appropriate assessment and planned interventions based on risk and need; the general failure to record in detail assessments and subsequent interventions; the limited inter-agency work, especially with education and social services; and the failure to use past relevant information (Arnull *et al.* 2005: 9). Given the focus on early intervention, the comments of Baker and colleagues on the use of Onset – the assessment tool for use by Youth Inclusion and Support Panels (YISPs) with 8–13 year-olds – also raise concerns:

> [ONSET] is closely based on *Asset,* having a similar structure and content. ... these results for *Asset* highlight two issues that may be particularly important for ONSET development ... First,

encouraging practitioners to focus on risks of future offending behaviour when allocating scores may be more difficult at this stage. ... Second, ensuring a clear link between assessments and plans could be difficult. Both issues suggest a need for thorough training and effective managerial oversight. (Baker *et al.* 2005: 68)

What Hannah-Moffat refers to as the third generation assessment tool – with, potentially, a fourth version (2005: 33–4) – may ameliorate the problems with Asset and Onset which have been outlined, but professional assessments which focus on risk in the aggregate may still respond less to risk of harm than to risk of offending. A full assessment may also be precluded if Asset or Onset are used by narrowly trained youth justice workers. Guidance aimed at encouraging better use of Asset evidences some awareness of this in stating that it will help 'multi-agency YOT management groups, and YOTs themselves, to make improved use of Asset data to manage resources and to make the case locally for access to essential services for young offenders' (Youth Justice Board 2004: para. 5.012).

Even with the new actuarially based assessment tools, professional judgements must still be made to decide whether the appropriate legal threshold criteria have been met – whether they be in statute or in guidance. Those decisions will determine what the outcomes might be and the level to which services might be provided but, as noted above, those thresholds cannot be established in a purely objective exercise.

Conclusions

This chapter began with a quote from an article by Rod Morgan, then Chair of the YJB. In reference to the continued politicisation of law and order and the emergence of criminal justice and security as major industries in academia and professional practice, that passage continued:

When brought together, these aspects of the contemporary scene result in curious twin-track developments. There are shadowlands of rhetoric and reality. We have the espousal, in pursuit of evidence-based policy, of the allegedly gold standard of randomised trails (RCTs) while other policy initiatives flourish in what appears to be evidence and research free zones. And lurking on the sidelines are both morally restorative ... and scientifically reductivist visions, some of the latter springing from genetics and suggesting earlier and earlier pre-crime interventions. (Morgan 2006: 3, 34)

Whilst science is portrayed as the basis of new policies and practices, the situation is, as Morgan argues, more complex than this. Early intervention, 'sold' as being based on sound knowledge of statistical risks of unwanted outcomes and on the scientific assessment of individual children and young people, has been heralded as a panacea for preventing poor outcomes. Scientific research seems to promise the possibility of accurate targeting of groups and individuals for preventative action.

However, there is, as we shall see in Chapter 7, less science in relation to the type and detail of intervention. Nor are there clear answers as to how those targeted can be forced or encouraged to participate in preventative programmes or, indeed, how those who would like to participate can ensure their participation. Law is perceived as a powerful instrument for enforcement and, indeed, 'encouragement', and it is assumed law can play a role. The next chapter will examine where law and the courts might or might not be engaged in implementing a policy of investment in children.

Notes

1 *Hansard* HC col. 1168 (12 February 1932).
2 *Re H (Minors) (Sexual Abuse: Standard of Proof)* [1996] AC 563; *Re H and R* [1996] 1 FLR 80), per Lord Nicholls of Birkenhead.
3 See http://www.portsmouthcf.org.uk/pcf/yisp.html (accessed 15.11.07).
4 See Farrington and Welsh (2007) at pp. 8–12 for detailed discussion of these methodologies.
5 There is an ESRC funded Research Priority Network entitled *Pathways into and out of Crime: Risk, Resilience and Diversity*. Links to a large number of research projects and conferences can be found at http://www.pcrrd. group.shef.ac.uk/.
6 See http://www.crimereduction.homeoffice.gov.uk/youth/youth56.htm (accessed 15.11.07).
7 See http://www.everychildmatters.gov.uk/deliveringservices/caf/ for current information about the CAF.
8 See www.youth-justice-board.gov.uk/PractitionersPortal/Assessments/ Asset.htm.

9 Youth Justice Board (2005) *Persistent Young Offenders: A Retrospective Study*.
10 See http://www.dfes.gov.uk/qualityprotects/.
11 See http://www.yjb.gov.uk/en-gb/practitioners/ReformingChildrens Services/ChildrensTrusts/.

Chapter 6

Law's role in investment

A local authority cannot finesse away their specific or particular duty by claiming merely to act under a general one. (Mr Justice Holman 2007)[1]

The House of Lords judgement ... is extremely disappointing ... It will encourage the view ... that pragmatic discussions can be made about pupils with no reference to legal restrictions and safeguards laid down by Government. (Barrie 2006: 6)[2]

Law and children

The purpose of the first half of this book was to examine those 'intangibles' – the ideologies, social constructions and moral precepts – which obstruct or encourage the passage and full implementation of legislation aiming to improve the lives and prospects of children and young people. Notions of family, assumptions about what children and young people 'are', and ideas around investment against future risks are the key factors here. The last chapter also examined the difficulties in applying science to the identification of risk factors related to outcomes for children and to the choice of target groups for risk-based intervention to provide support and services to children and their families. So far, however, law has been referenced only tangentially: the factors 'allowing' or 'necessitating' legal change or state expenditure were the focus of the interest in Part I, and new legislation was the implied aim of pressure for change. Yet, in one sense, legislation is not law; it is, rather, a hybrid of law and politics, a document in which government policy is put into legal language and concepts. So the role of law as a functional system which makes right/wrong, yes/no and guilty/not guilty decisions on ambiguities and conflicts does not end once policy documents have been drafted as Bills but, rather, begins once an Act is on the statute book. Having said that, the pressure groups and others who wish to influence the final content of legislation will be complicit in a process of transforming demands and interests into terms that are acceptable as legal communications (King and King 2006: 39).

Given the ideological difficulties facing intervention in, and spending on, families (see Chapter 4), this chapter will focus on whether and how law does or could help to 'deliver' appropriate investment in children. The quotations at the beginning of this chapter stress that there are conflicting trends and areas of uncertain law in relation to the investment theme. This chapter will focus on three issues in particular, although the discussion will, of necessity, need to be selective. Can the duties and support 'owed' to children be enforced through law, if necessary against the wishes of their parents, and even if children have committed criminal offences? Can those who want help from the state insist on assessment for, and delivery of, services? Can the take-up of voluntarily offered services best be encouraged through the use of a symbolic role for law or enforced through an instrumental role?

Legal criteria and concepts

Law's role will be circumscribed by the way in which legislation is being used as a strategy to further investment in children. There are three main strategies. First, statutory provisions can provide financial criteria and structures for the release of (more) resources for particular services; secondly, they can set up new administrative structures for protective or preventative intervention and the delivery of services, and, thirdly, they can lay down new criteria, duties and powers for intervention, access to resources and service delivery, as well as new offences and liabilities for 'negative' actions or inaction. Each of these strategies may result in lawyers and the courts being called upon to interpret the meaning and application of legal provisions, through negotiation or adjudication, and thereby justify and endorse the legality of decisions made and actions taken. Lawyers and courts are also called upon to advise and adjudicate in relation to the disciplinary measures provided in criminal and civil law to apply to those who fall short of the level of action and type of involvement envisaged by government policy.

Parliament's use of law to secure the welfare and future productive, law-abiding development of children has meant in practice that four main categories of legal criteria have been enshrined in legislation with the following functions:

- To structure and justify judicial decisions about aspects of a minor's upbringing in private disputes between parents and/or other care-givers.

- To permit or refuse compulsory intervention to protect, control or punish minors.

- To justify or deny public expenditure – by the NHS, educational and social care departments, for example – on services and programmes for children, young people and their families.

- To constrain or punish those whose behaviour obstructs achievement of the desired outcomes for a particular child or children generally.

Particular legal concepts are pivotal to the decisions of courts in relation to interventions designed to be preventative. Some of these have biblical, common law and Elizabethan Poor Law origins, and these lingering precepts from older moralities have contributed to inherent ambiguities in their meaning and application. On the other hand, the body of law relating specifically to the rights, duties and powers held by children or exercised in relation to children is relatively new,[3] and so 'old' ideas operate alongside newer concepts. Some of these concepts are used across child protection, education and health, and others are not.

Law's 'thinking'

There is another issue. Chapter 2 reviewed those ideas about children which have been most influential in Parliament over the last two centuries. Those ideas may or may not have been 'accurate' representations of 'real' children. Law, like politics, is a self-reproducing system (Luhmann 2004; Teubner 1993; King and Thornhill 2006) which cannot 'think' about real children and so law's constructions of children to 'fit' in with law's thinking, will also be influential in applying legislation to individual children and their families. Law uses a variety of images – or semantic artefacts – of children which may change over time and may not necessarily be compatible with each other. They are constructs for a purpose (see King and Piper 1995). One issue, then, is whether law will need to reconstruct the new images of children and youth which Chapter 2 examined.[4]

What is more, law – like politics – has no way of 'knowing' what is good or bad for children. Just as politics incorporates into its thinking dominant ideas about children and what is good for them, so law, if asked to adjudge on 'need' or 'harm', refers to 'truths' established by scientific systems of thinking. The means by which law is able to do this include the legal procedure of seeking and hearing expert evidence – the evidence of those professionals engaged in what might be loosely termed child welfare science (King and Piper 1995: Chapter 3). But, as we shall see, the 'truths' are not always reconstructed from child development or medical science; they may be those of politics or economics, themselves systems with their own particular communications and constructs.

To illustrate some of these difficulties, the next section will focus on 'safeguarding', specifically child protection and children's services, by the local authority, where the most important legal concepts are the welfare principle, 'in need' and 'significant harm', which can currently be found in the Children Act 1989, sections 1, 17 and 31, respectively.

Enforcing or denying duties

The Children Act 1989, notwithstanding the passage of the Children Act 2004, is still the major piece of legislation consolidating and reforming the law which allocates basic rights, duties and powers to parents and others in the upbringing of children. It places duties on local authorities – and on the new bodies set up by the Children Act 2004. The application of the new duties and powers in the Children Act 2004, which reorganise structures, specify outcomes, ring-fence money and place duties on public bodies, may need to be interpreted by legal and other professionals and may be reviewed or adjudicated upon by the courts, as they have done in relation to the 1989 Act duties. Two problematic issues which might arise are, first, the interpretation of legislation, rights conventions and cases which have cost implications and so deny or enforce expenditure for the benefit of children and, secondly, the use of courts to discipline children and their parents who do not choose to participate in opportunities offered.

Section 17

At this point in time, the evidence must come largely from the responses of the courts to cases brought under the 1989 Act. If we are focusing on the allocation of services to children and their families then section 17 of the Children Act 1989 is the most appropriate place to start. Section 17(1) of the Children Act 1989 states that:

> It shall be the general duty of every local authority (in addition to the other duties imposed on them by this Part)—
> (a) to safeguard and promote the welfare of children within their area who are in need; and
> (b) so far as is consistent with that duty, to promote the upbringing of such children by their families,
> by providing a range and level of services appropriate to those children's needs.

Section 17(10) clarifies that a child shall be taken to be in need if:

> (a) he is unlikely to achieve or maintain, or to have the opportunity of achieving or maintaining, a reasonable standard of health or development without the provision for him of services by a local authority under this Part;
> (b) his health or development is likely to be significantly impaired, or further impaired, without the provision for him of such services; or
> (c) he is disabled ...

Section 17 deals, then, with children 'in need' of services and incorporates a legal criterion for expenditure which has a long history, going back to at least the Elizabethan Poor Laws (Bainham 2005: 16–18) and which originally related to orphans and the destitute. It is essentially a legal device to legitimate the use of public funds to foster the welfare of children so that those administering the budget of the Poor Law Guardians (then) and the local authority or Children's Trust budget (now) are not sued for misuse of public money. Therefore, whilst the aim is to allow and encourage expenditure on children, there is a tension with the very different aim of rationing the use of public funds only for expenditure on legitimate purposes. The context is the political necessity of upholding a parsimony principle in relation to both local and national taxation. Within this context, section 17 is constructed as a general duty to children in need so that money can be spent on services which target groups of children with the particular needs indicated in the legislation.

Until recently, regulations have required the local authority to identify within their area these needs and specify their responses in a Children's Services Plan. As a result of the new overarching duties in sections 10 and 11 of the Children Act 2004 (section 25 and 26 for Wales), that plan has been replaced with the Children and Young People's Plan (Children Act 2004, section 17 and SI 2005 No. 2149 as amended by the SI 2007 No. 57), which must specifically relate to the five outcomes (see Chapter 3). That plan, if properly constructed as a result of the required consultation, and published and reviewed as required, is a means by which the local authority is able legitimately to structure its discretion so that services can be provided within the budget allocated or allowed by central government. Schedule 2 of the 1989 Act, which places on local authorities specific duties, such as taking steps to encourage children not to commit criminal offences, contains considerable discretion in that it is widely drawn and the duties are qualified by notions of what it is 'reasonable' so to do. Examples of the discretion accorded are to be found in the use of 'reasonable steps' (paras 1(1), 4(1) and 7), 'reasonably practicable' (paras 1(2)(b) and 10), 'may assess' (para. 3), 'may assist' (para. 5(1)), and 'as they consider appropriate' (paras 8 and 9(1)). The issue for the courts is then in determining the precise scope of these duties and powers and establishing criteria for reviewing the exercise of this discretion.

Assessment

There are three crucial issues concerning the assessment process: whether the law and guidance impose a duty to assess, whether an individual who asks for services for which an assessment is a prerequisite has a right to an assessment, and whether there is any remedy if a 'positive' assessment does not lead to suitable services.

The law in relation to the first issue is not totally clear. There is no explicit duty to assess 'need' in the Children Act 1989, although *The Framework for the Assessment of Children in Need* (DoH 2000; DfES 2006d) makes it clear that assessment should be undertaken, at least at the level of an initial exploratory review, to see if a fuller assessment is required. It would also appear that the courts expect local authorities to follow the *Framework* guidance when conducting assessments related to Children Act 1989 duties (see Chapter 5). In *R v Islington Borough Council ex parte Rixon* the court stated that a local authority has to comply 'in substance' with government guidance issued under section 7 of the Local Authority (Social Services) Act 1970,[5] and Lloyd Jones J made a similar statement in a more recent case:

> That document is issued under section 7 of the Local Authority (Social Services) Act 1970 which requires local authorities in their social services functions to act under the general guidance of the Secretary of State. Accordingly this guidance does not have the full force of statute, but its provisions are to be complied with unless local circumstances indicate exceptional reasons which justify a variation.[6]

Three important appeals involving the London Boroughs of Lambeth and Barnet, heard together by the House of Lords in 2003,[7] focused on section 17. The majority – as Cowan puts it – 'thought assessment was implied through section 17' (Cowan 2004: 334). For example, Lord Nichols of Birkenhead said that he was 'fortified' in his view that section 17 did impose a duty to assess a particular child 'by noting the consequences of the alternative approach' put forward by the local authority that, because section 17(1) does not impose a duty in relation to an individual child, there is no duty to assess the needs of a child in need: 'That cannot be right. That would go far to stultify the whole purpose of Part III of the Children Act 1989. The first step towards safeguarding and promoting the welfare of a child in need by providing services for him and his family is to identify the child's needs for those services.'[8]

The argument, then, is that the guidance does in effect impose a duty to assess, but that the duty does not give a child the right to be assessed. This is important given that it is known that the assessment of children – and so the possibility of accessing resources – is not consistent across local authorities (DfES et al. 2004). Recent research would also suggest little uniformity with regard to initial and core assessments of children in need or at risk, as well as in the subsequent provision of services (Masson et al. 2008: 25–30).

The legal situation is clearer in relation to the assessment of one category of children since the Children (Leaving Care) Act 2000 amended the Children Act 1989. The new section 23B(3) imposes a duty on the responsible local authority in relation to each eligible and relevant child '(a) to carry out an assessment of his needs with a view to determining what advice, assistance and support it would be appropriate for them to provide him under this Part; and (b) to prepare a pathway plan for him'. The 'eligible' children are those children aged 16 and 17 who have spent the requisite period as a child 'looked after' by the local authority, whether under a care order or under section 20 of the Children Act 1989, and the 'relevant' children are such children who left care when 16 or 17. A small number of cases have already been brought under that section and most hinge – as did the early case of *R (on the application of W) v Essex CC*[9] – on whether the local authority was right not to treat the applicant as a relevant or eligible child. In this case the court decided that W had been 'looked after', and so the authority did owe 'after care' duties and should assess W for that purpose. More recently, as the quotation at the beginning of this chapter shows, Holman J was more robust when dealing, in *H v Wandsworth and others*, with three cases concerning unaccompanied asylum-seeker minors where the local authorities concerned had, wrongly in relation to two of the young people, sought to avoid their duties by arguing they had been accommodated under section 17 and not section 20.[10] In these cases it would appear that local authorities, sometimes supported by the courts,[11] are attempting to narrow the category of children to whom the duty applies. In *Sutton*, however, Stanley Burnton J was very scathing of the standard of the assessment done by the local authority in relation to the section 20 duty.[12]

These different approaches can also been in a series of cases in relation to the distinction between section 23(2) and 23(6) of the Children Act 1989. The former section begins, 'A local authority shall provide accommodation and maintenance for any child whom they are looking after', and the latter includes the statement 'any local authority looking after a child shall make arrangements to enable him to live with (a) a person falling within subsection (4); or (b) a relative, friend or other person connected with him'. Previous cases took the view that if a child falls within section 23(6), the child is not accommodated by the local authority and so the authority does not incur the expense of the accommodation. The court could, of course, have taken a less restrictive approach. In a recent case involving the London Borough of Southwark,[13] the court did construe section 23(2) more broadly. In that case the authority unsuccessfully appealed a decision that the child was being 'looked after' by the local authority: the authority had contacted the claimant and asked her to take the child into her home that same day, and the court stated that 'no reasonable bystander' could have thought other than that the accommodation would be at the authority's expense.

These legal difficulties regarding assessment for duties under Part III contrast with the law in relation to children deemed to be at risk under Parts IV and V of the Children Act 1989. Section 47 mandates an assessment when there is 'reasonable cause to suspect' a child is suffering or will suffer significant harm, and, once care proceedings are under way, the courts may be involved in decisions about the form of assessment needed. In *Re L and H*, for example, the Court of Appeal ordered a residential assessment under section 38(6), which empowers the court to make such directions if it has made an interim care or supervision order.[14] However, this case should be set in the context of the more restrictive interpretation of the powers of the court under this section, made with explicit reference to the cost, established by the House of Lords in *Re G*,[15] a decision which has been criticised (Kennedy 2006).[16]

Services

The second issue – whether and when an individual has any redress if services are not provided when they adjudge themselves to need them – has been a major issue for children and their families. In particular, the legal issue is whether they can use the courts to pursue a grievance and receive a relevant solution in relation to assessment for, or the provision of, services under this section. In general, where legislation sets up new administrative processes and benefits then the legislation also sets up an administrative procedure to receive complaints and review decision-making. The courts have endorsed the view, in this area as in others, that the courts should not be the first resort of complainants.

The Children Act 1989 provides, in section 26, for the case review and grievance procedures for this part of the Act, which can be used by the child or his or her family and the courts have confirmed that this complaints procedure should normally be used before applying for judicial review of the operation of section 17.[17] In practice, it is sometimes possible for advocates to persuade the courts to grant leave to apply for judicial review without using the complaints procedure because of an emergency or a particular failing by the local authority. For example, in *R v Tower Hamlets LBC ex parte Bradford*,[18] the court allowed an application because the local authority had not complied with an undertaking to assess the needs of the child in question under section 17. Leave may also be given because the time limits for the complaints procedure have been breached, as in *R v Royal Borough of Kingston-upon-Thames ex parte T*.[19] If such leave is not given then time will be lost, and time is a real issue in relation to children. In the context of children's home closures, Lindsay goes as far as to argue that 'making a complaint under this statutory complaints procedure is often an exercise in futility', particularly if, as in an example he gives, the notice given for closure was three weeks (2006: 27).

However, even if children or their parents are given the 'right' to apply for judicial review, the court is limited in what it can then do. For example, in *Re T (Judicial Review: Local Authority Decisions Concerning Child in Need)*,[20] the assessment and decision-making process of the local authority was adjudged to be 'unreasonable' when applying the criteria established by the *Wednesbury* case.[21] The decision of the local authority was quashed, but the court reiterated that the process of judicial review does not allow a court to direct the local authority as to outcome.

Another legal remedy which can sometimes be used by those who have suffered a 'wrong' is an action in tort for negligence (see Bailey 2006) or an action for breach of a statutory duty. In *X (Minors) v Bedfordshire County Council* (1995), a child protection case, the House of Lords held that there was no cause of action for either of these remedies, and a case relating to nurseries and childminders at that time similarly failed to establish that a breach gives rise to civil liability.[22] However, *Z v UK*,[23] in the European Court of Human Rights, established that actions for negligence can be brought by a child against a local authority in relation to child protection actions or the lack of them, and the English courts have responded to this judgment (see Bainham 2005: 461–4 for subsequent cases in the Court of Appeal). 'The position that the law has now reached is that each case depends on its facts', but the case of *JD v East Berkshire Community Health Trust and others*[24] 'has marked a noticeable shift in the approach of the law' (Herring 2007: 625). That case upheld case law that had established that parents could not sue doctors or social workers for negligence in relation to the investigatory stage of child protection work because of the need not to constrain professionals in their investigations (at para. 85). However, it did establish that there was a duty of care to children.

Since then, the issues have been revisited in *Lawrence v Pembrokeshire*,[25] a case in which the claimant asked the court to reconsider the law, as the facts of the East Berkshire case had arisen before the implementation of the Human Rights Act 1998. Auld LJ determined that 'the advent of Art 8 to our domestic law ... does not undermine or weaken as a matter of public policy the primacy of the need to protect children from abuse ... from, among others, their parents' (para. 41). Further, in the recent child support case bought by

Mrs Rowley,[26] the Court of Appeal decided that it would not be 'just and reasonable' or consistent with the statutory scheme to impose a duty of care on the Secretary of State for Work and Pensions via the Child Support Agency (see Burrows 2007).

Another objective of the Children Act 2004 is that of increasing the co-operation between agencies in the hope that this will increase the provision of services and prevent children from 'falling through the net'. In review after review, the lack of 'joined-up' working has been perceived as the problem which has led to social work 'failures' and child deaths. The Children Act 1989 also encouraged co-operation through section 27, which specifies that a local authority can request the help of any of the listed authorities, and so the courts may be asked to decide whether partner agencies have properly co-operated with one another and the children's services authority. However, the provision mandates others to comply with a request only if 'it is compatible with their own statutory or other duties and obligations and does not unduly prejudice the discharge of any of their functions' (section 27(2)). The section has, therefore, proved largely ineffective: other legislation usually provides different criteria within which the partner agency must make decisions about services. Again, the *Lambeth* cases above pointed up this difficulty in relation to housing and the criteria for allocating publicly funded housing that are to be found in the Housing Acts. If more effective co-operation is to be achieved, it will have to be via guidance and ring-fenced money or legislation specifically addressing these conflicts: currently, law is unable to ensure this cooperation.

A general or specific duty?

Re T (2003 – see above) also stated that the duty of the local authority in section 22(3) of the Children Act 1989 to safeguard and promote the welfare of looked after children was a general duty which did not require a particular course of action. This issue of the nature of a general duty has been a crucial legal issue and one which has centred recently around the argument that the general duty in section 17 (which affords no individual a right to pursue an outcome in the courts because it is a duty to a target group and the courts deal with individuals) can become a specific duty once a child has been assessed as being 'in need'. All the children in the *Lambeth* and *Barnet* cases, noted above, had been assessed as in need and lacked suitable accommodation, but the majority judgment upheld the continuing nature of the general duty and the power of the local authority to set its own gate-keeping policies to ration the use of resources. The result of such case law is, according to Murphy, that there is 'Now ... very little accountability owed by the local authority in relation to children's services' (Murphy, 2003: 103) and so there is also very little for law to adjudicate.[27]

Some commentators have been very critical of the judicial approach, arguing that 'it is not an option for courts simply to defect from their obligations to protect vulnerable citizens against unlawful conduct of central government or local authorities, wherever scarce resources are at issue' (Palmer 2003: 309). The issue is, however, that the judiciary is very careful not to move into territory which it believes to belong to the executive and legislature. The result, argue France and Utting, is that 'a combination of scarce resources in the 1990s and a vague definition of "need" turned the legislation into an instrument for rationing, rather than furnishing better support' (2005: 77).[28]

Perhaps this is to be expected: section 17 remains essentially a mechanism to ensure the local authority's expenditure is not illegal. The deceptive use of the concept of a 'duty' and, according to the guidance issued in 1991, the 'deliberately wide' definition of 'in need' had led some to believe it would herald more and enforceable expenditure on preventative services (see Masson 2006: 235–6), but, as Williams points out:

> The Children Act 1989 drew deliberate lines of demarcation between judicial and administrative decision-making, conferring discretion on local authorities over provision of support and care, but assigning to the courts control over decisions about who can exercise parental responsibility and over certain disputes as to its exercise. Since the coming into force of the Human Rights Act ... the courts have shown their continuing adherence to this demarcation. (Williams 2007: 262).

So whilst some cases since the implementation of the Human Rights Act 1998 have successfully criticised decision-making processes as being incompatible with rights under the European Convention on Human Rights (ECHR),[30] generally speaking, legislation, with the co-operation of the courts, has operated to sideline any clear idea of the child with rights in relation to services. Law is either not thinking about the child or it is thinking about a child in the context of public policy and the use of scarce resources.

Explaining the law's stance on local authority duties

Law is sidelined

Much of the relevant legislation provides little opportunity for law to adjudicate within its competence: it leaves few conditional statements (see King 2006) on which law can make lawful/unlawful decisions. Law, then, has little to adjudicate or review. In *Youth Matters: Next Steps* the Government made clear that 'We are moving to a system where the accountabilities for delivering outcomes for young people are clearly placed at local level in keeping with *Every Child Matters*' (2006e: 26). The children's trusts will undertake 'a thorough needs analysis … [and] will then map existing provision against needs, identifying and addressing duplication and gaps' (ibid). The discourse and the method is that of management, not law, and such well documented decision-making will be very hard to challenge judicially. Risk-justified interventions also bypass legal notions: if guilt, due process and standards of proof are irrelevant to intervention then there is no role for law in deciding whether intervention is justified (Goldson 2005).

Further, the legislation stemming from *Every Child Matters* and *Youth Matters* establishes several review bodies which are based in management and politics, rather than in legal rights. For example, the Education and Inspection Act 2006 establishes an Office for Standards in Education, Children's Services and Skills, and a new HM Inspectorate of Education, Children's Services and Skills (sections 112–114). Chief Inspectors for Schools (abolished by the Act), as for the Prison Service, reporting to their relevant Secretaries of State, have often given high-profile publicity to conditions and professional practices which are deemed inadequate. This has sometimes, but not always, produced sufficient political pressure to lead to legislative change or greater resources. However, the new Inspectorate set up by the 2006 Act has its remit set and its effectiveness overseen by the new Crown Office, also established by the Act (sections 118–119).

No welfare principle

The cases above showed that, generally, the overriding concern of the courts is not to fetter the discretion of the local authority – either to manage its own resources or to protect children as it sees fit. However, where the welfare principle in section 1(1) of the Children Act 1989 operates, the courts can approach cases differently because the child's welfare must be paramount when the court makes decisions about the child's upbringing. That section does not apply to section 17 or any of the other sections in Part III of the 1989 Act, however. It does not apply for two reasons. First, according to the wording of section 1, it is the court – not the local authority – who must make the welfare of the child the determinative principle and, as we have seen, the court's review of the operation of section 17 focuses on the reasonableness or proportionality of the local authority's actions. Secondly, case law has clarified that, 'This duty cast upon the local authority to promote and safeguard welfare is not the same duty cast upon the court by section 1 to place welfare as the paramount consideration. Other considerations can and frequently do affect the local authority's approach.'[31]

This is important because, where the welfare principle does apply, the concept of best interests is determinative of the outcome and 'justice is done' if the decision can be justified in terms of the child's best interests. (For the history and operation of the welfare principle see Alston 1994; O'Halloran 1999; Parker 1994; Day Sclater and Piper 2001.) Interpreting the child's best interests in the family courts can, therefore, legitimate an outcome which trumps what might otherwise be regarded as injustice to adults. It is also the means by which law can take on board – can reconstruct – scientific knowledge about children, through using experts or through judicial training, that is external to law (see King and Piper 1995, Chapter 3). However, in section 17 cases, where the welfare principle does not operate, the 'truths' which influence the outcome are political or economic ones, not child welfare science. For example, in the *R (W) v Lambeth* case, Lord Scott decided in favour of the restrictive policy of the local authority (whereby homeless children would be fostered and so not live with their parent) even though fostering was more expensive than finding accommodation for the mother and child.[32] The economic principle that was endorsed was that costs would be lower in the long term because of the deterrent effect of the policy.

Even the welfare principle cannot, however, ensure what the judges might consider to be an optimum outcome: the court has little control, for example, over the implementation of agreed care plans. Reported cases reveal that 'relationships between local authorities and the courts have been characterised by mutual suspicion and antagonism' (Smith 2000: 373). In *Re S and W* the Court of Appeal roundly criticised Cheshire County Council for not having absorbed 'elementary principles of family law and practice' with regard to co-operation between the judge and local authority.[33]

Further, even section 31, where the court can make a care order if the child is found to be suffering significant harm attributable to his or her parents, is a means by which only the worst cases of cruelty or neglect are dealt with. The significant harm test justifies *non*-intervention where the harm is less than 'significant'. Those ideologies about the importance of autonomous families and the authority of parents that were examined in Chapter 3 have worked, therefore, to constrain intervention and ration expenditure to a relatively narrow category of children. Nor is there a consensus that the category should be widened. Guggenheim, for example, would argue that the category of children is still too wide and impinges too far on the autonomy of the family: 'The insistence by the children's rights movement that children's interests be separated from those of their parents ... is its most egregious error' (Guggenheim 2005: 13; see also King 2007).

The welfare principle is accompanied by a welfare checklist in section 1(3) of the Children Act 1989, designed to aid the courts in its assessment of where the child's best interests lie in relation, for example, to residence or contact. Arguably, however, the checklist points up the narrowness of the judicial exercise: in effect it produces a balance sheet of deficits and advantages, the decision being made in favour of one or other of the parties depending on who has most credit or least debit. It does not ensure all the debits are made good and, in particular, it cannot address investment in social and economic deficits (see King and Piper 1995: Chapter 1; Schiratzsk 2000).

The weight of the child's views

The child and his or her views may be legally irrelevant to an application centring on Part III duties and powers or similar provisions in the Children Act 2004. There was no clear image of the child underpinning the cases reviewed above: indeed there was often no image at all. The different conceptions of children in law and policy outlined in Chapter 2 have been almost irrelevant for law to fulfil its functions in relation to these public law provisions. This situation contrasts with the effect of provisions in the Children Act 1989 and the Children (Northern Ireland) Order 1995 which require the court, when applying the welfare checklist, to 'have regard to' the 'ascertainable wishes and feelings of the child' or to ascertain and 'give due consideration to' the child's wishes, 'in the light of his age and understanding'.[34] Where the welfare principle and the checklist do apply, the reasoning of the courts must include reference to the child's wishes and feelings. In practice, however, the process of 'ascertaining' and the impact of children's wishes may be limited.

The weight to be given to children's wishes generally and in particular circumstances had been the subject of reported cases from the English and Scottish courts long before the Children Act 1989 (Piper 1999d: 77; Scottish Law Commission 1992: 53). However, the incorporation of the 'wishes and feelings' requirement in a welfare checklist followed specific recommendations of the (English) Law Commission, which reflected the concerns of consultees about the 'dangers in giving them [children's views] too much recognition' (Law Commission 1988: para. 3.23) and were, in part, a response to the UK's imminent signing of the United Nations Convention on the Rights of the Child (UNCRC) and its subsequent 'duties' in relation to Article 12 focusing on the child's views (see Chapter 1). The Scottish Law Commission argued differently: 'The child's own views ... we believe, ought to be taken into account in their own right and not just as an aspect of welfare' (1992: para. 5.23). Similarly, Scottish law has diverged from the law in England, Wales and Northern Ireland in relation to the child's right to consent to adoption. The Adoption (Scotland) Act 1978, in section 12(8),[35] requires the agreement of children aged 12 or over to their adoption, whereas the Adoption Act 1976 and its successor, the Adoption and Children Act 2002, applying to England and Wales, and the Adoption (Northern Ireland) Order 1987 do not include such a requirement (see Piper and Miachichev 2003). However, the Republic of Ireland places less weight on the wishes of the mature child than occurs in the UK (O'Halloran 2001).

There are, however, duties on the local authority and other bodies to ascertain and consider the child's views in non-judicial processes. As passed, the Children Act 1989 imposed on local authorities a general duty to do so – 'as far as is reasonably practicable' – in relation to decision-making about 'looked after' children and specifically in relation to the review of cases and complaints by children.[36] Section 46 also requires the police to do so in relation to emergency police protection, and sections 61 and 64 impose similar duties on voluntary organisations and the proprietors of children's homes. This duty to ascertain and have regard to the wishes and feelings of the child has recently been extended. Section 53 of the Children Act 2004 inserts this requirement into sections 17, 20 and 47 of the Children Act 1989, which deal, respectively, with children in need, children who are accommodated by the local authority, and children who are being investigated as being at risk of significant harm. The Education Act 2002 also requires there to be consultation with pupils, with the views of a pupil likewise being 'considered in the light of his age and understanding' (section 176(2)). All these, however, are duties on professionals, not the courts. They are aimed at the social workers, police and other child and youth workers in their dealings with children, particularly when decisions have to be made. They are not matters for the court unless the tightly constrained applications noted above reach a judge. This does not mean they are unimportant, but they are simply not procedures directly under the control of the courts.

Furthermore, for over a decade, there has also been criticism of the time, expertise and importance given in practice to the task of ascertaining the wishes and feelings of the child in those legal proceedings where that task is required or encouraged. For example, if a care order is sought in relation to a child then section 41 of the Children Act 1989 mandates the appointment of a children's guardian to represent the best interests of the child and a solicitor to represent those interests in court. There are also procedures whereby a child could request and may be granted separate presentation by a solicitor of his or her views (which may not converge with the guardian's construction of the child's interests). Care proceedings are, however, one of a very limited number of proceedings which are specified proceedings for the purpose of the Act and which, therefore, attract this 'dual' form of representation for the child. The situation in private family proceedings is such that the opportunity for a child to have his or her wishes and feelings ascertained and put before the court is severely restricted both by the rules[37] and in the practice of professionals (see, for example, Lowe and Murch 2002; Piper 1997, 1999c, 2000). A recent report of HM Inspectorate of Court Administration (2005) found, for example, that a third of the court reports did not reach the appropriate standard, and the courts are reluctant to grant the child party status. The Department for Constitutional Affairs commissioned research on the matter (Douglas *et al.* 2006) and selectively used it to support its first proposal in a consultation paper, *Separate Representation of Children* (DCA 2006; the responses are reported in the paper published by the Ministry of Justice in 2007): 'A child should be made a party to proceedings only where there is a legal need to do so'. In any case, with the emphasis now on agreement-seeking in family law disputes, the child's views are inevitably marginalised if the mediation or negotiation is solely between parents without direct input from the child.

It would seem that the provisions of the Children Act 1989 are inadequate in ensuring that children are 'heard' in either public or private child law proceedings (Monk 2002; Fortin 2006a). Unhelpful and very divergent images of children still exist in law so that, 'in practice, children's voices are excluded or used selectively to resolve adult disputes' (Monk 2002: 48). In particular, Monk analysed the different approaches to children who are the subject of procedures relating to special educational needs (SEN) and exclusion (from school). In SEN cases, the child is constructed with reference to developmental psychology and so, within a medico-scientific discourse, is seen as 'ill' and in need of treatment, which requires resources. In school exclusion cases, the child is constructed as 'bad' and in need of punishment: the image incorporates longstanding ideas about acceptable and unacceptable pupil behaviour (Monk 2002: 50; see also Monk 2005). Courts are, therefore, implicated in this process of reaffirming what 'normal' pupils are (2002: 52), part of a process of 'identification of anomalies' which Jenks argues is 'integral to the establishment of social order' (Jenks 1996: 129). Rights to legal representation of children in practice have generally come into play only if there is parental or child 'failure', notably in care and criminal proceedings (Monk 2002: 54). However, argues Fortin, when children are enabled to bring their own application to court 'the domestic courts adopt an entirely different approach' in relation to European Convention rights (2006a: 304).

A role for rights

International Conventions

It has been argued that the Children Act 1989, with its focus on partnership between state and parent, left little room for the child or his or her rights: 'The outcome of the concern with the re-establishment of the family, was a denial of the rights-bearing child and instead in the context of private family law the focus became more on the family as an ideal than on the child' (Hendrick 2003: 203). Fortin also argued, before the implementation of the Human Rights Act (HRA) 1998, that the jurisprudence of the European Court had prioritised the family over the child by reinforcing 'the common view advocated by most legal systems throughout the world that the value of family life lies in its privacy from state interference; furthermore, that family privacy involves autonomy' (Fortin 1999: 369–70). She went further: 'Indeed, there is a considerable risk that incorporation of the Convention may encourage the increasingly laissez-faire approach adopted by English law regarding the regulation of family life' (ibid: 370).

The implementation of the HRA 1998 meant not only that all government legislation should be rights-compliant, but also that individuals can invoke, in the domestic courts, their rights under those articles of the European Convention on Human Rights (ECHR) which are specified in section 1(1) of the Act. In such proceedings, courts must take account of relevant European Court and Commission jurisprudence. Further, by section 6(1) of the HRA 1998, 'It is unlawful for a public authority to act in a way which is incompatible with a Convention right'. This has led to 'a reconfiguration in the discourse and norms of English judicial review' (Poole 2007: 1), pushed by the fact that the threshold for a successful judicial review of the reasonableness of decision-making will be the lower test of 'proportionality' if human rights breaches are involved (see Public Law Project 2006: 4). Proportionality requires a balancing exercise between the interests of the community/state and the protection of the interests/rights of an individual. One approach to weighting the state's action is to ask whether the state's objective is legitimate, whether the measure is suitable for achieving it, whether it is necessary, whether it is the least intrusive means of achieving the aim, and whether the end justifies the means overall (ibid).

Given the above review of relevant cases and the statement of Sedley J in *R v Somerset CC ex parte Dixon* that 'Public law is not at base about rights, even though abuses of power may and often do invade private rights; it is about wrongs – that is to say misuses of public power',[38] optimism here may not be appropriate. However, one might also take into account that, at least on one level, recent policy statements herald a new focus on children as citizens and, according to *Youth Matters: Next Steps,* the main theme of the earlier consultation paper was 'the engagement of young people in shaping social services' (DfES 2006a: Summary, p. 1). Further, *Every Child Matters* states that 'The Government wants to prevent situations where a child does not receive the help they need because of too rigid an interpretation of the privacy of the child and their family' (DfES 2003: 54). These developments, together with increasing reference to the principles of the United Nations Convention on the Rights of the Child (UNCRC), might provide scope for the construction of children as rights holders and lead to case law more beneficial to children and their families.

Unlike the ECHR, the UNCRC does not give the individual child any means by which he or she can use the courts to ensure the rights stated in the Convention are implemented. As international law – dealing with both welfare and autonomy rights – the effectiveness of the UNCRC at the level of policy and legislation depends on the political pressure on signatory states generated by the negative publicity resulting from non-compliance. At the level of judicial reasoning and professional practice, compliance with the articles in the UNCRC depends on the internalisation of their precepts, their incorporation in guidance and their influence evident in judicial principles. States must report periodically on their progress and the UNCRC Committee issues its concluding observations with any recommendations for improvement. The two reports submitted and examined in 1995 and 2002 have been critical of the UK. Nevertheless the Committee's observations in 2002 welcomed several positive developments, including the complete abolition of corporal punishment in schools and the withdrawal of reservations concerning economic exploitation and ensuring children deprived of their liberty have access to legal advice (Articles 32 and 37d) (see Dimmock 2007: 27). The next examination is in September 2008, and the Government in its third report has highlighted the 'Every Child Matters' programme, the target of ending child poverty by 2020 and increased participation rights as significant policy developments.

Changes in judicial thinking

Several high-profile cases have evidenced change, reflecting the influence of the UNCRC and ECHR. Thorpe LJ in the *Mabon* case referred to the 'obligations' imposed by Article 12 of the UNCRC as well as Article 8 of the ECHR, and noted that the provision being discussed was rights-compliant if there was, on the part of the judiciary, 'a keener appreciation of the autonomy of the child and the child's consequential right to participate in decision making processes'.[39] There is also evidence that other leading judges are taking a different approach to the views of children. The following, reproduced at length because of its importance in its reliance on a new image of the child as 'moral actor', is from the speech of Baroness Hale of Richmond in the recent *In Re D* case, which concerned an application to return a child to Romania:

As any parent who has ever asked a child what he wants for tea knows, there is a large difference between taking account of a child's views and doing what he wants. Especially in Hague Convention cases, the relevance of the child's views to the issues in the case may be limited. But there is now a growing understanding of the importance of listening to the children involved in children's cases. It is the child, more than anyone else, who will have to live with what the court decides. Those who do listen to children understand that they often have a point of view which is quite distinct from that of the person looking after them. They are quite capable of being moral actors in their own right. Just as the adults may have to do what the court decides whether they like it or not, so may the child. But that is no more a reason for failing to hear what the child has to say than it is for refusing to hear the parents' views.[40]

In this case, eight years old seemed to be the age at which views could not be ignored. Baroness Hale went on to state that children should be heard more frequently in Hague Convention cases than in past practice and reviewed the means by which such views could be ascertained. However, she also noted that, 'There is no reason why the approach which should be adopted in European cases should not also be adopted in others. The more uniform the practice, the better' (at para. 61). She then referred to a recent case Court of Appeal case – *In re H*[41] – which had suggested that the test for party status and separate representation of children 'should in future be more rather than less stringently applied' (ibid).

There are also cases evidencing a more proactive use of the ECHR: Munby J has drawn attention to the potential importance of this positive obligation on the state to respect both private and family life imposed by Article 8(1) of the ECHR (Munby 2005: 5), now reviewable in the domestic courts.[42] The ECtHR, in the *Botta v Italy* case, had pointed out that this positive obligation can extend to the state being required to prevent another individual from interfering with private or family life.[43] Palmer has noted, for example, case law which established that 'failure to provide accommodation for disabled persons within a reasonable period of time following assessments constitutes a breach of Art.8 ECHR' (Palmer 2003: 323–4),[44] and Munby noted that a child's Article 8 rights may be engaged 'if he is being brought up in surroundings that isolate him socially or confine or stultify him emotionally' (Munby 2005: 5). Such a right may be in conflict with a parent's right to family life, but the state may have a duty to intervene to ensure respect for the child's rights (ibid: 7). Such rights-based reasoning which takes full account of the child's rights would lead to a different balancing of interests (Fortin 2006a).

Several important rights-based judgements have focused on children and young people in Prison Service establishments – whether they be there as sentenced offenders or as children in mother and baby units. Munby J referred very broadly to 'human rights law' in the case brought by the Howard League for Penal Reform when deciding whether the obligations imposed by sections 17 and 47 of the Children Act 1989 applied to children in Prison Service establishments.[45] That decision led directly to new guidance being issued to all local authorities and governors of prisons and young offender institutions which quoted Munby J and promised further guidance to 'set out the arrangements and mutual responsibilities of the parties concerned for the assessment of children and provision of services under the Children Act 1989 by Local Authorities to children held in custody' (DfES 2004b: 2–3).

It is also made clear in a mother and baby case (*CF v Secretary of State for the Home Department* 2004)[46] that the local authority has a responsibility for all children within a prison in their area (see Munby 2004: 431–3). In particular, the duty of local authority children's services under section 47 of the Children Act 1989 to investigate if they have reasonable cause to suspect a particular child is suffering significant harm is no longer a duty which ends at the prison gate. Consequently, the Prison Service revised Prison Service Order 4950, which deals with the regime for juveniles, to incorporate a range of child protection measures.

The Howard League recently brought another successful case (*R (K) v Manchester City Council*)[47] in relation to the assessment of a child in custody as to whether that child would be 'in need' on release. Lloyd Jones J decided against the argument that the youth offending team (YOT) was the 'agency best suited to meeting the needs of K' and should do the assessment: 'The defendant authority is required itself to carry out an assessment. It is not entitled to delegate that function.' He further stated that YOTs can, and should, refer children to children's services, both under section 47 for a child at risk and under section 17 for child welfare.

The case brought by Ms Axon would also suggest that fears that the HRA 1998 might damage children's rights by strengthening the rights of parents are unfounded. *Axon*[48] was a challenge to the *Gillick* case and the subsequent guidance in relation to the confidentiality of competent minors when they seek medical advice, notably on contraception and abortion. Ms Axon argued that, post-HRA 1998, the guidance was an unjustified interference with her Article 8 parental rights and, further, that the *Gillick* judgement had not necessarily given the child confidentiality. However, Silber J 'read down' the cases in support of her claim and argued that the autonomy of a young person 'must undermine any Article 8 rights of a parent to family life'.[49] This approach has been criticised as not properly analysing the child's rights (see Taylor 2007; Fortin 2006b), but the case has nevertheless been viewed as a step forward for a child's right to autonomy in medical decision-making after earlier cases which had been seen as a retreat from *Gillick* (Douglas 1992; Taylor 2007).

Finally, the appointment of Children's Commissioners in the UK has been seen as indicating a more serious attempt to ensure that the interests and rights of children are upheld. The UN Committee on the Rights of the Child believes an independent 'children's champion' is crucial to the implementation of the Convention (see Williams 2005: 37), and the Joint Select Committee on Human Rights of the UK Parliament was very critical in its Ninth Report (2003) of the tardiness of the Government in appointing a Commissioner for England. The Welsh Commissioner had been established through legislation in 2000–02 and Commissioners for Scotland and Northern Ireland in 2003 (see Williams 2005). Section 1 of the Children Act 2004 remedied the deficiency, establishing that the (English) Commissioner should 'be concerned in particular' with the views and interests of children relating to the five outcomes specified elsewhere in the Act (section 2(3)). Section 2 also lists the rest of his functions and mandates that he must 'have regard to' the UNCRC when deciding what constitutes the interests of children. As Williams points out, the role of the English Commissioner differs from that of the Commissioners for Wales, Scotland and Northern Ireland and also gives the UNCRC a much weaker role (Williams 2005: 37–53). It is essentially a response to the *Every Child Matters* agenda rather than the rights-based arguments of the Parliamentary select committee (Williams 2007: 263).

Law as a giver of mixed messages?

Extraordinarily haphazard?

Law, for the reasons outlined earlier in this chapter, has rarely been able to enforce services for children. There have been cases which have upheld the status of children as worthy of being heard and allowed to take part in decision-making. Some of the cases reviewed above also show a new understanding by the judiciary of the needs and rights of children who are detained within Prison Service establishments: they can be said to expand the boundaries of traditional 'child law' which has excluded the child not viewed as a victim. Yet other cases reveal a lack of understanding of the needs of children, notably those who find themselves being questioned by the police or being given a statutory reprimand or warning.

It has been pointed out that only when children are themselves the litigants does the court consistently articulate their rights (Fortin 2006a: 300). Further, some of the 'successful' cases reviewed above did not base their reasoning on the child as rights holder. Another example can be found in the judicial interpretation of section 30(6) of the Anti-Social Behaviour Act 2003 which allows child curfews to be imposed in certain areas. This power was challenged in *Re (W) v Commissioner of Police of the Metropolis and another*[50] which held that the section did not give the police the power to use reasonable force to return a child home. Therefore, on the face, this was a victory for children's rights, but Hollingsworth points out that Brooke LJ made no reference to Convention rights at all (Hollingsworth 2006: 265). The reasoning in the case therefore gave no support for the child's entitlements under the ECHR and, in particular, did not make clear that children are 'persons' under the Convention (ibid: 268). This is a point that Sawyer has also pursued by arguing that the very fact that the locus of interest in children's legal rights has usually been in family law militates against the child being accorded a positive and separate legal identity and refers, instead, to more positive developments in European cases on citizenship rights (Sawyer 2006: 1, 12–13).

The tendency to reconstruct rights as something else is also seen, it is argued, in relation to Scottish Children's Hearings. McAra argues that 'the results of the most recent case to challenge the compatibility of the hearings system with the ECHR (*S v Miller* 2001 SLT 531) indicate that the judiciary has made strenuous efforts to reconstruct rights discourse in ways that do not undermine the established institutional ethos' (McAra 2005: 288). That case decided that the procedure was not compliant with Article 6 of the ECHR, and so the judgment established a right to have legal representation at a hearing, but McAra argues that the right was construed as 'a means of enhancing the participation of children and their families' and so fulfilling the traditional ideals of the system (ibid). Indeed, Williams has made the point that in England such participative rights within social work, educational and policy contexts – for example the advocacy arrangements introduced by the Children and Adoption Act 2002 (Williams 2007: 266) – seem to pose fewer problems, for political and legal reasons, than do children's legal rights to protection and services (ibid: 261).

Nevertheless, the developments above reveal new judicial thinking and a wider influence of the UNCRC. They would suggest that a higher profile for children's rights might tip the balance in judicial and administrative decision-making where there is room for a more positive approach to provision of services and support for children. But, as both Fortin (2006a) and Williams (2007: 262) have pointed out, the absorption of rights-based thinking in judicial reasoning about children has been uneven. Indeed, Fortin argues that 'The domestic courts have responded to the demands of the HRA in an extraordinarily haphazard manner when dealing with children's cases' (Fortin 2006a: 300).

Children and the police

In particular, whilst some cases noted above have shown gains for young offenders, children who offend have also seen their rights downgraded. One example concerns the 'final warning', part of the new statutory scheme introduced by sections 65 and 66 of the Crime and Disorder Act 1998. In the *Durham* case[51] the House of Lords decided that when imposing a reprimand or warning, the police are not required to obtain the consent of the child or young person who is being reprimanded or warned instead of being prosecuted for an offence. The issue in this particular case was that the 14-year-old had not been told that a final warning for indecent assault involved a registration requirement as a sex offender, and the court was being asked to decide whether the proceedings had been compliant with ECHR rights. Despite Baroness Hale of Richmond's questioning as to whether the proceedings were compatible with rights in the UNCRC, notably Article 40,[52] the procedure was held not to be unlawful.

The *Durham* case also reveals a propensity on the part of courts to reconstruct political truths, in the same way as was apparent in relation to the reconstruction of economic truths in the judicial review cases on section 17 summarised above. Lord Bingham's comments suggest that he has taken on board the government's account of the 'failure' of the cautioning system which reprimands and warnings replaced:

> As time passed, many cautions came to be given to young offenders in England and Wales (109,700 in 1998). But the procedure, as applied to young offenders, was seen to be subject to two major weaknesses. First, a significant number of persistent

young offenders were cautioned time after time. They inevitably came to appreciate that if they ignored one caution and offended again the likely consequence was that they would receive another caution, which they could again ignore with impunity, and so on. Thus the procedure did not achieve its intended object of stopping young offenders in their tracks before they had had time to become habituated to a life of crime.[53]

Parry has also used this case to highlight another deficit in upholding children's rights: 'There can be no better example of the potential prejudice occasioned to the interest of the juvenile suspect when assisted by the uninformed and incompetent appropriate adult' (2006: 386). No person under 17 (not 18 as for most other provisions for young offenders) can be detained and questioned in the police station unless he or she has an appropriate adult. This requirement and the role of the appropriate adult are set out in Code C of the Codes of Practice issued pursuant to the Police and Criminal Evidence Act (PACE) 1984. The intention is that the attendance of the adult will not only put the child or young person in the same position as an adult in relation to an understanding of the situation but that the adult will also have oversight of the welfare of the child and help with communication. However, after reviewing a series of cases where the court has been asked to exercise its discretion under section 78 of PACE to exclude unfairly obtained evidence on the grounds that the appropriate adult was incapable of giving the necessary support and advice, Parry concludes that there is a 'general indifference towards whether the appropriate adult can adequately protect the juvenile's interests' and a naïve belief in even the most 'appropriate' adult's ability to perform the complex role as assumed by the PACE Codes (Parry 2006: 385).

The Law Lords

Dickson has recently reviewed case law in order to assess how 'safe' human rights are in the hands of the Law Lords. They are applauded for their willingness to engage with human rights arguments in relation to customary international human rights law, equality law, asylum law and immigration law (Dickson 2006: 332–5). The Law Lords are also judged relatively positively in reading legislation such that it is compatible with the ECHR (ibid: 337–8) but four cases are given as exceptions, three of which relate to children and young people (ibid: 338, n. 62). After reviewing the negative aspects of their judgements, Dickson makes the following statements: 'Significant rifts have opened up between different groups of judges' and 'The views of Baroness Hale of Richmond have distinguished her very sharply from her brother judges' (ibid: 343 and 344).

There is certainly some evidence for the suggestion that Baroness Hale is currently ploughing a lone furrow in the House of Lords, hopefully one that encourages others to join her. In particular, Dickson refers to her 'passionate dissents' in *R v J*, where Baroness Hale upheld a conviction for indecent assault on a 13–14 year-old girl, and also in *Kehoe*.[54] In the latter case, resulting from the failure of the Child Support Agency (CSA) to collect the child support payments due from her ex-husband such that arrears of nearly £20,000 accrued, Mrs Kehoe argued that the statutory provisions which denied her the power to enforce the child support assessment were inconsistent with her access to a court and so did not uphold her Article 6 rights under the ECHR. The majority opinion did not accept this argument – Mrs Kehoe had no 'civil right' within Article 6(1) and so there was no requirement to address the issue of proportionality.

In a critical commentary, Wikeley notes that 'Baroness Hale of Richmond's speech in *Kehoe* is an erudite argument for placing children's rights at the heart of the child support debate' (Wikeley 2006: 291) and draws attention to her comment in her dissenting judgement: 'This is another case which has been presented to us largely as a case about adults' rights when in reality it is a case about children's rights' (*Kehoe* at para. 49; see Wikeley 2006: 287). The subsequent case of *Rowley*,[55] which also concerned the tardy and ineffective process of assessing and enforcing maintenance by the CSA, was, as noted above, an unsuccessful attempt to find a remedy via the law of tort (see Burrows 2007).

Wikeley has suggested that the reason for the different approach of Baroness Hale in *Kehoe* was that she set her opinion within the context of parents' obligations and children's rights as a whole (Wikeley 2006: 291), whereas 'the majority's interpretation meant that the child support legislation had to be read in splendid isolation' (ibid: 301). Burrows has made a similar point in that he sees the inclusion of a family lawyer in those arguing a case or judging it in the Court of Appeal or House of Lords as a crucial factor. In *Rowley* all the lawyers were administrative or tort law specialists, and so there was no family lawyer to provide a wider approach and one which focused on the welfare and rights of children and young people. Certainly in *R (Begum) v Headteacher and Governors of Denbigh High School*,[56] Baroness Hale was the only judge, as Edwards points out, who considered the *Gillick* principle or the more general principle of the adolescent's right to self-determination in the context of state education (Edwards 2007: 258). Not, of course, that a background in family law guarantees a rights-based approach: as we have seen, it may make the court more likely to focus on the dependency of children.

Other agendas

Despite a higher profile for 'rights talk' about children, the assumption of practitioners that the *Every Child Matters* programme creates a new children's rights agenda is, Fortin argues, 'simply untrue'. 'Margaret Hodge, then the Minister for Children, Young People and Families, expunged from the Bill, in the face of 'fruitless efforts' by MPs, every reference to the word "rights" bar one – the single reference to the word "rights" is when the Act refers by name to the UNCRC' (Fortin 2006b: 759). Williams agrees:

> *Every Child Matters, Youth Matters* and the Children Act 2004 all suggest a deliberate decision to eschew both the language and the concept of children's rights in favour of the pursuit of New Labour's 'five outcomes'. The result is that deficiencies in human rights awareness, and the suppression of rights-based reasoning, in decisions concerning children may be about to get worse, at least in England. (Williams 2007: 263)

This means that, at least in the short term, more rights for children to be able to use the law to access services, make their own decisions, and be treated appropriately are unlikely.

This review has necessarily concentrated on a very narrow range of issues, mostly connected with the provision of local authority services, but the detail has revealed processes by which both children and the law are sidelined. The courts are not being given the legislative materials which allow them more easily to ensure children receive the attention, the respect and the services they need. Instead, there are other serious issues around rights and the role of law for the success of a child-focused investment programme which concern law's involvement in implementing other policy agendas, notably the punitive aspects of the 'Respect' agenda. The courts have not been proactive in denying anti-social behaviour orders to applicant councils or in adding such orders to criminal orders on conviction of children and young people. These issues will be further examined in Chapter 8.

Notes

1 In *H v Wandsworth and others* [2007] EWHC 1082 (Admin) at para. 58.
2 In reference to the case of *Abdul Hakim Ali v The Lord Grey School* [2006] UKHL 14.
3 See, for example, Cunningham 1995: Chapter 6, 'Saving the Children 1830–c1920'; also Hendrick 1994. M. Freeman ('The Child in Family Law' in J. Fionda, *Legal Concepts of Childhood* (Oxford: Hart Publishing, 2001)) would leave the origins until the 20th century, offering the legislative landmarks in 1925, 1948 and 1969.
4 James and James (2004) offer a quite different perspective on the role of law and also international law in the process by which childhood is reproduced in the social order: see Chapters 3 and 4 in particular.
5 [1998] 1 CCLR 119 at 123J. See also the commentary by the Children's Legal Centre on the case of *R (on the application of B) v London Borough of Merton* [2003] EWHC 1689 in relation to the age assessment of unaccompanied children as a preliminary to an assessment of need: http://www.childrenslegalcentre.com/Templates/Internal.asp?NodeID=90214 (accessed 25.9.07).
6 *R (on the application of K) v Manchester City Council* [2006] EWHC 3164 (Admin) at para. 18.
7 *R (G) v London Borough of Barnet; R (W) v London Borough of Lambeth; R (A) v London Borough of Lambeth* [2003] UKHL 57, [2004] 1 FLR 454.
8 [2004] 2 AC 208 at para. 32.
9 [2003] EWHC 3175 (Admin).
10 *H, Barhanu and B v London Borough of Wandsworth, London Borough of Hackney, London Borough of Islington and Secretary of State for Education and Skills (Interested Party)* [2007] EWHC 1082 (Admin), [2007] 2 FLR 822.
11 See, for example, *R (on the application of M) v Hammersmith and Fulham LBC* [2006] EWCA Civ 917 where the court agreed that if the local authority had decided to use housing legislation to find accommodation for M, she did not qualify as having been 'looked after'.
12 *R (S) v Sutton London Borough Council* [2007] EWHC 1196 (Admin), [2007] 2 FLR 849.
13 *London Borough of Southwark v D* [2007] EWCA Civ 182.
14 *Re L and H (Residential Assessment)* [2007] EWCA Civ 213.
15 *Re G (Interim Care Order: Residential Assessment)* [2005] UKHL 68.
16 Section 4(1) of the Adoption and Children Act 2002 also imposes a duty to assess, on request, for the purpose of a person's need for post-adoption support services: see Harris-Short (2008: 46).
17 *R v Birmingham CC ex parte A* [1997] 2 FLR 841; see also Williams (1998).
18 [1998] 1 CCL Rep 294.
19 [1994] 1 FLR 798; see also Williams 2002.

20 [2003] EWHC 2151 (Admin), [2004] 1 FLR 601.

21 'If a decision on a competent matter is so unreasonable that no reasonable authority could ever have come to it, then the courts can interfere' (*Associated Provincial Picture Houses Ltd v Wednesbury Corporation* [1948] 1 KB 223, HL per Lord Greene).

22 *T v Surrey County Council* [1994] 4 All ER 577.

23 [2001] 2 FLR 612, ECtHR.

24 [2005] UKHL 23, [2005] 2 FLR 284.

25 [2007] EWCA Civ 446, [2007] 2 FLR 705.

26 *R (Rowley) v Secretary of State for Work and Pensions (Resolution Intervening)* [2007] EWCA Civ 598.

27 Tabled amendments to the Children and Young Persons Bill 2007–08 would provide clearer duties. For example, Earl Listowel proposed the following new subsection to section 23 of the 1989 Act: 'A local authority must provide a sufficient and diverse provision of appropriate placements within their local area' (accessed at http://services.parliament.uk/bills/2007-08/childrenandyoungpersonshl.html (14.12.07).

28 They note that Tunstill made the same argument in *Children and Society* in 1997 (Vol 19: 158–71).

29 She refers particularly to the case of *Re S (Minors) (Care Order: Implementation of Care Plan); Re W (Minors) (Care Order: Adequacy of Care Plan)* [2002] UKHL 10, [2002] 1 FLR 815 in which the House of Lords failed to uphold the Court of Appeal's attempt to exercise further judicial control over care plans post-hearing. See also Palmer (2003) with regard to sections 17 and 20 and Article 8 of the ECHR.

30 See, for example, *Re M (Care: Challenging Local Authority Decisions)* [2001] 2 FLR 1300; *Re L (Care: Assessment: Fair Trial) (Proceedings: Disclosure of Local Authority Decision-Making Process)* [2002] EWHC 1379 (Fam), [2002] 2 FLR 730.

31 *Re M (Secure Accommodation Order)* [1995] Fam 108 at 115.

32 [2004] 1 FLR 454 at para 118: see also Masson 2006: 239.

33 *Re S and W (Care Proceedings)* [2007] EWCA Civ 232, [2007] 2 FLR 275 at para. 25 per Wall LJ.

34 In section 1 and Article 3(3) respectively. Section 11(4)(a) of the Family Law Act 1996 extends the same requirement to proceedings related to divorce, but the section has never been implemented.

35 As amended by the Age of Legal Capacity (Scotland) Act 1991, section 2(3)(a). Section 2(3)(b) similarly amends section 18(8) in relation to freeing a child for adoption.

36 In sections 22(4), 26(2) and 26(3), respectively.

37 Family Proceeding Rules 1991, rule 9.5 relates to the representation of children in private family proceedings. The Practice Direction issued by the President of the Family Division (then Dame Elizabeth Butler-Sloss) in April 2004 states at para. 2 that, 'Making a child a party to the proceedings is a step that will be taken only in cases which involve

an issue of significant difficulty and consequently will occur only in a minority of cases'. Since then the Adoption and Children Act 2002, section 122 amended the Children Act 1989 to allow rules to be made making section 8 applications 'specified proceedings'.

38 1997 COD 323, QBD.

39 *Mabon v Mabon and others* [2005] EWCA Civ 634; [2005] 2 FLR 1011 at para. 26.

40 *In re D (a Child)* [2006] UKHL 51 at para. 57.

41 *In re H (a Child)* [2006] EWCA Civ 1247.

42 Section 7 of the HRA 1998 states: '(1) A person who claims that a public authority has acted (or proposes to act) in a way which is made unlawful by section 6(1) may—

(a) bring proceedings against the authority under this Act in the appropriate court or tribunal, or

(b) rely on the Convention right or rights concerned in any legal proceedings,

but only if he is (or would be) a victim of the unlawful act'.

43 *Botta v Italy* (1998) 26 EHRR 241 at para. 33. See also Munby 2005: 5.

44 See *Bernard v Enfield LBC* [2002] EWHC 2282, [2003] HRLR 4.

45 *R (on the Application of the Howard League for Penal Reform) v Secretary of State for the Home Department* [2002] EWHC 2497 (Admin), [2003] 1 FLR 484.

46 [2004] EWHC 111 (Fam), [2004] 2 FLR 517.

47 *R (on the Application of K) v Manchester City Council* [2006] EWHC 3164 (Admin).

48 *R (on the application of Sue Axon) v Secretary of State for Health and another* [2006] EWHC 37 (Admin).

49 At para. 130.

50 [2005] EWHC 1586 (Admin).

51 *R (on the application of R) v Durham Constabulary and another* [2005] UKHL 21, [2005] 1 WLR 1184, [2005] 2 All ER 369.

52 ibid at paras 24–49: see in particular her comment in para. 42: 'I have grave doubts about whether the statutory scheme is consistent with the child's rights under the international instruments dealing with children's rights'.

53 ibid at para. 4.

54 *R (Kehoe) v Secretary of State for Work and Pensions* [2005] UKHL 48; *R v J* [2005] 1 AC 562.

55 *R (Rowley) v Secretary of State for Work and Pensions (Resolution Intervening)* [2007] EWCA Civ 598.

56 [2006] UKHL 15.

Chapter 7

Investing in early intervention: addressing risk factors

It is better to catch the juvenile young, because it is better to help the improvable boy than to hang or flog the unimprovable man. (Frank Briant MP, *Hansard* (Commons) col. 1205, 12 February 1932)

Until the switch of policy focus, prevention tended to be a marginal component of service provision for children and families. (France and Utting 2005: 77)

Evidence-led interventions

The notion that 'prevention is better than cure' and the strategy of 'catching them young' are clearly not new ideas. Early preventative intervention has a long policy history – in child protection as well as juvenile offending – and a clear popular appeal. Nevertheless, the change in the direction of family and child-focused policy in the UK which has prompted this book should not be underestimated. Although, as earlier chapters have documented, the current investment and inclusion agenda has antecedents in much earlier policies to support children for the sake of the future health, wealth and security of the state, it is new in its high profile, its overarching rationales, its managerial ethos of audits and evaluation, and its explicit commitment to finding out 'what works'. As Cook has pointed out, Tony Blair's first speech as Prime Minister on 2 June 1997 included the following statements:

Unless government is pragmatic and rigorous about what does and does not work, it will not spend money wisely or gain the trust of the public ... We will find out what works ... We will back anyone ... if they can deliver the goods. We will evaluate our policies ... And where appropriate we will run pilots, testing out ideas so that we can be sure that every pound is well spent. (Cook 2006: 94)

In this policy context, investment in children not only saves money in the future but is carried out in a rigorously 'frugal' and scientific way. Further, such an approach is based on the belief that intervention through preventative programmes will improve outcomes for children and reduce the risk of poor outcomes and that, generally speaking, the earlier the intervention the better.

Evidence-led practice is currently immensely important in relation to interventions into the lives of children and young people. The Youth Justice Board (now YJB) has introduced a wide range of publications identifying Key Elements of Effective Practice (KEEPs), and the Department of Health in the UK developed an evidence-led framework for intervention taking account of the developmental and ecological perspective of the assessment framework (DoH *et al.* 2000). This was not new in the child protection field: *Messages from Research* (Department of Health 1995) had already brought together evidence pointing to a more preventative policy.

However, the review in Chapter 5 of research on developmental pathways, on onset of and desistance from offending, and on actuarially identified risk factors for a variety of poor outcomes noted doubts which have been raised about the application of research results. Some commentators have identified a need for qualitative research in order to better understand the quantitative data (Case 2006: 175–6); others have argued, in the context of criminal justice developments, that 'The case for evidence-led policy and practice has not been helped by a lack of methodological rigour, especially as claims of causality are difficult to unravel' (Painter 2005: 309).

As well as these concerns, there are further assumptions to be examined: that intervention leads to a more positive outcome than non-intervention, that 'science' ensures appropriate targeting of children and families, and that risk-based assessments of children and families lead to appropriate responses. Chapter 5 reviewed the science of risk prediction and issues around assessment: this chapter will focus on recent empirical research on the 'success' of offence- or other risk-based interventions to improve the life chances of those children and young people who are the target.

The development of evidence-led practice

Surprisingly, perhaps, the current encouragement of the use of research and monitoring to guide practice – the 'what works' agenda – is relatively recent. It has previously been customary to begin explanations of evidence-led practice with a reference to the 'nothing works' attitude which developed after Martinson's famous article of 1974. That 'mantra' was a misreading of an article in which he 'stated more cautiously that "instances of success... have been isolated, producing no clear pattern to indicate the efficacy of any particular methods or treatment" (1974: 49)' (Smith 2005a: 186), but it led, from the 1980s, in youth justice and criminal justice to a focus on finding out 'what works' with an increasing balance of evidence that some things do indeed work (see also Krisberg 2005: 145). For adult offenders, the policy developments have been termed the 'new rehabilitationism' (see Easton and Piper 2005: 290–1) and have justified a move, where feasible, from custodial to community punishment.

However, evidence-based practice has another history. That history lies in agendas for health services and, it is argued, in particular with the development by health academics in Canada of a process of critical appraisal of evidence for the validity and applicability of any form of intervention (McAuley *et al.* 2006: 322). As McAuley *et al.* point out, 'on the face of it it would be hard to argue with the intention of developing well-informed decision-making based upon the best available published research to provide the most effective services for children and families' (ibid: 323). However, they say, 'the collection of evidence is a complex social activity influenced by competing interests' (ibid): the amassing of evidence is by no means unproblematic. There is also a question as to whether a form of intervention based on health care – where research is based on positivist research methods – is suitable for the range of interventions into the family which the investment agenda envisages.

The strength of research evidence

With the increasing interest in preventative interventions, researchers have produced meta-analyses of large numbers of research studies which endeavour to draw general conclusions as to their effectiveness, especially in reducing offending. These studies are now summarised in several recent texts. Krisberg, for example, has pointed to the importance of the earlier analyses done by Lipsey and Palmer. Lipsey's first meta-analysis was of 400 studies (Lipsey 1992) with a further meta-analysis of the same database but restricted to 200 studies in which the target groups were relatively serious, frequent or violent offenders. Lipsey and Wilson (1998; see also Wilson and Lipsey 2007) concluded that there were positive results for juvenile justice treatment programmes, in some cases 20 to 37 per cent better than for youths in control groups, and so 'for Lipsey, it is not a matter of "does treatment of delinquency work?" but of defining the necessary conditions that maximise the effectiveness of various proven interventions' (Krisberg 2005: 150). Palmer's study examined 23 literature reviews of adult and correctional programmes and nine meta-analyses and concluded that behavioural and cognitive programmes all had consistently positive results (Palmer 1996).

The usefulness of these frequently referenced meta-analyses has been questioned. Smith applauds the fact that only studies which met minimum design standards were included in the analysis and so 'at its best, meta-analyses provide more systematic and objective assessment of the findings from a large number of studies than is possible through traditional methods of scholarly review' (2005a: 186). On the other hand, Lipsey excluded studies that were based only on a measure of before and after intervention but without any control group (ibid), an issue that we will return to later in relation to more recent programmes of intervention. Smith has also drawn attention to the fact that the average effect size across the studies reviewed is probably equivalent to a reduction in reoffending rates of about 5 per cent, an effect which, he argues, is small compared, for example, with the effects of psychotherapy for adults which are two or three times greater (Smith 2005a: 187). He also argues that 'the effects shown tend to be smaller where the methods of evaluation are more rigorous' and that 'the findings suggest anti-social behaviour is hard to change compared to other behavioural or psychological problems' (ibid).

A similar cautious message is to be found in a recent publication by NACRO in the UK: '[W]hat constitutes effective practice is still an area of considerable debate and the research evidence is frequently equivocal' (NACRO 2006a: 1). This Briefing draws attention to the use of the framework developed by Utting and Vennard (2000) which classifies initiatives into four categories on the strength of the evidence on which they are based: (1) what works; (2) what doesn't work; (3) what's promising; (4) what's unknown (ibid). It also notes that the preparatory materials produced by the YJB in relation to the Professional Certificate in Effective Practice acknowledge that, 'while evidence-based practice represents a new cultural approach for youth justice services to adopt, strictly speaking most approaches to preventing offending in the UK must be deemed "promising" or "unknown" rather than truly effective' (ibid). However, the meta-analysis by McGuire and Priestley (1995) suggests meta-analyses are useful in identifying styles of intervention that appear to be more effective (see below).

There is also now further work in reviewing intervention programmes aimed more generally at improvements in the life chances of children. For example, the edited collection by McAuley and colleagues (2006) reviews child welfare programmes.[1] Part 1 deals with general issues around the effectiveness of child welfare interventions and focuses on the UK and the USA, whereas Parts 2–5 examine different kinds of interventions, notably with vulnerable children, abused children and children in schools and community programmes. It is not easy to generalise about this wide variety of projects or the reviews of research in the UK under the auspices of both government department and research foundations or children's charities which the book lists (ibid: 15). The difficulty is in knowing *exactly* what is being done and whether findings can be compared across projects.

The McAuley collection acknowledges these difficulties. Pecora *et al.* (2006) set out a 21-point list of the challenges to be surmounted in measuring the effectiveness of interventions via child and family services, and they point out that this list is not exhaustive. They note, for example, that when follow-up studies of research have been completed, some of the positive results are shown to fade, and that there has been an overreliance on cross-section, snapshot or exit data instead of on longitudinal cohort data. Smith in her chapter likewise points out that 'few interventions have been systematically evaluated in any way, and even fewer evaluated in a scientifically rigorous way, such as by a randomised control trial' (Smith 2006: 48). She notes that 'the expectation is that short-term or intermediate improvements will indicate or predict better long-term outcomes, although there are many examples of short-term gains that have "washed out" over time', and that evaluations carried out in the UK have 'commonly been based on parents' perceptions of whether they or their child have benefited from the intervention' (ibid). Much of the literature is based on programmes in the USA and there is also a caveat given in relation to its relevance to the UK: there are differences in culture, including parenting behaviour, as well as differences in the main minority ethnic groups, education and the infrastructure of health delivery (ibid: 49). Smith's conclusions are harsh: '[A]s a result, within the UK, there is little "hard" evidence of the effectiveness of such interventions' and the results are, therefore, promising rather than conclusive (ibid: 57).

There are particular and fundamental problems in measuring risk and protection. France and Crow isolate several particular problems: audits are too long, the information is too complex, and there are no normative standards to judge whether risks are high or low (2005: 176). McAuley *et al.* point to the fact that there is no consensus on what constitutes valid evidence itself in this field, particularly in the context of the debate as to whether valid evidence can only result from randomised controlled trials and whether there should be qualitative or quantitative research (2006: 323). They conclude that there is a range of strengths and limitations in all the studies available, with a particular lack of good research on the effectiveness of core child welfare interventions (ibid: 325), that few interventions are systematically and rigorously evaluated, and that studies lack objective or standardised outcome measures (ibid: 326). They also refer to a dearth of longitudinal evaluations, confusions in the variables used, lack of specificity in research with regard to ages and ethnic contexts of their respondents, lack of a theoretical basis for analysis, and lack of information on user views (ibid: 327–8). Similarly, Dagenais *et al.* comment, in relation to their meta-analysis of Canadian programmes designed for children at risk of out-of-home placement, that they were 'forced to abandon [their] intention of calculating a global effectiveness score for these measurements because of methodological deficiencies' (2004: section 3.4). Their data suggested, however, that the programmes did not significantly affect the placement rate (ibid: section 4.1). Indeed Mair, in analysing probation practice in England and Wales, has asked whether 'what works' is 'a house built on sand' (Mair 2004), whilst Hood cautions that there is 'a danger that the question "What works?" has been too rapidly transformed into a prescription under the pressures to show that a difference can be made' (Hood 2004).

It is, therefore, very easy to find evidence of a pessimistic view of 'what works' and the strength of the research evidence on which it is based. It is also acknowledged that there is now a scarcity of experienced researchers in social science more generally and that 'the academic treadmill, driven by excessive accountability burdens, the Research Assessment Exercise and other factors, has reduced the originality and quality of much academic research and constrained interaction with various communities' (Commission on the Social Sciences 2003: 5; see also Genn *et al.* 2006).

This is not the whole picture but it is a necessary counterbalance to the excessively rosy assumptions about what research can currently tell us about the level of certainty of outcomes from preventative programmes.

Targeting the subject

A crucial issue is whether in practice it proves possible to target the 'right' children and intervene in their families. One solution – and one based on structural correlates of poor outcomes – is to target geographical areas rather than assess and target individual children and families. The areas targeted are those which evidence the highest number of indicators of deprivation or deficits in social capital – such as high unemployment, low educational attainment and high crime rates – which are linked to social exclusion and/or offending. Within the target areas, which statistically should have a large proportion of children and their families who need services and preventative programmes, the services offered are universal, and attendance is voluntary, so avoiding the issue of potentially undermining parental responsibility (see Chapter 4). Sure Start (see below) is one such area-based programme but, as Belsky (2007) has pointed out, area-based targeting cannot guarantee effective engagement with target children and families. The example he gives is of the selection of the Barbican area of London as a Sure Start area where its relatively rich inhabitants made more use of the Sure Start facilities than the most deprived who were the intended target (ibid).

In the Connexions programme there are also difficulties of ensuring the participation of those who are seen most to need the services (Barry 2005: 122), and monitoring of the take-up of opportunities by young people as part of the citizenship policies, notably extra-curricular 'volunteering' measures, has suggested that it is the more 'included' youngsters who have taken up such opportunities (ibid: 19) 'as value-added elements to their CV ... thereby marginalising the more marginalised even further' (Williamson 2005: 19). Another example can be found at the 'hard' end of the youth justice system where the Government has accepted that effective targeting has proved difficult in relation to their flagship Intensive Supervision and Surveillance Programme (ISSP) for young offenders at risk of custody (see below). The YJB is re-evaluating the eligibility criteria for the scheme to ensure that 'the right young people are being targeted' (YJB 2004: para. 4.2).

The crucial role of parents, and whether policies of partnership, voluntary take-up of advice and support, and re-organisation of local authority children's services are adequate to provide the right services to the right children and their families, is an issue referred to in previous chapters (see Chapters 4 and 6). Smith also focuses on the issues around parenting programmes in the UK which have been designed for, and targeted at, particular groups of children and their parents identified as in need, noting that 'these are not generally parents who "volunteer" for parenting programmes. This may go some way to explaining why many parenting programmes tend to report relatively low participation rates and high drop-out rates' (M. Smith 2006: 48–9). Referring to the research of Spencer (2003), she says that 'where such information is available, it is clear that there is social patterning in drop-out, with more disadvantaged parents less likely to complete the course' (ibid: 49). She also refers to the lack of information on the effectiveness of interventions in the UK designed for children and families in minority ethnic groups (ibid). '[W]e still have a lot to learn about how to design interventions or programmes that are acceptable to families, do not stigmatise and are seen as helpful, in order to engage parents effectively in interventions and maintain participation to avoid high drop-out rates' (ibid: 57).

These problems are now being acknowledged. Hilary Armstrong, then Minister for Social Exclusion, stated that, 'As people begin to take advantage of Sure Start, extended school activities and tax credits, and as they raise their aspirations, those who are not doing so are left further behind. We know that – we acknowledge it in the action plan.'[2] A recent report, *Children's Centres: ensuring that families most in need benefit* (Capacity and Esmee Fairbairn 2007) focuses on the running of four children's centres which are seen as models of good practice. It focuses particularly on identifying and publicising what they refer to as 'reach strategies' whereby the centres have achieved high visibility in, and the trust of, the communities in which they are situated. The result in these centres has been a high take up of services by those deemed most at risk of poor outcomes. The concern of the authors is that, despite the cash injection by the Government in 2007 of more than £4 billion into children's centres, early years education and childcare – which will include additional funds for outreach workers – some centres may face tapering funding which obliges them to attract middle class families who can afford to pay for services (ibid: 2; see also Childright 2007a: 29).

Non-intervention

The discourse of 'early interventions' takes intervention as a self-evident good, particularly for those children who most need the support and guidance, and assumes that intervention cannot, therefore, be harmful, but, as Knepper notes, 'the wisdom of early intervention is not as simple and obvious as the early interveners imply' (Knepper 2007: 114). There is emerging evidence that some interventions, notably in the lives of young offenders, may *not* be better than 'doing nothing'. A recent Scottish study of desistance from offending found that 'young people who were caught by the police were more likely to persist in their offending than those who offended at a similar level but who were not caught' (D. Smith 2006: 16). Smith goes on to say,

> These findings support the view that youth crime can be contained by avoiding the punishment and hence stigmatization of young people during their formative years. This fits with Moffitt's (1993) theory that much youth crime is committed by adolescence-limited offenders who will grow out of crime if they are not damaged by interventions from the criminal justice system. Particularly striking is the finding from the Edinburgh Study that the chances that a young person will stop offending altogether are sharply reduced by contact with the police. (ibid).

Young offenders and diversion

'Adolescents tend to test the limits of acceptable behaviour' (Bradford and Morgan 2005: 283): there are inevitably issues around responses to criminality and otherwise unacceptable behaviour, and policy has for at least two centuries veered between the poles of non-intervention (or intervention to divert to welfare-based measures) and severe punitive responses. Over the last decade the new statutory system of reprimands and warnings has provided a rule-based police intervention with young offenders, generally to be used only for the first two offences, after which prosecution is the outcome. Koffman and Dingwall (2007) have critiqued current practice as a

171

disproportionate response to minor offending and one which should not be described as diversion because, they argue, it pushes young offenders further into the system without necessarily delivering the benefits of rehabilitation measures. In this comment they echo that of Baroness Hale of Richmond in the *Durham* case:[3] 'The rigidity of the scheme undermines the emphasis given to diverting children from the criminal justice system, propels them into it and on a higher rung of the ladder earlier than they would previously have arrived there, and thus seriously risks offending against the principle that intervention must be proportionate both to the circumstances of the offender and of the offence' (at para. 42). The final warning scheme is, therefore, seen to be causing net-widening (Fox *et al.* 2006).

This critique appears as a reinvention of the wheel, given the extensive criticism in the 1970s and into the 1980s of interventionist policies which negatively 'labelled' young offenders and encouraged rather than constrained a 'career' into criminality. Researchers in other jurisdictions are also querying the current interventionist youth justice policies by reminding policy makers of earlier research and theory. For example, Harrikari and Pekkarinen (2006) draw attention to the comment of the Criminal Justice Committee of 1976 in Finland that most young offenders will cease criminal activity and so, 'From the perspective of recidivism, it would be better to totally refrain from punishing young offenders'. They compare that statement with the report of the Finnish Youth Crime Committee in 2004 that 'immediate and powerful intervention is a generally accepted and consistent starting point in preventing criminal activity of the youth'. They, and UK commentators, therefore argue that the seminal work of Lemert (1951) on labelling theory should be revisited. A NACRO Youth Crime Briefing has also pointed out that 'the desistence literature', such as that by Smith (D. Smith 2005a, 2006), 'emphasises the importance of the way that young people themselves understand their behaviour and how they experience youth justice interventions (NACRO 2007: 5). Dingwall and Gillespie (2007) also note that, while statistics appear to suggest that diversion is more effective than prosecution in terms of reconviction rates, those who are prosecuted may well have 'a more entrenched pattern of offending than those who are diverted'. There is also evidence that there may be some young offenders who admit guilt and accept a reprimand or a warning but who in fact are not technically guilty of the offence with which they are charged (see Hine 2007).

A recent report, *Tackling Anti-social Behaviour*, also provides evidence that sometimes, but not always, the least intrusive intervention is more effective. It found that there was further anti-social behaviour in 60 per cent of the cases in their sample of acceptable behaviour contracts which involved people under 18 years of age, whilst warning letters had most effect on young people, with around 62 per cent of those under 18 receiving no further interventions (Home Office 2006b: Executive Summary, para. 5 (e) and (f)).

System expansion

A common academic critique of diversion in the 1970s and 1980s was that it led to net-widening (see, for example, Landau 1981; Morris and Giller 1987: 137–54; Pratt 1989): more children were drawn into the system than 'needed' to be. A similar issue has been raised in the context of current policies. Bradford and Morgan state that 'the essence of this academic critique is that the reformed youth justice system is expansionist, dragging more children into a criminal justice system which, despite its socially inclusive protestations, is increasingly punitive' (2005: 286). There is also concern that the current policies around anti-social behaviour are blurring boundaries, with consequent net-widening (Hallam Centre for Criminal Justice 2006). Goldson (2007) also warns that risk-based early intervention, 'the cornerstone of contemporary young justice policy', can be triggered without an offence having been committed and therefore without any due process. He further argues that multi-disciplinarity, although it has merits in intervening in the lives of children who are multiply disadvantaged, has led to system expansion and increasingly interventionist powers.

When Professor Rod Morgan resigned as Chair of the Youth Justice Board in January 2007, he also endorsed the expansionism of the system when he said that it 'is being swamped by the growth of the number of children and young people in custody and the substantial increase in the numbers of children and young people being criminalised and/or prosecuted' (see Goldson 2007). Sutton, Utting and Farrington (2004: 5) have concluded that 'in particular, any notion that better screening can enable policy makers to identify young children destined to join the five per cent of offenders responsible for fifty to sixty per cent of youth crime is fanciful'. A difficulty, however, as Smith points out, is that, whilst these findings suggest that a policy of increased intervention by the juvenile justice system is unlikely to lead to a (significant) reduction in youth offending, intervention might still be appropriate for those offenders with 'deep-seated problems that will not recede as they reach maturity' and that serious offending 'has to be dealt with regardless of the consequences for the individuals involved' (Smith 2006: 16). Working out where those lines should be drawn is of course a key issue for the investment agenda.

Assessing key programmes

Whilst the pressure for an outcome-based policy began within the actuarial justice slant of the offending prevention programmes developed over the last few decades, the inclusion agenda of the New Labour Government introduced a much wider strand of outcome-based preventative programmes. Consequently, because many risk factors are common to all poor outcomes, some projects can be marketed as preventing social exclusion as well as offending. A wide range of initiatives has been developed: in the Government's response to the Audit Commission's report in 2004, the following activities are referred to as 'developing initiatives that will help the preventative approach' (YJB 2004: para. 6.0). These programmes are Connexions, the Children's Fund, Positive Activities for Young People, and the Parenting Fund. Subsequent paragraphs of that document refer to Sure Start programmes, the Extended Schools Programme, Youth Inclusion Support Panels (YISPs), the Children and Youth Support Fund in Wales, Crime and Disorder Reduction Partnerships, the Prevent and Deter programme and the All Wales Youth Offending Strategy (ibid: paras 6.1–6.4 and 6.7).

Of these initiatives, the high profile programme of the inclusion policy has been Sure Start and, in relation to financial support, tax credits, the New Deal and child benefit changes, together with further reform of the child support system. Policy documents have claimed success, sometimes limited, for these initiatives but, as one would expect from the above, the research evaluations of these projects give somewhat mixed messages. The list of such initiatives is very long, and what follows will simply be a brief summary of research on some of the programmes, listed alphabetically.

Children's Fund

The Children's Fund was set up in 2000 with two main objectives: the early identification of children at risk of social exclusion and the improvement of access to preventative services (see Martindale 2006: 49). Consequently, it funded new initiatives and commissioned research. The national evaluation, with its own website (to be found at www.ne-cf.org), led to series of conferences and reports in 2006. Between 2005 and 2008, £411.5 million was allocated to the Children's Fund; funding at £132 million pa was also allocated to cover the first three years of the mainstreaming of the Fund into children's trusts arrangements. According to a government document (HM Treasury and DfES 2007: 41), the Fund has helped:

- To develop responsive, specialist support tailored to the individual needs of the child and family
- To achieve positive outcomes with a range of children and parents; impacting on school attendance, behaviour, self-esteem, and relationships
- To improve skills, confidence and emotional well-being for parents
- To improve relationships and communication between families and professionals.

The Children's Fund Strategic Plan Guidance noted that projects should 'include opportunities to use learning to influence emerging developments for integrated children's services' (DfES 2006f: 2). Martindale examined the learning potential of Children's Fund initiatives in one area of Merseyside and, in particular, her research focused on the usefulness of Children's Fund initiatives in the development of children's trust arrangements (Martindale 2006). Early intervention services for children aged 5–13 years had been funded by the first wave of Children's Fund money from 2001–04, but then faced financial difficulties which were resolved by continued funding for the purpose of increasing understanding of the learning and mainstreaming potential of such initiatives. Clearly, such monitoring is important given that 2008 was the deadline for all local authorities to develop children's trusts to co-ordinate children's services.

However, Martindale's three key findings are that '(a) some learning has occurred which may be suitable for mainstreaming; (b) the scale of the learning has been exaggerated; (c) a number of challenges will require addressing if learning is to be mainstreamed' (Martindale 2006: 50). She points out, for example, that the Fund was aimed at services in areas of greatest deprivation and that the majority of learning that took place tended to remain within an organisation at the local level (ibid: 52). 'Short-term funding was seen to have encouraged services to look inward rather than to make links with each other. This is because services have to brand themselves as unique in order to gain refunding' (ibid: 53). This is not to say that the projects funded by the Children's Fund have been a waste of resources, but it does point up that 'the lessons are, of course, more qualified' (Martindale 2006: 55). Ideas cannot just unproblematically be rolled out across even a whole borough, let alone a whole country.

Communities that Care (now Rainer CtC)

The Communities that Care (CtC) early intervention programme, currently being implemented in around 30 communities in England, Wales and Scotland, was first developed in the USA (see Farrington and Welsh 2007: 171–3). Farrington suggested the UK should use that programme (see Farrington 1997; France and Crow 2005), and the Joseph Rowntree Fund (JRF) set up CtC as a registered charity which funded three pilot projects. CtC has since been taken over by the Rainer Foundation. It is, therefore, not a government initiative but one supported by, and fully linked into, DfES (now DCFS) and YJB policy. The CtC website explains the research-based approach:

> Using a school survey and a step by step approach, Communities that Care makes it possible to map factors in the lives of local children that are making it more – or less – likely they will experience: school failure, school-age pregnancy and sexually transmitted diseases; or become involved in: drug abuse; violence and crime.[4]

To underline the dual focus on research and involvement of young people, the first national survey of risk and protective factors relating to offending, commissioned by the YJB, was undertaken by the CtC using self-report surveys with young people (YJB 2001; see also Beinhart et al. 2002; for a later survey see Sutherland et al. 2005).

The evaluation of the impact of CtC on levels of risk and protection has proved somewhat difficult to measure (JRF 2004a: 1). In early research, the reduction in risk factors by one project was not definitely attributable to the influence of CtC; it was thought that in the second project the new interventions might be making a difference; but in the third there was no evidence of impact (ibid). Whilst the development of CtC programmes had been part of a Government aim to increase community capacity, one problem with the projects has been implementation and the use of local leadership (ibid). The aim of CtC was to bring together local community representatives with professionals to design an action plan for that area to reduce risk factors: 'CtC is therefore not simply a service delivery programme, but a process leading to the identification of a programme of work, and method of facilitating the delivery of well co-ordinated services that reduce risk and increase protection' (JRF 2004a: 2). Whilst more recent results from monitoring individual projects show promising reductions in risk factors, the strength of CtC might, rather, be in building up knowledge about local communities, its use of self-report data by children and young people and the potential of risk audits to improve policy-making (see Crow *et al.* 2004; Utting and Langman 2005, 2006).

Connexions

The Connexions strategy for inter-agency working with young people began with the Connexions partnerships piloted during 2001 and operating throughout England by 2002–03. Each young person was allocated a Connexions personal advisor, the target group being young people aged 13–19 and particularly those aged 16 and 17 who were not in, or were at risk of disengaging from education, employment or training (JRF 2004b: 2). The Joseph Rowntree Fund supported research, conducted in three of the 47 partnership areas, which identified a need for roles to be clarified, better systems of referral, improved communication between agencies, more consistently applied systems of information sharing and case conferencing, and better systems of support and supervision for management of personal advisors (ibid: 4). However, the research was done at a very early stage of the development of Connexions.

The *Every Child Matters* agenda has changed the organisational entity which was Connexions: from April 2008; funding was transferred from the Connexions' partnerships to local authorities, although there is still a live website – Connexions Direct – giving information and advice to young people aged 13–19.[5] Guidance has been given to local authorities on Connexions 'branding' (DfES 2007a) and reports circulated on issues involved in incorporating Connexions within children's trust services (ECOTEC 2006).

Education: SEAL and extended schools

Education is of course a major plank of New Labour policy and the wide range of initiatives cannot be summarised here. Instead, two very different developments which feed into the wider social inclusion agenda will be reviewed: SEAL and extended schools.

SEAL (social and emotional aspects of learning), another US import (see, for example, Elias *et al.* 1997), is an approach aimed at developing the social, emotional and behavioural skills of children in primary schools. SEAL for Key Stages 1 and 2 has been part of the Primary National Strategy's behaviour and attendance pilot, which has run since 2005 in 500 schools. The latest guidance, comprising a set of publications, asks 'Why is it important to develop these aspects of learning in the primary curriculum?' and answers with the following bullet points:

- They underlie almost every aspect of our lives.
- They enable us to be effective learners.
- They enable us to get on with other people.
- They enable us to be responsible citizens. (DfES 2007b: 1)

There is also a secondary school SEAL programme, rolled out across all schools since September 2007, with details on the SEAL website.[6] The latest guidance for secondary schools takes on board the results of the secondary SEAL two-year pilots which involved six LEAs. Staff as well as pupils must also be involved in this programme. This programme clearly has multiple aims: if effective, students will achieve more effective learning and become better citizens.

The Extended Schools Programme is somewhat different in its role in the inclusion and prevention agenda. The Extended Schools Prospectus was published by the Government in 2005 and set out the Extended Schools Support Service to which all children and their families are to have access by 2010 through their schools, though not necessarily on the school site itself. The Sure Start centres taken over by the local authority and the new child centres to be set up under the ECM (Every Child Matters) agenda will take on a co-ordinating role. Set out in the 'Five Year Strategy for Children and Learners' is a core offer of extended services which would include parenting support for primary schools, other forms of multi-agency support, study support and community use of school facilities and family learning activities. Furthermore, by 2010 all parents of children aged 5–11 will be offered school-based child care between 8 a.m. and 6 p.m. all year round, while secondary schools will be open from 8 a.m. to 6 p.m. offering a range of activities for young people (YJB 2004: para. 6.1).

The most recent research findings (DfES 2007c) suggest that 'progress in full service extended schools was around double the rate of the national average between 2005 and 2006. At Key Stage 4, the percentage of pupils achieving 5+ A*–Cs at GCSE increased by just over 5%, compared to 2.5% increase nationally over the same period.' Programmes 'were also having a range of other impacts on outcomes for pupils, including engagement with learning, family stability and enhanced life chances'.[7]

Final Warning Schemes

Sections 65–66 of the Crime and Disorder Act (CDA) 1998 in effect introduced the presumption that children and young people under 18 will not normally be prosecuted for the first two known offences. If a young offender admits the offence and the police have sufficient evidence for a prosecution, he or she will normally receive a reprimand and then, for a subsequent offence, a warning. The aim is to divert the young offender from court and prosecution but to attach a rehabilitation or restorative justice intervention to a final warning as a form of early intervention to prevent reoffending.

The findings of early research suggested that these interventions 'led to an improvement in [young offenders'] thinking and behaviour and their attitudes to offending' (Audit Commission 2004: 19). However, whilst 13 aspects of the lives of the young offenders were surveyed, only 30 per cent said they experienced improvements in 'thinking and behaviour' and 18 per cent in 'attitudes to offending', with less than 10 per cent experiencing improvements in relation to family, neighbourhood, employment and training aspects of their lives (ibid: Exhibit 5, para. 28). The Audit Commission consequently suggested that there needed to be 'a more tailored approach that uses resources in a more targeted way' (ibid: 19)

Much of the research has focused on the use of a warning as a vehicle for restorative justice approaches. The policy of the YJB is that the warning should, if possible, be given at a restorative conference, and guidance on the administration of such meetings states that youth offending teams (YOTs) should contact the victim (Home Office/Youth Justice Board 2002: 16). The research by Hoyle *et al.* (2002) on an earlier similar initiative found that *how* the process was done was crucial in helping the offender to understand and regret the effects of his or her offending. Holdaway *et al.* made a similar point in relation to victim-offender mediation in their evaluation of the work of pilot youth offending teams: that restorative justice is a set of values and so the intervention is not simply rolling out a collection of techniques which are not fully understood or contextualised (2001: 39).

The national evaluation of 'final warning' projects for the YJB found that, whilst parents and the young offenders were generally positive about the process (Holdaway and Desborough 2004: 6), 31 per cent of young offenders on the programmes reoffended within a year of finishing the programme (ibid: 37) and many schemes had a low number of referrals (ibid: 6). The authors concluded that, to be successful, 'The requirement is a giving of a high priority by Yot managers to the Final Warning; their careful planning of the delivery of warnings; closer liaison between Yots and projects delivering Final Warnings; a research-led, systematic approach to the assessment of offenders and, subsequently, the design and delivery of intervention programmes' (ibid: 43).

Health

Health services for children are an integral part of the *Every Child Matters* agenda: section 10(2)(a) of the Children Act 2004 mandates children's services to improve the well-being of children relating to 'physical and mental health and emotional well-being', and Strategic Health Authorities and Primary Care Trusts are statutory partners in this enterprise, sharing the duty to safeguard with other Special Health Authorities and other NHS trusts (sections 10(4) and 11(1)). The failures in health and social care and resulting enquiries led to changes in the organisation of health services for children, as they have done in relation other child protection services. In particular, a National Service Framework (NSF) for children, young people and maternity services was published in 2004 (DoH and DfES), setting out a 10-year programme to improve children's health and providing 11 separate standards for social and health services. Further, a *Statement of intent: Improving health services for disabled children and young people and those with complex health needs* was issued by the Department of Health in 2005.

The provision of and clear access to health services appropriate to children and young people is crucial to the current and future well-being of children but, as with the equally important provision of education, there are too many initiatives for this book to review and assess to the extent they deserve. Suffice it to say that the baseline for improvement is in some instances low, as reported by the Healthcare Commission's recent 'improvement review' of services for children in hospital. Using the 2003 Hospital Standard as the yardstick and previous reviews highlighting areas for improvement for the focus, the review asked five questions about aspects of hospital services for children. Only a quarter of hospitals surveyed received an overall score of 'excellent' (4 per cent) or 'good' (21 per cent); 70 per cent scored 'fair' and 5 per cent were 'weak' (Healthcare Commission 2007: 3). In particular the review found that 'the broader needs of children were not being recognized or given proper priority' and that 'Safeguarding children remains a major area of risk and many children are having worse experiences of hospital than they should' (ibid: 28; see also *Childright* 2007b: 8–9).

It is particularly encouraging that *The Children's Plan* (DCFS 2007) places a high priority on better services to support disabled children and their families. The Plan states the Government's intention to undertake a review of the Child and Adolescent Mental Health Service (CAMS) and to produce a new Public Service Agreement for Health Service Standards (ibid: Chapter 1).

Intensive Supervision and Surveillance Programme (ISSP)

Yet again, this is an import from the USA where such programmes are well established. The first full schemes were set up in 2001 in England and Wales with 41 schemes operational by early 2003 (Moore 2004: 161). The programme represents a heavy investment by the YJB (ibid: 159) which publicised the fact that the ISSP is based on the 'best evidence as to what will reduce the frequency and seriousness of offending' (YJB 2002: 5). Clearly this is not an early intervention programme in the sense that it aims to catch children before they offend, but the aim is to intervene, earlier and intensively, in the criminal 'careers' of the most 'at risk' 10–17 year olds, but focused on 15–17 year olds – with very controlling surveillance, such that fewer young people go on to ever more serious offending and receive custodial sentences. A key objective set by the YJB is that the underlying problems of young people on the programme are also tackled (YJB 2002; see also YJB 2003). ISSP is an initiative, as Moore points out, which builds on the much earlier intermediate treatment (IT) projects for young offenders, the IMPACT scheme for young adults on probation, and the requirements added to supervision orders (now imposed under the Powers of Criminal Courts (Sentencing) Act 2000, sections 63–68) (Moore 2004: 160–1).

ISSP was originally accessed only via three routes – as a condition of bail supervision, as part of a community penalty or as part of the community supervision element of a custodial order – but the eligibility criteria have since been widened to focus on those who have been charged or warned at least four times in the previous 12 months. A programme includes 25 hours of compulsory educational or other activity, whilst section 88 of the Anti-social Behaviour Act 2003 empowers the court to require that a child or young person lives with a local authority foster parent for a period up to 12 months as part of a supervision programme. These criteria and practices raise again the issue of effective targeting and the possibility of net-widening (Moore 2004: 164–5).

The development of ISSP in the UK has been evaluated since its inception with a final report issued in 2005 (Gray *et al.* 2005). One of the researchers has cautioned that, based on US experience, it may be difficult for all these diverse aims to be met in one programme (Moore 2004: 162). Early evaluation of the schemes found that 'failure' to reach all the objectives, particularly in reducing reoffending rates, was the result of the fact that 'Most innovative programmes in youth justice are handicapped by unrealistic expectation about what can be achieved. Almost by definition, persistent offending behaviour is extremely resistant to change' (Little *et al.* 2004: 228–9). Reviewing the earlier research, Moore draws attention to the differences in outcomes and effectiveness depending on whether the programme has a 'treatment' component or not, and notes that reoffending rates could well be higher because of the intensive surveillance component which might increase the visibility of offending (Moore 2004: 169–70).

The Final Report, which extended the reconviction study to 24 months, did find a reduction in offending in comparison with the period before the young person was placed on the ISSP: 'The frequency of offending in the ISSP sample went down by 40% over one year and by 39% over two years. The seriousness of any further offending went down by 13% in both one and two years after ISSP' (Gray *et al.* 2005: 9). However, the researchers also found a similar level of improvement in the comparison group and suggest that 'One reason for this may be that the perceived high demands of DTO [post-detention] ISSP are counter productive' (ibid). The overall proportion of young people reoffending after the ISSP was also very high (91 per cent), not surprising given the sample of prolific offenders. The researchers focused, therefore, on the need to differentiate between the sub-groups researched. They found that 'young women performed significantly better than young men on ISSP' and that the 'greatest improvements were achieved when there was suitable matching between eligibility and the use of ISSP; young people who were not eligible for the programme did not show any benefit. However, those who were "persistent and serious" experienced a significant reduction in offending frequency' (ibid). However, the research suggested that the impact of ISSP on the different sub-samples became less over time and 'statistically significant results at 12 months disappeared at 24 months in many instances' (ibid).

New Deal for Communities

The Government's New Deal for Communities (NDC) programme[8] – 'the £2 bn jewel in the government's regeneration crown' (Salmon 2007) – was launched in 1998 as part of the National Strategy for Neighbourhood Renewal, and the last of the programmes will end in 2011. Seventeen pathfinder NDC partnerships were set up in 1998 and there are now 39. The initiative, overseen by the Department for Communities and Local Government, as it then was, aimed to put local residents at the heart of the decision-making, and an important target, reiterated in a recent Green Paper entitled A *New Deal for Welfare: Empowering People to Work* (DWP 2006), is to get more people in disadvantaged groups into employment. In response to this Green Paper, the Joseph Rowntree Fund argued that current policies are still inadequate and that there will be 'lots of lone parents in poverty for years to come', important because 'almost half of the children in poverty are in lone parent households and a third are in lone parent households who are not working' (JRF 2006: 7). The NDC is, therefore, of relevance not only to young adults who are 'workless' but also to the children of these people.

There is an independent national evaluation of NDC, Phase 1 reporting in 2005 and Phase 2 running 2006–09.[9] The Phase 1 report found that residents in the partnership areas were more aware of the NDC and more positive about their neighbourhoods and that, by 2004, there was also evidence that changes were beginning to occur in relation to longer-term outcomes, such as employment:

> unemployed people in NDC areas were 1.1 times more likely to exit unemployment benefits, and 1.6 times more likely to exit sickness/disability benefits, than claimants living in the rest of the country; evidence from across the evaluation points to there being positive outcomes for individuals in relation to unemployment. (Office of the Deputy Prime Minister 2005: Executive Summary)

Prevent and Deter

Prevent and Deter (P&D) is one of the three strands of the

Government's Prolific and Priority Offenders Strategy, launched in 2004. Its official aim is to prevent the most at-risk young people from becoming the most prolific offenders of the future. The lead agencies are the police, the National Probation Service and the Prevent and Deter section of youth offending teams. It is therefore firmly located within the criminal justice system for adults but is focused on prevention. The aim of P&D is 'to identify those on the cusp of a prolific offending lifestyle to prevent them from becoming the persistent offenders of the future' (NACRO 2006b: 1). P&D therefore has two different target groups, the priority being active offenders or young people already on youth justice interventions. The other group comprises those who are at risk of becoming involved and who are seen to require intensive targeting. As NACRO points out, the focus on this second group requires preventative activities to be viewed in a much wider context and become a matter for mainstream children's services. That would be in line with the *Every Child Matters* agenda and is to be welcomed (NACRO 2006b: 2). However, NACRO's own research suggests that there is little consistency across England and Wales in terms of the criteria being used, and some areas have no set criteria. The YJB guidance suggests the use of Asset with a threshold entry score of 20–30 being used in practice. NACRO has summarised the difficulties that have come from the implementation of this programme as arising from the difficulty of developing and sustaining multi-agency panels, the lack of extra funding from central government, and a lack of clarity regarding entry and exit from P&D. There has also been wide variation in the elements of P&D that have been the focus of area schemes (NACRO 2006b: 7).

Some of these deficiencies have been acknowledged. Recent new guidance aiming at more effective interventions notes that, 'For some time, many CDRPs [Crime and Disorder Reduction Partnerships] have struggled to identify and deliver the added value of the P&D scheme and in particular the Youth Justice Interventions (YJI) strand' (Government Office for London and the YJB 2006: 3).

Respect Action Plan: components

At the beginning of 2006 the new Respect Action Plan was issued by the Home Office which set out powers to 'promote respect positively; bear down uncompromisingly on anti-social behaviour; tackle its causes; and offer leadership and support to local people and local services' (Home Office 2006b: 1). Building on earlier powers such as ASBOs, the new Plan aims to 'intervene earlier in families, homes and schools to prevent children and young people who are showing signs of problems from getting any worse' (ibid: 7). It is, therefore, presented as part of the early intervention raft of programmes, and Chapter 2, headed 'Activities for Children and Young People', argues that 'the future depends on unlocking the positive potential of young people' (ibid: 8). The proposed action includes building on existing activities, such as the National Youth Voluntary Service, Sport Youth Opportunity Cards, Children's Centres, Extended Schools, and incorporating 'a new approach to the most challenging families' with proposals for new parenting programmes and a national network of intensive family support schemes (ibid: 21).

However, in line with the respect and responsibility theme running through the Government's policies, the paper argues that 'respect cannot be learned, purchased or acquired, it can only be earned' (ibid: 30). Consequently it also focuses on enforcement and changes to ASBOs as well as the introduction of a new intervention order. McDonald queries whether there will be sufficient resources to fund the positive aspects of the action plan such as an expansion of youth mentoring (McDonald 2006: 196) and argues that, by 'demonising the very children that the Government is trying to regulate and control with their strategies and early intervention', the action plan 'would appear to be creating the very problem that it is seeking to tackle' (ibid: 198; see also Chapter 8 below).

Sure Start

Home Start was an earlier initiative in parent support, set up as a national organisation in England in 1981. Taking self- and agency referrals, Home Start provided parent volunteers to give practical support to families, often in their own homes but also in local centres which might be multi-use premises. In 2004 the organisation received government funding. Meanwhile, the first 524 Sure Start local programmes were set up in 1999 as area-based programmes with substantial investment by the Government in the early years.

These early Sure Start programmes also aimed to provide core services of family support and good quality child care experiences. As the Sure Start web page notes: 'The concept itself is not a new one, it is about building on existing good practice, rather than starting afresh'. [10] In a special supplement on *Every Child Matters*, one national newspaper referred, not necessarily negatively, to Sure Start as 'care, coffee and kindness'.[11] Most of these programmes are now Sure Start Children's Centres for children up to four years of age: there are now around 1,000 Sure Start Children's Centres at local authority level with the Government committed to delivering a Sure Start Children's Centre for every community (a total of around 3,500) by 2010. There is also now a considerable administrative resource framework for delivering services, including a partnership of private sector and public sector organisations, called 'Together for Children' to support local authorities in running centres.

Sure Start Local Programmes (SSLPs) have been evaluated nationally using interviews with mothers of over 12,000 children aged nine months and of nearly 4,000 children aged 36 months in SSLP areas with a comparison group in other communities. The outcome measures were mothers' reports of community services in the local area, family functioning and parenting skills, child health and development and verbal ability at 36 months (see Belsky *et al.* 2006: 1476). The results of these evaluations have been given considerable publicity because they did not show a very clear success rate. The differences between the SSLP areas and comparison areas were limited, with quite small differences. The beneficial effects were on non-teenage mothers, but there were adverse effects on children of teenage mothers under some of the outcomes. The overall conclusion was that SSLPs 'seem to benefit relatively less socially deprived parents (who have greater personal resources) and their children but seem to have an adverse effect on the most disadvantaged children' (ibid).

The aim of Sure Start to give children a sure start in life and break the cycle of disadvantage was the result of policy-making based on evidence (Tunstill *et al.* 2005: 158–9). The research, therefore, gives the warning that it must not be assumed that all early intervention 'works' (Belsky 2007). Rather, what needs to be valued is 'building knowledge' (Tunstill *et al.* 2005) and, in particular, knowledge about the reasons why there had been positive – but small – effects found in the Sure Start data in relation to one or two factors but not others. The extensive research completed as part of the Millennium Cohort Study, which provides important general data on many aspects of children's lives including childcare, also provides detailed control data (see Hansen and Joshi 2007).

The Nurse–Family Partnership Programme

This 'health-led parenting project' is another initiative imported from the USA, pioneered by David Olds in Colorado, where it has been extensively evaluated over three decades (see, for example, O'Brien 2005). The 15-year evaluation of the original Elmira trial cohort researched by Olds found that, compared with the control group, children in their research group (Group 4) had significantly fewer arrests, convictions, and violations of probation; that Group 4 adolescents born to unmarried women with low socio-economic status reported significantly fewer instances of running away, significantly fewer sexual partners and consumed alcohol on fewer days during the six months before the interview (Olds *et al.* 1998; see also Olds 2005).

The UK scheme will cost £7 million and is a two-year programme. Family nurses, who have trained and worked as health visitors or midwives, are given an enhanced role with specific targeted young mothers. By early 2007, 10 pilot sites had been identified and tenders received (Lewis 2007),[12] and these are now in operation. The London Borough of Tower Hamlets is one of the pilot areas where, according to the website, the scheme provides 'extra help for 100 young mums … from family nurses … Each will work with 25 families and will work with the mum and baby until they [the children] are two years old. The families will be visited at least once a fortnight and sometimes weekly.' The targeted mums-to-be are 16 to 28 weeks pregnant and are aged under 20.[13]

The answer is in the detail?

Early intervention can be a wasteful use of scarce resources. Research evidence would suggest that actuarial calculations of risk factors may be the result of perfectly done research but that alone will not guarantee success, even if a way of accessing and bringing on board the relevant target children and families is found. The message or research so far is that the detail of what is to be done and how is crucial and that, despite the focus on 'what works', there is not enough discussion of *exactly* what works *for whom* and *when*.

Dosage

What has been seen as particularly important is that the intervention is both sustained and followed up. For example, the National Audit Office report on custodial and community disposals for youth offenders points out the ineffectiveness of disrupted, disjointed and unfinished educational programmes (2004: para. 13). This is sometimes referred to as the 'dosage': 'perhaps an incongruous term given the rejection by the "What Works" literature of a medical model of offending' (NACRO 2006a: 3). Dosage is one of the seven principles referred to as the 'McGuire principles'; the other six principles are risk classification, criminogenic need, intervention modality, responsivity, programme integrity and the community base (see, for example, McGuire and Priestley 1995; McGuire 1997, 2001).

The idea is that the intensity and duration of the intervention should be of such an amount that it will be enough to activate change. Again, the stress is on assessment to ensure that the level of dosage is right for the particular individual young person (ibid). For example, the FAST programme, using the school as a site for community-based engagement with parents and children, requires six 'doses' and this is seen as crucial to success (McDonald 2006).

Timing

'The earlier the better' – both in terms of effectiveness and the cost savings from the intervention – has been the received wisdom: 'If a youngster is left to go wrong … It will cost society £250,000. Proper health visiting and midwifery for a minus-nine month to two year old will cost a tenth of that … The earlier we intervene, the better the value for money for the taxpayer as well.' That statement by Graham Allen MP[14] suggests a widespread, but unhelpful, belief that almost any intervention, if early enough, will 'save' a child and also save a considerable amount of money. Recent research would suggest that a reduction in such confidence would, in the long run, make improved outcomes more likely. To quote Belsky (2007), 'The child is father to the man – *depending*'. Ideas about the 'stability' of aspects of a child's developmental characteristics are over-emphasised, and so early intervention may not be the most effective timing. Policy-makers, he argues, should not be so 'hung up' on the notion that the early years of a child's life are always the most critical (ibid).

The critique of the youth justice interventions might also suggest non-intervention, or later intervention, in the lives of some children and young people, whilst Forrester (2007) has argued that intensive and early intervention 'family preservation' services – to prevent a child being taken into care – may also be counter-productive. Research does not always show clear differences in outcome, and it is also accepted that children entering care usually come from families with severe problems who are not accessing available programmes (ibid). There is also the caveat that there should perhaps not be a later interventions cut-off point: 'The problems associated with youth transitions do not conclude at neat, age-specific points and, therefore, age-related policies (such as Youth Offender Teams, Connexions Service and the New Deal for Young People) do not 'fit' harmoniously with the realities of the extended transitions of young adults' (Webster *et al.* 2006).

Local knowledge

One focus has been the 'new localism' (Painter 2005: 310). It is argued that there is a need to produce programmes as a result of detailed consultation with users, including older children, and programmes that, consequently, respond to local needs. As Oliver Heald MP said in a parliamentary debate on social exclusion, 'I have visited many projects that help the socially excluded and one lesson I have learnt is that it is not possible to make sweeping decisions from on high … Solutions to social exclusion must come from the bottom.'[15] This 'lesson' must, however, be read alongside the importance of having a clearly set out and detailed programme with good leadership (see below).

Multi-modal

Intervention modality refers to the fact that deemed programmes are likely to be more effective if they are 'multi-modal', that is they employ a variety of techniques to address a range of needs as assessed in the young person (NACRO 2006a: 4). Early evaluation of the 'On Side' project found that a key issue is this multi-faceted 'holistic' approach because most young people have got numerous and complex needs (NACRO 2003a: 1). That particular project is based at HMYOI Portland and was designed to help identify what the key elements of an effective resettlement service with 15–18 year-old offenders should be and gave the now familiar message that services must be co-ordinated to address the wide range of complex needs of the most serious offenders (for an update see NACRO 2006d). The personnel are then crucial to success.

Krisberg, in reviewing examinations of the most effective juvenile justice programmes in the USA, points to the six critical components of successful programmes outlined more than two decades ago in 1984 by Altschuler and Armstrong (Krisberg 2005: 150). They had argued that the best programmes use 'continuous case-management', that a broad range of highly individualised services are provided for the young person and monitored, and that educational and vocational components are also required. This means that, as the Joseph

Rowntree Foundation reported in its evaluation of Communities that Care, there needs to be the presence of effective strong leadership, which means early and comprehensive induction for new partners and staff, with skilled project co-ordinators (2004a: 1–3). Therefore, training and support for key workers is crucial.

Smith also sounds a warning note in relation to research on pilot or 'one-off' projects:

> Evaluation of flagship programmes is a poor guide to the effects of the system because the system does not deliver the flagship programmes to most young offenders most of the time … This is because the quality of the programmes will always be variable, because programmes launched by energetic and enthusiastic staff will not always remain at their peak. (Smith 2005a: 192)

A blueprint

Perhaps the most important point that the reviews of research and evaluation make is that what is needed is a clearer 'blueprint' for action. For example, NACRO has pointed out that the McGuire principles (see above) are extremely broad. They may provide a framework for intervention but they do not give the details of how exactly one should work with young people (NACRO 2006a: 4). A number of commentators have argued that it is partly for this reason that 'What Works' has tended to prioritise structured cognitive behavioural programmes (see for example Smith 2005a: 188; Krisberg 2005: 151) at the expense of other forms of intervention because they do provide a clearer idea of what precisely to do (NACRO 2006a: 5; see, also, Bottoms et al. 2001). A calculation of dosage also requires an attention to the selection and detail of the approach of the programme. So the FAST programme, theorised as increasing social capital, works as a systemic and very prescriptive multi-family group programme, with repetition of activities, a very structured and timed programme, and trainers to monitor the 'integrity' of the programme (McDonald 2006). Ryan and Schuerman make a similar point when drawing lessons from their review of family preservation programmes in the USA: 'It is important we step back and explore the individual components that comprise the interventions' (2004: 372).

Others argue that in order for the blueprint to be worked out, the research needs to be more rigorous; that there should always be, for example, control groups so that it can be clearer what exactly are the inputs that lead to the desired outputs (Belsky 2007).

Personnel and practice

Several of the studies reviewed above emphasised how important an influence on the success or failure of programmes are the attitudes and approach of professionals. Fitzgibbon also points to the danger that 'deskilled practitioners working under increasing resource constraints' might inflate the levels of risk presented and refer to inappropriate programmes (2007: 87). It has been acknowledged that the *Every Child Matters* programme requires new ways of joined-up working resulting from 'cross-cutting' initiatives and the development of Children's Trusts. However, a *Guardian* survey of 400 professionals[16] in October 2005 found that two-thirds believed that frontline staff 'did not fully understand what integrated services would mean to them. The case loads they carry leave them little time for looking at the bigger picture', and only 20 per cent believed that integrated care was a practice concept understood in health (Dean 2005).

Theoretical and empirical evidence would suggest that practice may not have changed so much as policy would suggest. Some practitioners appear not to subscribe to dominant notions of risk-based practice and are addressing needs and accessing resources for children. Field (2007) found, for example, that social workers practising within youth offending teams reconfigured welfare in terms of intervention to prevent offending, although their version of 'welfare' was now more conditional.

Conclusions

It is argued that the evidence-based policy agenda presents a 'technicist view' of the process of policy-making, implementation and evaluation, exacerbated by the plethora of 'What Works' 'toolkits' which 'offer simple "off the shelf" ... guides to practice' (Cooke 2006: 103). Even the focus on community involvement is more problematic than presented. It is a 'dynamic and contested' context which raises questions about the evidence base: 'whose knowledge is it and where does it come from, where does it apply and to what end was it generated?' (ibid: 104). From this perspective, 'Never too early', the title of chapter 10 of the book by Farrington and Welsh (2007: 159), gives a misleading message about the certainty of what we know.

The research does *not* suggest that the *Every Child Matters* agenda is too ambitious: there is enough science to merit the initiatives. However, I have a real fear that the current overly optimistic interpretation of the messages of research may lead to unthinking and unprincipled application of inappropriate and ill-targeted interventions. Many of the research reports reviewed above stress the need for careful planning, for trained staff, for an understanding of objectives and for careful yet exploratory targeting. It is also of concern that many interventions are still based on dichotomised images of victims and offenders. As Case points out, 'The reconstruction of "youth" and "adolescence" as pejorative labels and touchstones for punitive restrictive and increasingly invasive state responses' is a distraction and hides the vulnerable child from the view of Parliament and practitioner (Case 2006: 172; see also Muncie and Hughes 2002). Furthermore, he argues, 'the tacit (and occasionally explicit) implication is that it is the general public who are, in fact, at risk from young people's responses to "risk factors"' (Case 2006: 172). It is the public who are presented as the most vulnerable: 'both from young people's rational, calculating choices to offend and from their inability to resist those influences that predetermine their offending' (ibid: 173). The needs and fears of adults – where they take precedence over the needs of the child – will undermine attempts to intervene positively in a child's life. What is also crucial is that there develops an integrated image of the child. The final chapter will review the importance of these images in current developments.

The approach reflected in the title of a recent Communities that Care publication – *A Guide to Promising Approaches* (Utting and Langman 2006), now in its second edition – would seem to be the way forward. There are many *promising* approaches and programmes: if treated as promising rather than prescriptive of assured success then there will be careful implementation of clearly specified programmes which can be properly evaluated, and then modified as appropriate. *The Children's Plan*, published by the government at the end of 2007 suggests that more than decade is being allocated for a continuation and intensification of the investment, social inclusion and prevention policies outlined in this book. This timescale should address many of the concerns this chapter raises. However, the next chapter reviews some developments which might reduce significantly the effectiveness of the more optimistic research pointers.

Notes

1 The impetus for the book was a meeting of international child welfare research experts in Windsor, UK in 2001, organised by the Department of Health (McAuley *et al.* 2006: 11).

2   *Hansard* HC coll. 453–4 (11 January 2007).
3   *R (on the application of R) v Durham Constabulary and another* [2005] UKHL 21; see Chapter 6.
4   http://www.communitiesthatcare.org.uk/thectcprocess.html.
5   http://www.connexions-direct.com/ (6.11.07).
6   http://bandapilot.org.uk/secondary/.
7   See http://www.teachernet.gov.uk/wholeschool/extendedschools/research/.
8   See www.neighbourhood.gov.uk/page.asp?id=617; see also www.ndcnetwork.co.uk.
9   See home page of the evaluation at http://extra.shu.ac.uk/ndc/.
10 See http://www.surestart.gov.uk/surestartservices/settings/surestart childrenscentres/ (accessed 26.10.07).
11 *The Guardian*, 11 October 2006.
12 Ivan Lewis, Parliamentary Under-Secretary, Department of Health, *Hansard* HC col. 808W (6 February 2007).
13 http://www.thpct.nhs.uk/news/index.aspx?pid=125&newsid=307.
14 *Hansard* HC col. 460 (11 January 2007).
15 ibid col. 470.
16 See www.cyc-net.org/features/viewpoints/c-protectvulnerable.html (accessed 28.10.2005).

Chapter 8

The right mix of parents, policy, science and law?

I must frankly own, that if I had known, beforehand, that this book would have cost me the labour which it has, I should never have been courageous enough to commence it. (Isabella Beeton, Preface, *The Book of Household Management*)[1]

So wrote Mrs Beeton at the beginning of her book published in 1863. So, probably, would write all authors: writing a book is like giving birth, and the immediate reaction to both events is to say 'Never again'. But this book has been particularly problematic for me. It is built on my research and thinking over many years, but it has been written at a time of huge social anxiety and during what must count as a political experiment in investing more in children's futures. *The Children's Plan*, published in December 2007, aims to take the Government's investment in children project, with a particular focus on education, health and safety, and family relationships and well-being, through to 2020. This, of course, is subject to the effects of a threatened recession and general elections: a Labour administration, currently under Prime Minister Brown, may not see out the new Plan, and the extent to which the Conservatives would continue an investment in children agenda were they asked to form a government is far from clear.

At this point in time, the effectiveness of early intervention investment is also not at all clear. The results of earlier research findings have already been published – some have been reviewed in previous chapters – and further research is in the pipeline. That may give a better indication as to whether the experiment will ultimately succeed or fail in improving the experience of both childhood and adulthood. It might not, however, because this project must essentially be long-term, and decades of underinvestment in children cannot easily and quickly be remedied.

The investment approach to legitimating expenditure

The Labour administrations of the last 10 years have repeatedly expressed their desire to improve the lives of children: in terms of publicly and explicitly expressed policy aims, this is a critical change. The issue is whether these new explicit agendas of inclusion and investment have the potential to release sufficient and effective resources over a sustained period of time to promote the optimum development of happy children who progress to good adulthoods.

As Chapters 3 and 4, in particular, showed, the new policy agendas are infused with a Third Way political ideology and its focus on 'responsible citizenship', and are legitimated by promises of future gains. There are obvious advantages to such an approach, with its use of agreements and voluntary parental involvement rather than court orders: it precludes or delays the use of 'hard-end' intervention in the lives of children and can more easily justify increased public expenditure on children. Those specified geographical areas and groups of children and families who are targeted by social inclusion policies, including those relating to crime prevention, receive extra resources without the stigma produced by targeting individuals, and access to risk-reducing interventions may tackle structural inequalities of support, opportunity and skills and so improve the child's life chances. They may also lead to referral to mainstream social services and child protection teams and familiar conceptions of best interests, whilst the encouragement of citizenship in children through positive responses to 'investment' initiatives can help develop their maturity (Dobbs and Moore 2002).

Policies have produced encouraging developments over the last decade. For example, the risk of persistent poverty for those children living in lone-parent families, rented accommodation and workless households 'declined markedly by 2002–5 when compared to the earlier time periods' (DWP 2007a: 14; see also DWP 2007c); the proportion of children living in a home that does not meet the set standard of decency fell from 41 per cent in 1996 to 23 per cent in 2005 (DWP 2007: 16); the number of children admitted to hospital for at least three days as a result of unintentional injury has shown a gradual reduction since 1990 (ibid: 14); and there has been increased stability of placements for 'looked after' children (ibid: 34). More is also promised: spending on education, including provision for Sure Start centres in every community, will increase from £77.7 billion to £92 billion (HM Treasury 2007: Summary and para. 5.32); further measures to tackle the 'poverty trap' – 'when those in work have limited incentives to move up the earnings ladder because it may leave them little better off' – are planned (ibid: para. 5.21), and there will be more money for health services for children, including an additional £60 million for targeted mental health work in schools and an extra £280 million from the DCSF to provide 40,000 short breaks for severely disabled children (ibid: para. 5.33).

The Government published *The Children's Plan* to outline policy up to 2020 (DCFS 2007) and incorporating the above promises and more. It was preceded by a nationwide consultation with teachers, children's professionals, universities, colleges, the voluntary sector, parents, and children and young people, feeding into three working groups for nought to seven year-olds, eight to 13 year-olds and 14 to 19 year-olds, involving experts 'from schools, colleges, children's services, health partners, the criminal justice system, the wider public, and the voluntary and private sectors' (Ed Balls, July 2007).[2] The day after its publication, in an article headed 'The Children's Plan: blueprint for a generation', the *Daily Telegraph* announced that 'The Children's Plan will herald the biggest shake-up of policies for young people in a generation, covering education, health, the family and law and order' (12 December 2007). In some ways this statement is misleading – many of the policies are developments of policies already in place – but the bringing together of policies from across departments, the longer timescale for action, and the use of schools on which to 'peg' a much larger range of services are what makes this a very different approach from any seen before in the UK.

As one would expect, Ed Balls, speaking in July 2007 as the new Secretary of State for the new Department for Children, Schools and Families, was optimistic about the future:

After decades of underperformance, we have turned the tide. We have rising standards – more than 58 per cent of 15-year-olds achieved five or more good GCSEs in 2006, compared to only 45 per cent in 1997. There is new investment, with 35,000 more teachers, 172,000 new classroom assistants, more than 1,100 new schools and more than 1,300 Sure Start children's centres. Teenage pregnancy rates are at a 20-year low. Re-offending rates among young people are down, and 600,000 children have been lifted out of poverty.[3]

But, the new minister continued, 'Significant challenges remain, however, which require us to change and to renew', and a fellow Cabinet Minister cautioned that, 'In the kind of market economy we live in and the kind of world we live in, it is much harder than we thought to make a difference to child poverty' (Ed Miliband, quoted in Wintour 2007: 10).

This book has been about those difficulties and, in particular, difficulties posed by ideologies of family, notions of childhood, and the reliance on science to produce solutions and provide the necessary confidence to commit resources. It has reviewed developments which make the current investment policies possible at this point in time. However, there are serious potential difficulties in undertaking to abolish child poverty and to ensure good outcomes for children through a policy which is legitimated by a notion of a sound investment for the future, particularly if a recession leads to the reduction of all investment:

- If, in order to retain the support of the electorate, the investment is conditional, children and young people who do not fulfil the conditions – who do not grasp the 'opportunities' offered by the new policies – may face more detrimental consequences than under previous policies.

- If outputs must be measurable to ensure the electorate is kept onside, then this may affect the likelihood of reaching desirable longer-term outcomes.

- If there is no investment 'income' for several years, in other words if there is no clear, measurable and favourable outcome of investment for some time, the future of investment strategies is put in doubt.

- The new criteria and structures for accessing resources may face the same hurdles as previous structures: the extent of and justification for expenditure may not alone change either professional and public attitudes or the operation of law.

- An investment approach tends to require governmental 'micro-management' and audit to ensure the confidence of the investors – the electorate – but this may detrimentally constrain and demoralise professionals on the 'frontline'.

• The current investment agenda relies heavily on research studies for its justification: science may not be able to continue to produce research which can do so.

The problem of problematic science

The dependence on science for both the formulation and legitimation of policies of social inclusion and investment in children policies was evidenced in Chapter 5 by many examples of policy documents and politicians referring to 'what we know' – and so what 'we' must do. The most recent Comprehensive Spending Review endorsed that valorisation of scientific research results in its announcement that the Government would increase the total public investment in science from £5.4 billion in 2007–08 to £6.3 billion by 2010–11 (HM Treasury 2007).

The difficulty is, as we have seen, that knowledge is not as 'solid' as it is sometimes made out to be, and that knowledge is still partial in relation to the effectiveness of particular programmes for particular people and for particular purposes. It is, then, difficult to be confident about outcomes given the fact that some of the early research findings seem to defy logic: why didn't the extra 'help' – for example via Sure Start centres – always make a positive difference? The comment of Mrs Beeton, this time from her chapter on 'The rearing, management and diseases of childhood', is again apt:

> We turn to the foetor and darkness that, in some obscure court, attend the robust brood who, coated in dirt, and with mud and refuse for playthings, live and thrive, and grow into manhood, and, in contrast to the pale face and flabby flesh of the aristocratic child, exhibit strength, vigour, and well-developed frames, and our belief in the potency of the life-giving elements of air, light, and cleanliness receives a shock that, at first sight, would appear fatal to the implied benefits of these, in reality, all-sufficient attributes of health and life.

There is much that she didn't, and we don't, know about the mechanisms linking the factors which science has identified.

With the answer appearing to lie in the detail – and with a need for more qualitative research to provide that detailed understanding – there is still more money to be spent on research, and, more importantly, it will take time to establish what does and does not work in a way that saves money in the long run. That timescale is dangerous, especially when set in the context of the 'responsibilising' strand of current political ideologies which is applied to minors as well as their parents. The continuance of investment nationally will depend on maintaining public confidence in science even when the results are not immediately forthcoming. In relation to individual children and young people, the continuance of positive investment in them (as opposed to no investment or to investment in punishment and injunctive measures) may depend too heavily on their ability to 'play ball' and to be the responsible citizen within the time limits and within the chances given.

Images of children: 'time to stop knocking the young'?[4]

Given the above concerns, the images of children which have been influential in legitimating expenditure are very important. Dominant images not only justify the continuance (or discontinuance) of child-friendly policies but also influence their implementation. The images at the two ends of a continuum still have resonance and legitimate quite different aspects of some current policies: at one end are children as innocent and victimised and, at the other, children as evil and dangerous (see Chapter 2). However, the dominant images of children and young people which currently underpin investment and inclusion policies might suggest that the wheel has come full circle over the last two centuries. The responsible citizen-child in whom Parliament now wants to invest looks very like the disciplined and responsible child espoused by the campaigning Sunday School Movement at the beginning of the 19th century.[5] There is also evidence of the re-emergence of the early 20th century 'child in trouble', with policies to help and encourage young offenders to leave offending behind and move on towards respectable adulthood, and, to complete this very divergent mix of images, a faint image of the child with rights.

Analysis of divergent images is not simply of academic interest, as has been acknowledged by Lockyer and colleagues. In the context of an analysis of whether the administrative structures for dealing with children who offend and children in need of protection should be separate, as in England, or joined, as in the Scottish Children's Hearing system, they have concluded that what is most important is that, 'whether or not systems are integrated, conjoined, separated or overlapping, *our thinking about young people does need to be integrated and holistic*' (Lockyer, Hill and Stone 2006: 300, emphasis added). Without that, the tendency has been for the more 'negative' images to influence detrimentally the implementation of positive policies for children and young people, and that is now a real fear in relation to investment policies.

Recent legislation in relation to online exploitation (see Chapter 2), which shows very contradictory images of children as victims, as adolescents to be controlled or as responsible young people, is evidence of the confused policy which can result from divergent images existing in parallel. The new image of the child as responsible for 'responsible sex' – just as with the image of the child responsible for ensuring that he or she is a responsible future citizen – has many benefits for children but does not by itself give access to resources or rights, whilst the other images endorse a policy priority given to the regulation and surveillance of children. Different and competing images can nullify the good and amplify the bad: the rapid rise in the use of ASBOs is an example of this. With punitive images of children 'waiting in the wings', the processes for carrying through positive policies are – to mix metaphors – on very shaky foundations. The minute a child or young person 'fails' – through not complying with a voluntary contract, by not taking up ways of being involved in the community or joining positive programmes, by failing to heed the significance of the 'final' warning given by the police, or by failing to complete the activities specified by the YOT or Youth Offender Panel – then the child as victim or as citizen disappears and is replaced by other images which justify control and punishment.

A prime example is the fact that the Government has been able to resist criticism from the UNCRC in order to effectively lower the age of criminal responsibility: until the passage of section 34 of the Crime and Disorder Act 1998, the presumption was that children between 10 and 14 were not criminally liable. What we have now are very divergent tests of competence in criminal and family law (Keating 2007: 187 *et seq.*). The test in family law stems largely from the *Gillick* judgment (see Chapter 2) with its emphasis on the maturity of an adolescent, whilst in criminal law the rigid *cut-in* point of 10 years is justified by an image of even the young child as a mini-adult capable of deliberate wrongdoing.

There is some evidence that government ministers might now have some understanding of the deleterious knock-on effect of the more negative set of images:

I think one of the things we have to do as a government is talk about young people in a much more positive fashion … We have to give a much more accurate impression of the vast majority of young people who do the right thing in society, and want to make the most of themselves, and not to give the impression that most young people are about to commit acts of antisocial behaviour. (Ed Miliband, Cabinet Minister, quoted in Wintour 2007: 1)

If this signals a real change of direction then the resulting new dominant image of the child or young person could well be the most important factor in the success of a child-based investment policy.

Another development might also be seen as evidence of potentially crucial changing thinking about children. The Government established in 2007 a new Joint Youth Justice Unit which merges the responsibilities of the former Youth Justice and Children Unit in the Ministry of Justice with those of the Young Offender Education team at the former DfES (now DCFS). The intention is that the dual aim of protecting the public but also ensuring that young offenders achieve the five outcomes specified in *Every Child Matters* can be better managed within the new Unit, which will also sponsor the YJB (Youth Justice Board) for England and Wales. This would appear to be a compromise position given the conflicting views on the placing of the YJB. Allen's report, *From punishment to problem-solving: A new approach to children in trouble*, asked, amongst other things, for 'new organisational arrangements, with the Children's Department in the Department for Education and Skills in the lead' (Allen 2006), but other researchers have not supported a move of youth justice services to what is now the DCFS. 'It is our view that it can be more difficult to target resources to youth justice in a welfare setting than it is in a criminal justice one because youth justice becomes marginalised in this context. We feel, therefore, that we would be in danger of losing the gains made by making youth justice a specific service if it were moved back into child services' (Hallam Centre for Community Justice 2006: 3). The desire to have children envisaged first and foremost as children, not offenders, conflicts with an acknowledgement that, so far, it has been politically easier to justify expenditure to control offending. How exactly the new Unit operates is going to be crucial.

Another potentially helpful development is the movement of the Respect Unit from the Home Office, with its clear law and order ambiance and images of 'the hooded enemy to be Asbo'd', to the new DCFS with its *Children's Plan*: 'As the emphasis shifts from punishment to prevention, expect a breath of fresh air' (Toynbee 2007: 1).

A more proactive role for rights?

The issue of how children are perceived is closely linked to the issue of children's rights. The dependent child image has been of little use to raise the profile of children's rights that go beyond protectionist rights. Yet, the 'responsibilisation' policy which is so crucial a part of the investment agenda, and in particular that relating to offending by children and young people, has not produced any image of a rights-holding young citizen either. Gray argues that the focus on responsibilisation and 'the individualisation of social risks' has 'done little to either boost young offenders' sense of social worth or change their material circumstances' (Gray 2007: 410). She proposes that, in order to achieve a more equitable distribution of economic rewards and resources, 'a solution may lie in the propagation of a "transformative" rights-based agenda'.

Gray is not the first to make such a call: she refers, for example, to the appeal by Scraton and Haydon (2002: 311) for greater use of the UNCRC. However, she argues specifically for reform that requires 'fundamental changes' in the distribution of resources such that young offenders – the focus of her interest – would 'have the right to enjoy' a particular standard of health, education and employment provision. As we saw in Chapter 6, this is generally not treated as a right, and where the courts are asked to interpret legislation they are generally reluctant to do so in ways which give children rights. Chapter 6 showed some encouraging signs of change in this respect but rights alone will not achieve a better world for children (see King 1997: Chapter 7).

Williams argues for a different approach. Instead of seeing children's rights as incompatible with the public law principles underpinning the provision of services, she points to the potential of extra-judicial processes for integrating UNCRC principles into child-friendly policies (Williams 2007: 283). 'There is evidence that within the scheme of "executive" devolution in Wales ... efforts are being made to internalise institutional children's rights obligations within executive and non-governmental policing mechanisms' (ibid: 287). In particular she refers to the statutory and audit commissions, the Family Justice Council and the reporting under the UNCRC (ibid:

284–7). If lawyers engaged with these processes, there would be 'greater absorption of human rights principles into public service delivery' (ibid: 287; see also Williams and Croke 2008).

Parental autonomy: thus far and no further?

Chapter 4 focused on the means by which the autonomy of the family, historically a barrier to investing in children's lives, has been whittled away at the edges to allow state intervention to protect and educate children. However, one issue in particular in the recent past, that of smacking, reveals the continuing power of 'the family' and its ability to block policy change which might improve the lives of children. Despite the successful abolition of corporal punishment in all schools, the issue of physical chastisement by parents has proved a much more contentious one, going, as it does, to the very heart of the conflict between parental autonomy and state power which was discussed in Part I of this book. Until section 58 of the Children Act 2004 came into force in 2005, the law was as contained in section 1(7) of the Children and Young Persons Act 1933, which provided that the offence of wilful assault, ill-treatment or neglect established by section 1(1) (and so also other offences of assault) 'does not affect the right of any parent to administer punishment to their child'. This reflected a common law defence of 'reasonable chastisement', which has itself been distinguished by cases called upon to establish whether particular actions, implements and outcomes were reasonable.

That case law was challenged by the judgment of the European Court of Human Rights in *A v UK*,[6] when the applicant, a nine-year-old who had been beaten by his step-father with a garden cane, successfully argued that the state had failed to protect him from ill-treatment, which was a violation of his Article 3 rights not to be subjected to inhuman or degrading punishment. This necessitated some change in the law, but the Government, anxious to keep the issue as low key as possible, notwithstanding the criticism of the UNCRC Committee and pressure groups, ruled out the possibility of abolishing the defence completely: '[I]t would be quite unacceptable to outlaw physical punishment of a child by a parent. Nor, we believe, would the majority of parents support such a measure. It would be intrusive and incompatible with our aim of helping and encouraging parents in their role' (Department of Health (DoH) 2000b: para. 2.14). But, as Keating points out, 'It seems reasonable to have expected rather more analysis than this of the arguments for and against abolition' (Keating 2006: 399). She also criticizes the fact that, three years later, after the investigation into the death of Victoria Climbié, when child protection was a political issue, 'Every Child Matters had nothing to say at all about smacking' (ibid: 395).

The result of these competing pressures was the compromise contained in the Children Act 2004. The defence of reasonable chastisement was abolished and replaced with the concept of 'reasonable punishment': there is a defence when the punishment amounts to common assault but not when it results in actual bodily harm. The 'ill-fated attempts in Scotland' to ban the smacking of children under three may have contributed to the Government's lack of courage (Keating 2006: 405) but, as Fortin has commented, it is 'regrettable that the Government is not prepared to promote attitudinal changes amongst parents' (Fortin 2001: 246). Certainly Lord Laming, who argued for the compromise eventually enacted, was concerned to be seen as supportive of parents:

> In my view, the choice before us is either to respect the respon-sibilities of parents; to seek to work with them constructively in partnership; to pursue policies and practices which are based on encouragement, help and support – or to go down a route which is based upon threat and coercion.[7]

Others employed arguments reminiscent of those used long ago (see Chapter 1), seeing 'danger' in not upholding parental autonomy. Earl Howe, for example, argued that 'The state should not interfere in the way in which parents bring up their children unless real abuse or violence has occurred. Loving parents should be entitled to use moderate physical punishment if they deem it to be justified in their children's best interests' and concluded that 'my belief is that the risks of changing the law considerably outweigh the risks of keeping the law as it is'.[8]

Whilst section 58 applies to Wales, the Welsh Assembly is to be applauded for opposing its passage and subsequently introducing a number of National Plans which confirm its view that physical punishment is unacceptable (see Hamilton 2007: 12). Further, the Children's Commissioners for England, Wales and Northern Ireland have all stated that they do not think that section 58 ensures adequate protection in relation to Article 3 (ibid). Similarly, in Scotland, where section 51 of the Criminal Justice (Scotland) Act 2003 introduced the concept of 'justifiable assault', the Children's Commissioner said that the concept is 'an affront to the child's human dignity' (see Hamilton

2007: 13). However, although research by the Crown Prosecution Service on a sample of cases since the implementation of section 58 reveals some problems in practice (see CPS 2007), the Government does not intend to legislate further to outlaw smacking: the responses by parents to the Government's review of section 58 were not in favour of a ban (see DCFS 2007b).

The issue of smacking therefore provides a clear example of the limits to which the state can currently go in the UK to protect children when parents oppose a policy. Policy therefore seeks to encourage partnership between parents and state and to package advice and intervention as help and support.

New support for parents and families: partnership with parents is a unifying theme of the Children's Plan. Early years settings, primary and secondary schools have done much in recent years to work with parents but the Plan seeks a step-change in the involvement of parents in their child's learning and in more general support to parents and families. (Ed Balls, press notice 2007/0235)[9]

However, as noted in earlier chapters, law is increasingly being used as a threat in the background of partnership and support, in relation both to parents who are not 'good enough' parents or who are not adequately supervising the socialisation of their children into law-abiding citizens.

In the context of child protection, commentators have alerted us for over a decade to the fact that the partnership between social workers and parents which is enjoined by guidance to the Children Act 1989 is not perceived as voluntary by those parents who are aware that a lack of co-operation will mean that legal measures of compulsion will be sought and that their lack of co-operation will be a factor in the case against their parenting (Kaganas 1995; Lindley and Richards 2000). Masson's research on emergency protection orders (EPOs) found, for example, that local authorities might make an agreement with the parents to place the child in a day nursery or accommodate the child under section 20 of the Children Act 1989 rather than applying for an EPO (Masson 2005: 77–81). The parents might not understand the implications of making an agreement, often under considerable pressure, which, if not kept, would be used in evidence against them in court. As one solicitor responded: 'Often you get to court and proceedings have commenced, the social services department say, "Well we have had a written agreement and mum and dad didn't stick to it, it was breached"' (Masson 2005: 82). The new legal aid provisions to encourage parents to take legal advice before local authorities seek care orders[10] are a further 'encouragement' to parents to agree voluntary measures of care.

Law also operates as a threat for parents of children who publicly behave in anti-social or criminal ways (see Chapter 4). For example, the use of 'contracts' in conjunction with referral orders, or in relation to anti-social behaviour and parenting support, have no legal force in themselves but are increasingly linked to legal measures. Further, the statutory provisions introduced by a range of Acts between 1991 and 2004 have provided for penalties to be paid by parents and for orders whose breach can lead to a criminal sanction. Parents can now be responsible for fines and be bound over to keep the peace (Criminal Justice Act 1991, sections 57–58 and Criminal Justice and Public Order Act 1994, Schedule 9, para. 50), and they can be the subject of parenting orders (POs). These were introduced in England and Wales by sections 8–11 of the Crime and Disorder Act (CDA) 1998 and in Scotland by section 102 of the Antisocial Behaviour etc. (Scotland) Act (ABSA) 2004. Parenting orders are triggered in England and Wales when the child or young person is made subject to a child safety order, an anti-social behaviour order or a sex offender order created, respectively, by sections 11, 1 and 2 of the CDA 1998, is convicted of a criminal offence or fails to comply with a school attendance order (under the Education Act 1996, sections 443–444: CDA 1998, section 8(1)(d)). In Scotland the order is subject to three conditions relating to behaviour, conduct and welfare (see Cleland and Tisdall 2005).

Parenting orders, it is argued, have 'set up a new relationship between parents and the state, mediated by the court' (ibid: 412), one where Scottish parents who have refused to accept parenting support voluntarily, or English parents who have failed to complete parenting contracts, can legitimately be labelled and be forced to receive 'support'. As Cleland and Tisdall note, quoting the Scottish Executive's consultation paper, the line between 'good' and 'bad' parenting is easily crossed: 'Bad parenting can have devastating effects. It is these parents – those who deliberately or recklessly fail their children – at whom POs are aimed' (ibid). What Lord Templeman 'famously explained' in a case in 1988 may no longer apply: 'The best person to bring up a child is the natural parent. It matters not whether the parent is wise or foolish, rich or poor, educated or illiterate, provided the child's moral and physical health is not endangered'[11] (see Jackson 2006: 67). It does now seem to matter whether the parent can find, accept and implement advice on parenting and also take on board a wider idea of what moral health involves.

These developments are also of concern because they may not only alienate the parents with whom the state must work in partnership – to do otherwise is expensive and politically risky – but may also be diverting attention and resources from the socio-economic factors which underlie exclusion and lack of aspiration. Gillies notes that 'There was no sign in my research of the irresponsible, indifferent parent letting her children run wild described in the government's anti-social behaviour initiatives' (2008: 107). Instead, she found parents putting 'considerable mental and physical effort into retaining basic resources and preventing a slide into destitution' but still being 'unable to ensure that their children grow up without experiencing and understanding deprivation' (ibid: 111). For many mothers in her sample, their life experiences meant that 'school was often viewed as a harsh, perilous world in which children were successful if they avoided attention from teachers' (ibid: 104). Home became their priority, not investment in education (ibid), and yet they 'forged an extremely positive identity around mothering' (ibid: 112). Without the insight from qualitative research such as this, policy will not only be based on unjust judgements of parents but will also be ineffective.

The law and order agenda

Chapter 6 reviewed cases which evidenced a greater commitment by the courts to children's rights to protection, autonomy and representation contained in both the UNCRC and the ECHR. However, policy documents suggest that the agency of children has been transformed, not so much into rights, but rather into opportunities to make choices and an 'empowerment' to do so (Monk 2002: 54). Citizenship has focused on the ability to seek and find advice, on the making of choices based on the information sought, on the taking up of opportunities and on engaging in civic work. If children make 'wrong' choices or 'fail' to make any positive choices then various forms of discipline or punishment are triggered but, argues *Childright*, whilst it 'is perfectly legitimate to promote responsibility … it is not equally legitimate to withhold rights until a young person can demonstrate that responsibility' (*Childright* 2005: 3). The judicial decisions which accord children respect and services also contrast with the large volume of more 'negative' activity by the courts which has resulted from the legislation providing the courts with more 'conditional statements' (see above) to adjudicate in relation to anti-social and criminal behaviour.

Previous chapters have also emphasised the importance of 'community' in inclusion and investment policies, but that policy may not work to the advantage of children and young people. 'Analyses of child care legislation have tended to consider the triangle of relationships between the state, parents and children ... our conclusion is that analyses must now consider a square, not a triangle. The new point ... is the community' but, Cleland and Tisdall go on to argue, the values represented by the 'community' element are 'profoundly worrying' because they encourage punitive treatment of children engaging in anti-social behaviour (Cleland and Tisdall 2005: 413). This has become apparent in England and Wales because of the overlap of the social inclusion and Respect agendas. That latter programme has included positive programmes to prevent anti-social behaviour, but the 'negative' control aspects of the programme – the increased focus on orders and contracts – have produced issues for the courts. In particular, the courts have been asked to deal with applications for anti-social behaviour orders (ASBOs), available for anyone over 10 years of age, and to sentence on breach of such orders. This has produced a significant workload. Up to the end of 2004, 52 per cent of orders were given to 10–17 year-olds despite the initial unwillingness of the government to use ASBOs for juveniles at all and then only for those over 12 (see Burney 2005: 97–8).

Arguably, the judiciary has played a significant role in the increasing use of ASBOs: 'While it is the local authorities and the police who are instructive in determining ASBO *applications*, it is the judiciary who primarily define their legitimacy, their purpose and scope, and their function in law' (Donoghue 2007: 428). Bateman has also argued that magistrates give insufficient attention to the legal requirement only to impose an order if it is 'necessary', assuming – wrongly – that alternatives have been tried already (Bateman 2007: 313–20). Further, the appeal courts have dismissed claims brought under the ECHR. The *McCann* case in relation to Article 6 – the right to a fair trial and the issue of the standard of proof – did not lead to a unanimous judgment, but Lord Hope's view that 'these restrictions are imposed for preventative reasons not punishment' prevailed.[12] This ruling means that the proceedings remain as civil ones, although the courts must be 'sure' that the evidence supports the claim, a test akin to the criminal standard. The McCanns were brothers aged 13, 14 and 16, and the conditions imposed excluded them from the neighbourhood of their home. The court said, however, that the appropriate balance 'requires the scales to come down in favour of the community' (see Burney 2005: 84–9).

Yet these assumptions are not based on evidence of the effectiveness of ASBOs. In recent research the Audit Office found that over half of those in their sample group breached their order, and a third did so on two or more occasions (Home Office 2006b: Executive Summary, para. 5h). About 46 per cent of the cases sampled concerned young people aged under 18 (ibid: para. 5b), and this growing area of work for the sentencing courts prompted the Sentencing Advisory Panel (SAP) to issue a consultation paper on the sentencing of young offenders for breach (SAP 2007: para 78 *et seq.*). That paper notes that the approach towards sentencing adults which it outlines, whereby levels of seriousness are determined by harm and persistence, applies equally to 'youths' (ibid).

Others have pointed to the decrease in rights for young people as a result of the introduction of, and changes to, ASBOs. Burney has criticised, in particular, the 'naming and shaming' allowed by the courts, which she argues has strengthened popular ideas 'of a country at the mercy of 12 year old tearaways' (Burney 2003: 475), reflecting and strengthening an unhelpful image of children as 'dangerous youth'. Cobb has also traced the incremental reduction in anonymity rights for minors over the last decade, and the Government's espousal in practice of shaming as a means of increasing public surveillance (Cobb 2007: 360–1). However, the case of *Stanley v Metropolitan Police*[13] exonerated publicity practices from censure under Article 8(1) of the ECHR (Burney 2005: 96–7; see also Taylor 2006), although the EU Commissioner on Human Rights has criticised the 'aggressive publication of ASBOs, through, for instance, the door step distribution of leaflets containing the names and addresses of children subject to ASBOs' (Gil-Robles 2005: 37; see also Donoghue 2007: 420–1). The message from the Judicial Studies Board echoes that of the Government, however:

> Given the nature of the proceedings, i.e. that the under 18 year old is being accused of anti-social behaviour in the community, it is in the community interest that any order will be enforced in order to protect the community. Unless the nuisance is extremely localised, enforcement of the order will normally depend upon the general public being aware of the order and of the identity of the person against whom it is made. (undated: section 3.6)

Yet the Children and Young People's Act 1933, section 39, as amended by the Youth Justice and Criminal Evidence Act 1999, gives the court a discretion to forbid identification in any civil or criminal proceedings, and section 44 of the 1933 Act mandates any court dealing with a minor to have regard to the child's welfare (see NACRO 2007). However, the argument by which the courts have justified overriding the child's anonymity under this provision has been by legitimating the taking into account of the deterrent effect of publicity on the young defendant. According to Brown LJ, 'These deterrents are proper objectives for the court to seek';[14] the effect is beneficial in reducing the young person's offending. Cobb argues that Brown LJ's assumption about the value of shame 'illustrates the law's position as a particularly dominant source of expertise in the construction of "truths"', a construction, he argues, achieved 'in the absence of even the most basic evidence' to support the approach taken. In effect, law has rejected knowledge about labelling in favour of the 'neo-conservative commonsense of shame' (Cobb 2006: 361–2).

What this evidences is the potential of law and order initiatives to take precedence over more positive initiatives and to influence the way all children are viewed. The amendment to section 44 of the Children and Young Persons Act 1933 by the Criminal Justice and Immigration Act 2008 will solidify this trend. New subsections 1A and 1B will be inserted into section 44 to make clear that the 'principal aim' of the youth justice system, to prevent offending by persons under 18, must take precedence over the duty to have regard to the child's welfare.

No linear progression?

It would be good if we could document – in the tradition of liberal historians – a clear linear progression from one image of the child through to another, and from one clear policy framework to another, but that is not going to happen. With particular reference to youth justice policy, Muncie has argued:

> The 'new' never replaces the old. In the twenty-first century discourse of protection, restoration, punishment, responsibility, rehabilitation, welfare, retribution, diversion, human rights and so on exist alongside each other in some perpetually uneasy and contradictory manner. (Muncie 2004: 249; see also Cobb 2007: 369)

The difficulty is that all those intangibles reviewed in the first part of this book – images of children, conceptions of family, fears about the future – influence the balance given to particular conceptions and constructions at particular points in time and space. So Chapter 1 of this book argued that the time and place is very important. There may currently be global movements and dominant discourses, but how they play out in any jurisdiction depends on the detail of developments and ideas. McAra (2005) uses recent Scottish developments in dealing with young offenders to make this point. She argues that, whilst the elision of social inclusion, community safety and youth justice agendas – with resultant pressure for change – is occurring in Scotland as in the rest of the UK, the pressures have been mediated by localised political and cultural processes and so there has not been 'a *seismic* shift within the broader juvenile justice system' (ibid: 287). In Scotland, she argues, penal-welfare values continue even though the Children (Scotland) Act 1995 enabled Children's Hearings to place public protection above the best interests of the child where the child presented a significant risk to the public. It matters how those working with children and structuring policy at the local level work out in practice the micro-level of policy.

What also matters is that their 'clients' should be seen, first and foremost, as children and adolescents *now*, because the most problematic aspect for children of the investment and inclusion agendas is, arguably, their future focus; legitimation of public expenditure on children via a discourse of investment can construct childhood as nothing but a training ground. The fear is that children *when children* are being neglected:

> The multi-million pound Children's Agenda mainly funds buildings, committees, and other infrastructures and not direct care of children. … There are risks that the System's over-concentration on monetary wealth and poverty and on children's future earning potential could turn children into hostages to the future, and paradoxically impoverish their present Lifeworld, restricting their citizenship, their enjoyments and relationships, freedoms and rights during their early years. (Alderson 2008: 117)

There is also a fear that too little attention will be paid to young adults (Jones 2008: 103–5): a focus on investment in children for the future seems to bring back the very child/adult distinction which the 'death of childhood' studies decried (see Chapter 2).

The Children's Plan does, however, have indications that childhood itself may at least be part of the new policy focus:

> Good health is vital if children and young people are to enjoy their childhood and achieve their full potential ... No one can guarantee wellbeing and health for every child, but as a society *it must be our aspiration for children and young people to have a good childhood*, and live free from the avoidable causes of poor health and unhappiness. We want to see each child and young person feeling well prepared for the next phase of growing up at each stage of their journey to adulthood ... By 2020 *we want to see: ... all children able to enjoy an active childhood*, with safe places to play independently. (DCFS 2007: 18, 19; emphasis added)

This is a welcome development although one which will need careful management, given the problems outlined in the first part of this book.

In January 2007, Hilary Armstrong, then Minister for Social Exclusion, set out her 'key principles of reform' in the Government's plan to tackle social exclusion: first, 'better identification of the problems and who is suffering them, followed by early intervention ... it makes moral and financial sense to invest in prevention'; secondly, 'we must identify what works'; thirdly, 'we want to promote more effective multi-agency prevention'; fourthly, 'we need to focus on personalisation and rights and responsibilities'; fifthly, 'we must support achievement and manage underperformance ... if local authorities and service providers deliver the goods, the Government should leave them alone'.[15]

This book aimed to identify the underlying and long-standing 'intangibles', the ideologies and social constructions around family and child, as well as more recent assumptions about science, investment and management, which make some of Armstrong's key principles – 'identification', 'prevention' and 'rights and responsibilities' – problematic concepts. But this book has also identified developments which are favourable to children and young people in that, politically, there are the 'right' components for change. If governments continue to provide a rhetoric and the resources which support the valuing of, and investment in, children and young people, but at the same time 'leave alone' those who can best implement positive policies into practice, then the UK may yet rise to the top of the league tables for child well-being.

Notes

1 See http://www.mrsbeeton.com/ for links to all chapters of the book.
2 *Hansard* HC col. 1323 (10 July 2007).
3 *Hansard* HC col. 1319 (10 July 2007).
4 The headline for an article by Patrick Wintour, reporting on comments by Ed Miliband, on the front page of the *Guardian* (23.07.2007).
5 See, for example, Dick 1980; Lacquer 1976; Thompson 1968.
6 *A v UK* (1999) 27 EHRR 611.
7 *Hansard* HL col. 534 (5 July 2004).
8 *Hansard* HL col. 554 and 555 (5 July 2004).
9 http://www.dfes.gov.uk/pns/DisplayPN.cgi?pn_id=2007_0235 (accessed 28.12.07).
10 Family Help (Lower), Public Law, introduced in October 2007: see http://www.legalservices.gov.uk/docs/forms/Controlled_Work_1_Public_Law_Version1_October_2007_(244kb).pdf (accessed 28.12.07).
11 *Re KD (A Minor) (Ward: Termination of Access)* [1988] AC 806 at 812.
12 *McCann v Crown Court at Manchester* [2002] UKHL 39.
13 *R v Stanley and others v Metropolitan Police Commissioner* [2004] EWHC 222 (Admin).
14 *R v Winchester Crown Court ex parte B* [2000] 1 Cr App R 11 at 13; see also *T v St Albans Crown Court* [2002] EWHC 1129, para. 22.
15 Hilary Armstrong, *Hansard* HC coll. 458–9 (11 January 2007).

References

Ainley, P. (1999) *Learning Policy – Towards the Certificated Society*. Basingstoke: Macmillan.

AITC (Association of Investment Trust Companies) (2003) *Survey*, http://www.aitc.co.uk/press_centre/default.asp?id=2700 (accessed on 25.9.06).

Alden, M. (1908) *Child Life and Labour*. London: Headley Bros.

Alderson. P. (2008) 'When Does Citizenship Begin? Economics and Early Childhood', in J. Williams and A. Invernizzi (eds) *Children and Citizenship*. London: Sage.

Alexander, R. and Hargreaves, L. (2007) *Community Soundings: Report on the Primary Review regional witness sessions*. Cambridge: Cambridge University Press.

Allen, R. (2006) *From Punishment to Problem Solving: A New Approach to Children in Trouble*. London: Centre for Crime and Justice Studies, King's College, London.

Alston, P. (1994) 'The best interests principle: towards a reconciliation of culture and human rights', *International Journal of Law and the Family*, 8 (1): 1–25.

Archard, D. (1993) *Children, Rights and Childhood*. London: Routledge.

Arnull, E., Eagle, S., Gammampila, A., Archer, D., Johnston, V., Miller, K. and Pitcher, J. (2005) *Persistent Young Offenders: A retrospective study*. London: Youth Justice Board.

Audit Commission (1996) *Misspent Youth: Young People and Crime*. London: Audit Commission.

Audit Commission (2004) *Youth Justice 2004: A review of the reformed youth justice system*. London: Audit Commission.

Atkinson, A. (2003) 'Social Europe and Social Science', *Social Policy and Society*, 2 (4): 261–72.

215

Bailey, S. (2006) 'Public authority liability in negligence: the continued search for coherence', *Legal Studies*, 26 (2): 155–84.

Baker, K. (2004) 'Is *Asset* really an asset? Assessment of young offenders in practice' in R. Burnett and C. Roberts (eds) *What Works in Probation and Youth Justice: Developing evidence-based practice*. Cullompton: Willan.

Baker, K., Jones, S., Merrington, S. and Roberts, C. (2005) *Further Development of Asset*. London: Youth Justice Board.

Banks, P., Gallagher, E., Hill, M. and Riddell, S. (2002) *Young Carers: Assessment and Services*, Health and Community Care Research Findings No. 23, Scottish Executive Central Research Unit. Edinburgh: The Stationery Office.

Barnsdale, L., MacRae, R., McIvor, G., Brown, A., Eley, S., Malloch, M., Murray, C., Popham, F., Piacentini, L. and Walters, R. (2006) *Evaluation of the Airdrie Sheriff Youth Court Pilot*. Edinburgh: Scottish Executive.

Barrie, L. (2006) 'Abdul Ali: The impact of the House of Lords judgment on the right to education under Article 2 Protocol 1 ECHR', *Childright*, cR 226: 6–7.

Bateman, T. (2007) 'Ignoring necessity: the court's decision to impose an ASBO on a child', *Child and Family Law Quarterly*, 19 (3): 304–21.

Beck, U. (1992) *Risk Society: Towards a New Modernity*. London: Sage.

Beckett (2007) *Child Protection, An Introduction*, 3rd edn. London: Sage.

Behlmer, G. (1982) *Child Abuse and Moral Reform in England 1870–1908*. Stanford: Stanford University Press.

Beinart, S., Anderson, B., Lee, S. and Utting, D. (2002) *Youth at Risk? A national survey of risk factors and problem behaviour among young people in England, Scotland and Wales*. London: Communities that Care.

Belsky, J. (2007) 'Lessons learned and some new issues' Paper presented at the conference *Early Interventions – Panacea or Policy Hype?* Brunel University 15 June.

Belsky, J., Melhuish, E., Barnes, J., Leyland, A., Romaniuk, H. and the National Evaluation of Sure Start Research Team (2006) 'Effects of Sure Start local programmes on children and families: early findings from a quasi-experimental, cross sectional study', *BMJ*, 332: 1476–8.

Berger, P. and Luckman, T. (1966) *The Social Construction of Reality*. New York: Doubleday.

Bilston, B. (undated) *The History of Child Protection*, http://www.open2.net/healthliving/health_socialcare/history.html (accessed 16.10.06).

Boeck, T., Fleming, J., Hine, J. and Kemshall, H. (2006) 'Pathways into and out of crime for young people' *Childright*, cR 228: 18–21.

Booth, C. (1902–03) *Life and Labour of the People in London*, 17 vols. London: Macmillan.

Booth, W. (1890) *In Darkest England and the Way Out*, 1st edn. London: International Headquarters of the Salvation Army.

Borge, A., Rutter, M., Cote, R. and Tremblay, S. (2004) 'Early childcare and physical aggression: differentiating social selection and social causation', *Journal of Child Psychology and Psychiatry and Allied Disciplines*, 45 (2): 367–76.

Bottoms, A., Gelsthorpe, L. and Rex, S. (2001) 'Concluding Reflections' in A. Bottoms, L. Gelsthorpe and S. Rex (eds) *Community Penalties: Change and Challenges*. Cullompton: Willan.

Bradshaw, J. (2001) 'Child Poverty under Labour' in G. Fimister (ed.) *Tackling Child Poverty in the UK: An end in sight?* London: Child Poverty Action Group.

Bradshaw, J. and Mayhew, E. (eds) (2005) *The Well Being of Children in the UK*, 2nd edn. London: Save the Children.

Brannen, J. and Storey, P. (1998) 'School meals and the start of secondary school' *Health Education Research*, 13 (1): 73–86.

Brown, G. (2002) 'Budget Statement', *House of Commons, Hansard*, April 17.

Buckingham, D. (2000) *After the Death of Childhood: Growing up in the age of the electronic media*. Cambridge: Polity Press.

Burnett, R. and Appleton, C. (2004) 'Joined-up Services to Tackle Youth Crime', *British Journal of Criminology*, 44: 35–54.

Burnett, R. and Roberts, C. (eds) (2004) *What Works in Probation and Youth Justice: Developing evidence-based practice*. Cullompton: Willan.

Burney, E. (2003) 'Talking tough, acting coy: crime control and social control', *The Howard Journal*, 43: 203–11.

Burney, E. (2005) *Making People Behave: Anti-social Behaviour, Politics and Policy*. Cullompton: Willan.

Burrow, J.A. (1986) *The Ages of Man: A Study in Medieval Writing and Thought*. Oxford: Clarendon Press.

Cabinet Office (1999) *Professional policy making for the twenty-first century*, Report by the Strategic Policy Making Team. London: Cabinet Office, HM Government.

Cabinet Office (2006) *Reaching Out: An action plan on social exclusion*. London: Cabinet Office, HM Government.

Calder, M. (2003) 'The Assessment Framework: A Critique and Reformulation', in M. Calder and S. Hackett (eds) *Assessment in Child Care, Using and Developing Frameworks for Practice*. Lyme Regis: Russell House Publishing.

Campbell, B. (2006) 'The Disrespect Agenda', Paper presented at Reconstruct conference, London, 13 October.

Cannan, C. (1992) *Changing Families, Changing Welfare*. Hemel Hempstead: Harvester Wheatsheaf.

Capacity and Esmee Fairbairn (2007) *Children's Centres: Ensuring that families most in need benefit*. London: Capacity and Esmee Fairbairn.

Case, S. (2006) 'Young People "At Risk" of What? Challenging Risk-focussed Early Intervention as Crime Prevention', *Youth Justice*, 6 (3): 171–9.

217

Childright (2005) 'Which Youth Matters? Comments on the Government Green Paper', *Agenda*. Colchester: Children's Legal Centre, University of Essex.

Childright (2007a) 'Building on Progress: Government Policy for Families in the Next Ten Years', June. University of Essex: Children's Legal Centre.

Childright (2007b) 'Agenda: Health Services for Children', April. Colchester: Children's Legal Centre, University of Essex.

Cleland, A. and Tisdall, K. (2005) 'The challenge of anti-social behaviour: New relationships between the State, Children and Parents', *International Journal of Law, Policy and the Family*, 19 (3): 395–420.

Cobb, N. (2007) 'Governance through publicity: Anti-social Behaviour Orders, young people, and the problematization of the right to anonymity', *Journal of Law and Society*, 34 (3): 342–73.

Collier, R. (2001) 'A hard time to be a father?: reassessing the relationship between law, policy, and family (practices)', *Journal of Law and Society*, 28 (4): 520–45.

Commission on the Social Sciences (2003) *Great Expectations: The Social Sciences in Britain*. Reading: Academy of Learned Societies for the Social Sciences.

Cook, D. (2006) *Criminal and Social Justice*. London: Sage.

Cox, R. (1996) *Shaping Childhood*. London: Routledge.

Cunningham, H. (1995) *Children and Childhood in Western Society Since 1500*. London and New York: Longman.

Crawford, A. (2003) 'Contractual governance of deviant behaviour', *Journal of Law and Society*, 30 (4): 479–505.

Creasey, R. and Trikha S. (2004) *Meeting parents' needs for information: evidence from the 2001 Home Office Citizenship Survey*, Home Office Online Report 48/04. London: Home Office.

Cretney, S. (1998) *Law, Law Reform and the Family*. Oxford: Clarendon Press.

Cretney, S. (2003) *Family Law in the Twentieth Century, A History*. Oxford: Oxford University Press.

Crew, L. and Collins, P. (2006) 'Commodifying children: fashion, space, and the production of the profitable child', *Environment and Planning*, 38: 7–24.

Cross, G. (2002) 'Valves of desire: a historian's perspective on parents, children and marketing', *Journal of Consumer Research*, 29 (3): 441–7.

Crow, I., France, A., Hacking, S. and Hart, M. (2004) *Does Communities that Care Work? An evaluation of a community-based risk prevention programme in three neighbourhoods*. York: Joseph Rowntree Foundation.

CWDC (Children's Workforce Development Council) (2007) *Common Assessment Framework for Children and Young People: frequently asked questions*. London: CWDC.

Curtis Committee (1946) *Report of the Care of Children Committee*: presented by the Secretary of State for the Home Department, the Minister of Health and the Minister of Education, Cmd. 6922. London: HMSO.

Dagenais, C., Begin, J., Bouchard, C. and Fortin, D. (2004) 'Impact of intensive family support programmes: a synthesis of evaluation studies', *Children and Youth Services Review*, 26 (3): 249–63.

Dahrendorf, R. (1987) 'The erosion of citizenship and its consequences for us all', *New Statesman and Society,* 12 June, 13.

Davenport Hill, M. (1855) *Practical Suggestions to the Founders of Reformatory Schools* (Written in a letter to Lord Brougham 1855; reprinted 1878 in a collection by R. and F. Davenport-Hill (eds) *The recorder of Birmingham: a memoir of Matthew Davenport Hill, with selections from his correspondence.* London: Macmillan.

Day Sclater, S. and Piper, C. (2000) 'Remoralising the family: family policy, family law and youth justice', *Child and Family Law Quarterly,* 12 (2): 135–51.

Day Sclater, S. and Piper, C. (2001) 'Social exclusion and the welfare of the child', *Journal of Law and Society*, 28 (3): 409–29.

DCA, DfES and DTI (2005) *Parental Separation: Children's Needs and Parents' Responsibilities – Next Steps,* Cm. 6452, Report of the Responses to Consultation and Agenda for Action. London: Stationery Office.

DCSF (Department for Children, Schools and Families) (2007) *The Children's Plan: Building brighter futures,* Cm. 7280. London: Stationery Office.

Dean, M. (2005) 'How to better protect vulnerable children', *The Guardian,* 28 October.

DfE (Department for Education) (1992) *Choice and Diversity: a new framework for schools*, Cm. 2021. London: HMSO.

DfES (Department for Education and Skills) (2003) *Every Child Matters,* Cm. 5860. London: Stationery Office.

DfES (2004) *Every Child Matters – Next Steps – The Response.* London: DfES.

DfES (2004b) *Safeguarding and promoting the welfare of children and young people in custody,* Local Authority Circular LAC 2004(26). London: DfES.

DfES (2005a) *Common Assessment Framework for Children and Young People, Implementation Guidance for Directors of Children's Services in Local Areas Implementing during March 2005 – March 2006.* London: DfES.

DfES (2005b) *Youth Matters,* Cm. 6629. London: Stationery Office.

DfES (2005c) *Every Child Matters Outcomes Framework,* Version 2, http://www.everychildmatters.gov.uk/aims/outcomes/.

DfES (2005d) *Statutory guidance on inter-agency co-operation to improve the wellbeing of children: children's trusts.* London: DfES.

DfES (2005e) *Realising Children's Trust Arrangements,* RR 682, National Evaluation of Children's Trusts, University of East Anglia in association with the National Children's Bureau. London: DfES.

DfES (2006a) *Care Matters: Transforming the Lives of Children and Young People in Care,* Cm. 6932. London: Stationery Office.

DfES (2006b) *Parenting Support: Guidance for Local Authorities in England.* London: DfES.

DfES (2006c) *The Common Assessment Framework for children and young people: Practitioners' guide, Integrated working to improve outcomes for children and young people.* London: DfES.

DfES (2006d) *Working together to safeguard children: a guide to inter-agency working to safeguard and promote the welfare of children.* London: Stationery Office.

DfES (2006e) *Youth Matters: Next Steps.* London: DfES.

DfES (2006f) *Developing Preventative Services: Children's Fund Strategic Plan Guidance.* London: DfES [The updated version of this guidance now covers 2005–08.]

DfES (2007a) *Connexions Branding Guidance.* London: DfES.

DfES (2007b) *Social and Emotional Aspects of Learning – A quick Guide to these materials.* London: DfES.

DfES (2007c) *Evaluation of the Full Service Extended Schools Initiative,* Research Brief and Report 852. London: DfES.

DfES (2007d) *Every Parent Matters.* London: DfES.

DoH (Department of Health) (1991) *The Children Act 1989: Guidance and Regulations, Volumes 1–10.* London: Department of Health.

DoH (Department of Health) (1995) *Child Protection: Messages from Research.* London: HMSO.

DoH (2000b) *Protecting Children, Supporting Parents: A Consultation Document on the Physical Punishment of Children.* London: Department of Health.

DoH (Department of Health) (2005) *Statement of intent: Improving health services for disabled children and young people and those with complex health needs.* London: Department of Health.

DoH, Home Office, Department for Education and Employment (1999) *Working Together to Safeguard Children.* London: Stationery Office.

DoH and DfES (2004) *National Service Framework for Children, Young People and Maternity Service,* Gateway ref. 3779. London: Department of Health.

DoH (Department of Health) with the Home Office and the Department for Education and Employment (2000) *Framework for the Assessment of Children in Need and Families.* London: Stationery Office.

Deloitte (2005) *Christmas Retail Survey 2005.* London: Deloitte & Touche LLP.

deYoung, M. (2007) ' "To catch a predator": narratizing sexual danger on a popular American television show,' Paper presented to the SLSA conference, Canterbury, England, April.

Dingwall, G. and Gillespie, A. (2007) 'Diverting Juveniles, Diverting Justice?' [2007] 2 Web JCLI, http://webjcli.ncl.ac.uk/2007/issue2/dingwall2.html.

Dick, M. (1980) 'The myth of the working class Sunday School', *History of Education,* 9 (1): 27–41.

Dickson, B. (2006) 'Safe in their hands? Britain's Law Lords and human rights', *Legal Studies,* 26 (3): 329–46.

Dickson, N. (1999) 'UK Politics, What is the Third Way?' *BBC News,* 27 September, http://news.bbc.co.uk/1/hi/uk_politics/458626.stm (accessed 7.8.2007).

Diduck, A. (2003) *Law's Families*. London: Butterworths.

Diduck, A. (2005) 'Shifting familiarity', *Current Legal Problems*, 58: 235–54.

Dimmock, S. (2007) 'Reporting on children's rights to the UN Committee on the Rights of the Child', *Childright*, cR 239: 26–30.

Dingwall, R., Eekelaar, J. and Murray, T. (1984) 'Childhood as a social problem: a survey of the history of legal regulation', *Journal of Law and Society*, 11 (2): 207.

Dobbs, L. and Moore, C. (2002) 'Engaging communities in area-based regeneration: the role of participatory evaluation', *Policy Studies*, 23 (3/4): 157–72.

Donoghue, J. (2007) 'The hudiciary as a primary definer on Anti-Social Behaviour Orders', *The Howard Journal*, 46 (4): 417–30.

Douglas, G. (1992) 'The retreat from *Gillick*', *Modern Law Review*, 55 (4): 569–76.

Drakeford, M. and Butler, I. (2007) 'Everyday tragedies: justice, scandal and young people in contemporary Britain', *Howard Journal*, 46 (3): 219–35.

Drakeford, M and Vanstone, M (2000) 'Social Exclusion and the Politics of Criminal Justice: a Tale of Two Administrations', *Howard Journal*, 39 (4): 369–81.

Duncan, T., Piper, C. and Warren-Adamson, C. (2003) 'Running rings round law? An ecological approach to teaching law for child-centred practice' *Social Work Education*, 22 (5): 493–503.

DWP (Department of Work and Pensions) United Kingdom National Action Plan on Social Inclusion – 2001–03, www.dwp.gov.uk.

DWP (2006) A *New Deal for Welfare: Empowering People to Work*. London: DWP.

DWP (2007a) *Opportunity for all: Indicators update 2007*. London: DWP.

DWP (2007b) *Joint birth registration: promoting parental responsibility*, Cm. 7160. London: Stationery Office.

DWP (2007c) *Low-Income Dynamics 1991–2005 (Great Britain)*. London: DWP.

ECOTEC (2006) *Connexions Moving Towards Children's Trusts: A Report to the Department for Education and Skills*. London: ECOTEC.

Edwards, R. (2003) 'Introduction, social capital, families and welfare policy', *Social Policy and Society*, 2 (4): 305–8.

Edwards, S. (2007) 'Imagining Islam … of meaning and metaphor symbolising the jilbab – R (Begum) v Headteacher and Governors of Denbigh High School', *Child and Family Law Quarterly*, 9 (2): 247–68.

Edwards, S. and Halpern, A. (1992) 'Parental responsibility: an instrument of social policy', *Family Law*, 22: 113–18.

Eekelaar, J. (1991) 'Parental responsibility: state of nature or nature of the state', *Journal of Social Welfare and Family Law*, 13 (1): 37–50.

Eekelaar, J., Dingwall, R. and Murray, T. (1982) 'Victims or threats? Children in care proceedings', *Journal of Social Welfare Law*, 4 (1): 68–82.

Elias, M.J., Zins, J.E., Weissberg, R.P., Frey, K., Greenberg, M., Haynes, N., Kessler, R., Schwab-Stone, M. and Shriver, T. (1997) *Promoting Social and Emotional Learning*. Alexandria, Virginia: ASCD.

Etzioni, A. (1993) *The Spirit of Community: Rights, Responsibilities and the Communitarian Agenda*. London: Fontana.

Farrington, D. (1977) 'The effects of public labelling', *British Journal of Criminology*, 17: 122–35.

Farrington, D. (1997) *Understanding and Preventing Youth Crime*. York: Joseph Rowntree Foundation.

Farrington, D. (2007) 'Childhood risk factors and risk-focused prevention', in M. Maguire, R. Morgan and R. Reiner (eds) *The Oxford Handbook of Criminology*, 4th edn. Oxford: Oxford University Press.

Farrington, D., Osborn, S.G. and West, D.J. (1978) 'The persistence of labelling effects', *British Journal of Criminology*, 18: 277–84.

Farrington, D. and Welsh, B. (2007) *Saving Children from a Life of Crime*. Oxford: Oxford University Press.

Feeley, M. and Simon, J. (1992) 'The new penology: notes on the emerging strategy of corrections and its implications', *Criminology*, 30 (4): 449–74.

Ferguson, H. (2004) *Protecting Children in Time, Child Abuse, Child Protection and the Consequences of Modernity*. Basingstoke: Palgrave Macmillan.

Fergusson, R. (2002) 'Rethinking youth transitions: policy transfer and new exclusions in New Labour's New Deal', *Policy Studies*, 23 (3/4): 173–91.

Field, F. (1989) *Losing Out: The Emergence of Britain's Underclass*. Oxford: Blackwell.

Field, S. (2007) 'Practice cultures and the "new" youth hustice in (England and) Wales', *British Journal of Criminology*, 47: 311–30.

Fionda, J. (1998) 'R v Secretary of State for the Home Department ex parte Venables and Thompson: The age of innocence? – the concept of childhood in the punishment of offenders', *Child and Family Law Quarterly*, 10 (1): 73–83.

Fionda, J. (2005) *Devils and Angels: Youth, Policy and Crime*. Oxford: Hart Publishing.

Fitzgibbon, D. (2007) 'Risk analysis and the new practitioner', *Punishment and Society*, 9 (1): 87–97.

Forrester, D. (2007) 'Early intervention to prevent care entry', Paper presented at the conference *Early Interventions – Panacea or Policy Hype?*, Brunel University, 15 June.

Fortin, J. (1999) 'Rights brought home for children', *Modern Law Review*, 62 (3): 350–70.

Fortin, J. (2001) 'Children's rights and the use of physical force', *Child and Family Law Quarterly*, 13 (3): 243–64.

Fortin, J. (2006a) 'Accommodating children's rights in a post human rights Act era', *Modern Law Review*, 69 (3): 299–326.

Fortin, J. (2006b) 'Children's rights – substance or spin?', *Family Law*, 36: 759–66.

Fox, D., Dhami, M. and Mantle G. (2006) 'Restorative Final Warnings: policy and practice', *Howard Journal of Criminal Justice,* 45 (2): 129–40.

France, A. and Crow, I. (2005) 'Using the "risk factor paradigm" in prevention: lessons from evaluation of Communities that Care', *Children and Society,* 19 (2): 172–84.

France, A. and Utting, D. (2005) 'The paradigm of "risk and protection-focused prevention" and its impact on services for children', *Children and Society,* 19 (2): 77–90.

Fraser, G. (2007) 'Sheds burned as vandals go on rampage', *Edinburgh Evening News,* 5 July.

Freeman, M. (2000) 'The end of the century of the child?', *Current Legal Problems,* 53: 505–58.

Garside, R. (2004) 'Crime, persistent offenders and the justice gap', Crime and Society Foundation, Discussion Paper No. 1. London: Centre for Crime and Justice Studies, Kings College.

Genn, H., Partington, M. and Wheeler, S. (2006) *Law in the Real World: Improving our Understanding of How Law Works,* Final Report. London: Nuffield Foundation.

Giddens, A. (1998) *The Third Way: The Renewal of Social Democracy.* Cambridge: Polity Press.

Giddens, A. (1999) 'Risk and responsibility', *Modern Law Review,* 62 (1): 1–10.

Giddens, A. (2000) *The Third Way and Its Critics.* Cambridge: Polity Press.

Gillies, V. (2005) 'Meeting parents' needs? Discourses of "support" and "inclusion" in family policy', *Critical Social Policy,* 25: 70–90.

Gillies, V. (2008) 'Perspectives on parenting responsibly: contextualizing values and practices', *Journal of Law and Society,* 35 (1): 95–112.

Gil-Robles, A. (2005) *Report by the Commissioner for Human Rights on his Visit to the UK.* Strasbourg: Council of Europe.

Goldson, B. (2007) 'Should we intervene in children's lives early: all that glisters is not gold: problematizing early intervention in the youth justice sphere', Paper presented at the conference *Early Interventions – Panacea or Policy Hype?* Brunel University, 15 June.

Goldson, B. and Peters, E. (2000) *Tough Justice – Responding to Children in Trouble.* London: Children's Society.

Gordon, L. (1988). *Heroes of Their Own Lives: The politics and history of family violence – Boston 1880–1960.* New York: Viking.

Government Office for London and the YJB (2006) *Prevent and Deter: Youth Justice Interventions Operational Guidance.* London: YJB.

Gray, P. (2005) 'The politics of risk and young offenders' experience of social exclusion and restorative justice', *British Journal of Criminology,* 45 (6): 938–57.

Gray, P. (2007) 'Youth justice, social exclusion and the demise of social justice', *Howard Journal,* 46 (4): 401–16.

Gray, E., Taylor, E., Roberts, C., Merrington, S., Fernandez, R. and Moore, R. (2005) *ISSP: The Final Report.* London: YJB.

223

Guggenheim (2005) *What's Wrong with Children's Rights?* Cambridge, Mass: Harvard University Press.

Haas, H., Farrington, D., Killias, M. and Sattar, G. (2004) 'The impact of different configurations on delinquency', *British Journal of Criminology*, 44: 520–32.

Hall, C, McClelland, K. and Rendall, J. (2000) *Defining the Victorian Nation: Class, Race, Gender and the British Reform Act of 1867*. Cambridge: Cambridge University Press.

Hallam Centre for Community Justice (2006) Response to "From Punishment to Problem Solving: A New Approach to Children in Trouble" (Sheffield: Sheffield Hallam University)', http://www.shu.ac.uk/research/hccj/downloads/538.pdf.

Hamilton, C. (2007) 'Smacking children: has the Government implemented the judgement of the European Court of Human Rights in *A v UK*?', *Childright*, cR 238: 10–13.

Hannah-Moffat, K. (2005) 'Criminogenic needs and the transformative risk subject: hybridisations of risk/need in penality', *Punishment and Society*, 7 (1): 29–52.

Hansen, K. and Joshi, H. (eds) (2007) *Millennium Cohort Study Second Survey: A User's Guide to Initial Findings*. London: Institute of Education, London University.

Harrikari, T. and Pekkarinen, E. (2006) 'Youth Curfews in Finnish Post-Welfare Society – Indicators of Generational Change?', paper presented to the SLSA Annual Conference, 29 March, Stirling, Scotland.

Harris-Short, S. (2008) 'Making and breaking family life: adoption, the state and human rights', *Journal of Law and Society*, 35 (1): 28–51.

Haydon, D. and Scraton, P. (2000) '"Condemn a little more and understand a little less": the political context and rights implications of the domestic and European rulings in the Venables-Thompson Case', *Journal of Law and Society*, 27 (3): 416–48.

Healthcare Commission (2007) *Improving Services for Children in Hospital*, Improvement Review. London: Commission for Healthcare Audit and Inspection.

Hendley, M. (1995) '"Help us to secure a strong, healthy, prosperous and peaceful Britain": The social arguments for compulsory military service in Britain, 1899–1914', *Canadian Journal of History*, 30 (2): 261.

Hendrick, H. (1994) *Child Welfare, England 1872–1989*. London: Routledge.

Hendrick, H. (2003) *Child Welfare, Historical Dimensions, Contemporary Debate*. Bristol: The Policy Press.

Hendrick, H. (ed.) (2005) *Child Welfare and Social Policy*. Bristol: The Policy Press.

Henricson, C. (2008) 'Governing parenting: is there a case for a policy of review and statement of parenting rights and responsibilities?', *Journal of Law and Society*, 35 (1): 150–65.

Hier, S. and Greenberg, J. (eds) (2007) *The Surveillance Studies Reader*. Maidenhead: Open University Press, McGraw-Hill Education.

Higate, P. (2001) 'Suicide', in J. Bradshaw (ed.) *Poverty: the outcomes for children*. London: Family Policy Studies Centre.

Hill, M., Lockyer, A. and Stone, F. (eds) (2006) *Youth Justice and Child Protection*. London: Jessica Kingsley Publishers.

Hine, J. (2007) 'Young people's perspectives on Final Warnings', Web JCL, 2, 1, http://webjcli.ncl.ac.uk/2007/issue2/hine2.html.

Hine, J. France, A., Dunkerton, L. and Armstrong, D. (2006) *Risk and resilience in children who are offending, excluded from school or who have behaviour problems*, Pathways into and out of Crime: Risk, Resilience and Diversity: Project 1, Report, http://www.pcrrd.group.shef.ac.uk/reports/project_1.pdf.

HM Treasury (2000) *Prudent for a Purpose: Building Opportunity and Security for All, 2000 Spending Review: New Public Spending Plans 2001–2004*, Cm. 4807. London: Stationery Office.

HM Treasury (2001) Children at Risk Cross-Cutting Review, http://www.hm-treasury.gov.uk/Spending_Review/spend_ccr/spend_ccr_child.cfm (accessed 21.8.07).

HM Treasury (2004) *Child Poverty Review*. London: HM Treasury.

HM Treasury (2005) *Budget 2005: Investing for our Future: Fairness and opportunity for Britain's hard-working families, Economic and Fiscal Strategy Report*, HC 372. London: Stationery Office.

HM Treasury (2007) *Meeting the Aspirations of the British People*, 2007 Pre-Budget Report and Comprehensive Spending Review, Cm. 7227. London: Stationery Office.

HM Treasury and DfES (2007) *Aiming High for Children: supporting families*. London: Stationery Office.

HM Treasury, Department for Education and Skills, Department for Work and Pensions, Department for Trade and Skills (2004) *Choice for Parents, the Best Start for Children: a ten year strategy for childcare*. London: HM Treasury.

Hoggett, B. (1989) 'The Children Bill: the aim', *Family Law*, 19: 217–22.

Holdaway, S. and Desborough, S. (2001) *Final Warnings: The National Evaluation of The Youth Justice Board's Final Warning Projects*, RDS Occasional Paper No. 69. London: Home Office.

Holland, P. (1996) ' "I've just seen a hole in the reality barrier!": Children, childishness and the Media in the Ruins of the Twentieth century' in Pilcher, J. and Wragg, S. (Eds) *Thatcher's Children*. London: Falmer Press.

Hollingsworth, K. (2006) '*R(W) v Commissioner of Police for the Metropolis and Another* – Interpreting child curfews: a question of rights?', *Child and Family Law Quarterly*, 18 (2): 253–68.

Hollingsworth, K. (2007) 'Responsibility and rights: children and their parents in the youth justice system', *International Journal of Law, Policy and the Family*, 21 (2): 190–219.

Home Office (1997) *No More Excuses: A New Approach to Tackling Youth Crime in England and Wales*, Cm. 3809. London: Stationery Office.

Home Office (1998) *Supporting Families: a consultation document*. London: Stationery Office.

Home Office (2001) *Criminal Justice: the way ahead*, Cm. 5074. London: Stationery Office.

Home Office (2003) *Respect and Responsibility – taking a stand against anti-social behaviour*, Cm. 5778. London: Stationery Office.

Home Office (2003b) *2001 Citizenship Survey*. London: Home Office.

Home Office (2004) *Youth Justice – Next Steps: Summary of Responses and Government Proposals*. London: Home Office.

Home Office (2004b) *Confident Communities in a Secure Britain – The Home Office Strategic Plan 2004–2008*. London: Home Office.

Home Office (2004c) *Children and Families: Safer from Sexual Crime: The Sexual Offences Act 2003*. London: Home Office.

Home Office (2006a) *The Final Warning Scheme*, Home Office Circular No. 14/2006. London: Home Office.

Home Office (2006b) *Tackling Anti-Social Behaviour,* National Audit Office 'Value for Money' Report by the Comptroller and Auditor General, HC 99 2006–07.

Home Office (2007a) *Guidance on the Use of Acceptable Behaviour Contracts and Agreements*. London: Home Office.

Home Office (2007b) *Review of the Protection of Children from Sex Offenders*. London: Central Office of Information.

Home Office/Youth Justice Board (2002) *Final Warning Scheme, Guidance to the Police and Youth Offending Teams*. London: Home Office.

Hood, R. (2004) 'Foreword', in R. Burnett, and C. Roberts (eds) *What Works in Probation and Youth Justice: Developing Evidence-based Practice*. Cullompton: Willan.

Horwarth, J. (2006) 'The Children Act 2004: safeguarding whom from what?', Paper presented at Reconstruct conference, London, 13 October.

Hoyle, C., Young, R. and Hill, R. (2002) *Proceed with Caution: An evaluation of the Thames Valley Police initiative in restorative cautioning*. York: Joseph Rowntree Foundation.

Hudson, B. (2003) *Justice in the Risk Society*. London: Sage.

Hunt, J. (2005) 'Combating social exclusion: the EU's contribution', *Journal of Social Welfare and Family Law*, 27 (1): 113–20.

Jackson, E. (2006) 'What is a Parent?', in A. Diduck and K. O'Donovan (eds) *Feminist Perspectives on Family Law*. London: Routledge Cavendish.

James, A. (2008) 'Care and Control in the Construction of Children's Citizenship', in J. Williams and A. Invernizzi (eds) *Children and Citizenship*. London: Sage.

James, A. and James, A.L. (2004) *Constructing Childhood*. Basingstoke: Palgrave Macmillan.

James, A. and James, A.L. (2008) 'Changing Childhood in England: reconstructing discourses of "risk" and "protection" in children's best interests', in A. James and A.L. James (eds) *European Childhoods: Culture, Politics and Participation*. Basingstoke: Palgrave Macmillan.

Jenks, C. (1996) *Childhood*. London: Routledge.

Jenks, J. (2005) 'Childhood and Transgression', in J. Qvortrup (ed.) *Studies in Modern Childhood: Society, Agency and Culture*. Basingstoke, Palgrave Macmillan.

Jenson, J. (2004) 'Changing the paradigm: family responsibility or investing in children', *Canadian Journal of Sociology*, 29 (2): 169–92.

Jepson, S. (2007) 'Shameless Mick lands a job after a week with Widdecombe', *Derby Evening Telegraph*, 18 August, 3.

Jones. G. (2008) 'Youth, Citizenship and the Problem of Dependence', in J. Williams and A. Invernizzi (eds) *Children and Citizenship*. London: Sage, pp. 97–107.

Jones, L. and O'Loughlin, T. (2003) 'A Child Concern Model to Embrace the Framework', in M. Calder and S. Hackett (eds) *Assessment in Child Care, Using and Developing Frameworks for Practice*. Lyme Regis: Russell House Publishing.

Jordan, B. (2000) *Social Work and the Third Way, Tough Love and Social Policy*. London: Sage.

JRF (Joseph Rowntree Foundation) (1999) *Findings: The interaction between housing policy and educational problems – a case study*. York: JRF.

Judicial Studies Board (2005) *Youth Court Bench Book*, section 2, Sentencing guidelines for youths, http://www.jsboard.co.uk/downloads/ycbb/ycbb_section2.pdf.

Judicial Studies Board (undated) *Reporting Restrictions: Magistrates' Courts* http://www.jsboard.co.uk/publications/rrmc/index.htm (accessed 12.9.07).

Kablenet News (2007) 'Council uses web to fight yobs', *Government Computing*, 27 July. London: Kable, http://www.kablenet.com/.

Kaganas, F. (1995) 'Partnership Under the Children Act – An Overview', in Kaganas, King and Piper (eds) *Legislating for Harmony: Partnership Under the Children Act 1989*. London: Jessica Kingsley.

Kaganas, F. (1996) 'Responsible or feckless fathers? *Re S (Parental Responsibility)*', *Child and Family Law Quarterly*, 8 (2): 165–73.

Kaganas, F., King, M. and Piper, C. (eds) (1995) *Legislating for Harmony: Partnership Under the Children Act 1989*. London: Jessica Kingsley.

Kaganas, F and Piper, C. (2002) 'Shared parenting – a 70% solution?', *Child and Family Law Quarterly*, 14 (4): 365–79.

Kaganas, F. and Diduck, A. (2004) 'Incomplete citizens: changing images of post-separation children', *Modern Law Review*, 67: 959–81.

Kaufmann, Franz-Xaver (1996) *Modernisierungsschübe, Familie und Sozialstaat*. München: R. Oldenbourg Verlag.

Keating, H. (2006) 'Protecting or punishing children: physical punishment, human rights and English law reform', *Legal Studies*, 26 (3): 394–413.

Keating, H. (2007) 'The "responsibility" of children in criminal law', *Child and Family Law Quarterly*, 19 (2): 183–203.

Kehily, M.J. and Montgomery, H. (2003) 'Innocence and Experience' in M. Woodhead and H. Montgomery (eds) *Understanding Childhood, an Interdisciplinary Approach*. Milton Keynes/Chichester: The Open University/John Wiley.

Kennedy, R. (2006) 'Assessing life after *Re G*', *Family Law*, 379–84.

Kilkelly, U. (2000) 'The child and the European Convention on Human Rights', *The International Journal of Children's Rights*, 8 (3): 299–301.

Kilkelly, U. and Lundy, L. (2006) 'Children's rights in action in using the UN Convention on the Rights of the Child as an auditing tool', *Child and Family Law Quarterly*, 18 (3): 331–50.

Kincaid, J. (1992) *Child-Loving: The Erotic Child and Victorian Culture*. New York: Routledge.

King, M. (1995) 'Partnership in Politics and Law: a new deal for parents?' in King, Kaganas and Piper (eds) *Legislating for Harmony: Partnership Under the Children Act 1989*. London: Jessica Kingsley Publications.

King, M. (1997) *A Better World for Children: Explorations in Morality and Authority*. London: Taylor and Francis.

King, M. (2007) 'The right decision for the child', review article: M. Guggenheim, What's wrong with children's rights?, *Modern Law Review*, 70 (5): 857–71.

King, M. and King, D. (2006) 'How the law defines the special educational needs of autistic children', *Child and Family Law Quarterly*, 18 (1): 23–42.

King, M. and Piper, C. (1995) *How the Law Thinks About Children* (2nd ed). Aldershot: Arena.

King, M. and Thornhill, C. (2006) *Luhmann in Law and Politics: Critical Appraisals and Applications*. Oxford: Hart Publishing.

Kitson-Clarke, G. (1962) *The Making of Victorian England*. London: Methuen.

Knepper, P. (2007) *Criminology and Social Policy*. London: Sage.

Koffman, L. (2008) 'Holding parents to account: tough on children, tough on the causes of children?', *Journal of Law and Society*, 35 (1): 113–30.

Koffman, L. and Dingwall, G. (2007) 'The Diversion of Young Offenders: A Proportionate Response?', Web JCL, 2, I.

Krisberg, B. (2005) *Juvenile Justice: Redeeming our Children*. London: Sage.

Law Commission (1982) *Family Law: Illegitimacy*, Law Com. No. 118. London: HMSO.

Laqueur, T. (1976) *Religion and Respectability: Sunday Schools and Working Class Culture*. New Haven: Yale University Press.

Landau, S. (1981) 'Juveniles and the police: Who is charged immediately and who is referred to the juvenile bureau?' *British Journal of Criminology*, 21 (1): 27–46.

Law Commission (1985) *Family Law, Review of Child Law: Guardianship*, Working Paper No. 91. London: HMSO.

Law Commission (1988) *Family Law, Review of Child Law Guardianship and Custody*, Law Com. No. 172. London: HMSO.

Le Grand, J. (1998) 'The third way begins with CORA', *New Statesman*, 6 March.

Lemert, E. (1951) *Social Pathology. A Systematic Approach to the Theory of Sociopathic Behaviour*. New York: McGrawhill Book Company.

Lindley, B. and Richards, M. (2000) 'Working Together 2000 – how will parents fare under the child protection process?', *Child and Family Law Quarterly*, 12 (3): 213–28.

Lindsay, M. (2006) 'The law relating to children's home closures', *Childright*, cR 226: 25–7.

Lipsey, M. (1992) 'Juvenile Delinquency Treatment: A meta-analytic inquiry into the variability of effects', in T.C. Cook, H. Cooper, D.S. Cordray, H. Hartmann, L.V. Hedges, R.L. Light, T.A. Louis and F.M. Mosteller (eds) *Meta-Analysis for Explanation*. New York: Russell Sage.

Lipsey, M. and Wilson, D. (1998) 'Effective Intervention for Serious Juvenile Offenders: A Synthesis of Research', in R. Loeber and D. Farrington (eds) *Serious and Violent Juvenile Offenders: Risk Factors and Successful Interventions*. Thousand Oaks, CA: Sage.

Lister, R. (2005) 'Investing in the Citizen-workers of the Future', in H. Hendrick (ed.) *Child Welfare and Social Policy*. Bristol: The Policy Press, pp. 449–62.

Little, M., Kogan, J., Bullock, R. and Van der Lann, P. (2004) 'ISSP: An experiment in multi-systemic responses to persistent young offenders known to children's services', *British Journal of Criminology*, 44: 225–40.

Lockyer, A., Hill, M. and Stone, F. (2006) 'Conclusions', in M. Hill, A. Lockyer and F. Stone (eds) *Youth Justice and Child Protection*. London: Jessica Kingsley, pp. 284–301.

Lord Chancellor's Department (1995) *Looking to the Future: Mediation and the Ground for Divorce*, Cm. 2799. London: HMSO.

Lowe, N. and Murch, M. (2001) 'Children's participation in the family justice system – translating principles into practice', *Child and Family Law Quarterly*, 13 (2): 137–58.

Lubcock, B. (2008) 'Adoption support and the negotiation of ambivalence in family policy and children's services', *Journal of Law and Society*, 35 (1): 3–27.

Luhmann, N. (2004) *Law as a Social System*. Oxford: Oxford University Press.

Lyman, R. (1957) *The First Labour Government 1924*. London: Chapman and Hall.

Lyon, J., Dennison, C. and Wilson, A. (2000) *Tell Them so They Listen: Messages from young people in custody*, HORS Study 201. London: HMSO.

Macleod, M. (2000) 'The Childright interview: Mary MacLeod, Chief Executive of the National Family and Parenting Institute', *Childright, cR* 167: 14–16.

Madge, N. (2003) *Is England child-friendly enough?*, Briefing Paper. London: National Children's Bureau.

Madge, N. (2006) *Children These Days*. London: National Children's Bureau and the Policy Press.

Mair (2004) 'The Origins of What Works in England and Wales: A House Built on Sand?', in G. Mair (ed.) *What Matters in Probation*. Cullompton: Willan.

Maloney Report (1927) *Report of the Departmental Committee on the Treatment of Young Offenders*, Cmnd 2831. London: HMSO.

McAra, L. (2005) 'Modelling penal transformation', *Punishment and Society*, 7 (3): 277–302.

McAuley, C., Pecora, P. and Rose, W. (2006) 'Effective Child Welfare Interventions: Evidence for Practice', in C. McAuley, P. Pecora and W. Rose (eds) *Enhancing the Well-being of Children and Families through Effective Interventions, International Evidence for Practice*. London: Jessica Kingsley.

McCarthy, P., Laing, K. and Walker, J. (2004) *Offenders of the Future? Assessing the Risk of Children and Young People Becoming Involved in Criminal or Antisocial Behaviour*, Research Report 545. London: DfES.

McDonald, I. (2006) 'The "Respect Action Plan": something new or more of the same?', *Journal of Social Welfare and Family Law*, 28 (2): 191–200.

McGuire, J. (ed.) (1995) *What Works: Reducing Offending: Guidelines from Research and Practice*. Chichester: Wiley.

McGuire, J. (2001) 'What Works in Correctional Intervention? Evidence and practical implications', in G. Bernfeld, D.P. Farrington and A. Lescheid (eds) *Offender Rehabilitation in Practice: Implementing and Evaluating Effective Programs*. Chichester: John Wiley.

McGuire, J. and Priestley, P. (1995) 'Reviewing "What Works": past, present and future', in J. McGuire (ed.) *What Works: Reducing Offending, Guidelines for Research and Practice*. Chichester: Wiley.

McVie, S. and Norris, P. (2006) *Neighbourhood Effects on Youth Delinquency and Drug Use*, Edinburgh Study of Youth Transitions and Crime Report No. 10. Edinburgh: Centre for Law and Society, The University of Edinburgh.

Martindale, A.-M. (2006) 'Mainstreaming learning from the Children's Fund: as easy as A, B, C?', *Journal of Social Welfare and Family Law*, 28 (1): 47–57.

Martinson, R. (1974) 'What Works? – Questions and answers about prison reform', *The Public Interest*, 35: 22–45.

Masson, J. (2005) 'Emergency intervention to protect children: using and avoiding legal controls', *Child and Family Law Quarterly*, 17 (1): 75–96.

Masson, J. (2006) 'The Climbié Inquiry – Context and Critique', *Journal of Law and Society*, 33 (2): 221–43.

Masson, J. (2008) 'The State as Parent: The Reluctant Parent? The Problems of Parents as Last Resort', *Journal of Law and Society*, 35 (1): 52–75.

Masson, J., Pearce, J., Bader, K. with Joyner, O., Marsden, J. and D. Westlake (2008) *Care Profiling Study*, Ministry of Justice Research Series 4/08. London: Ministry of Justice.

Miliband, D. (2005) 'Social Exclusion: The Next Steps Forward', Speech, 2 November, http://www.davidmiliband.info/sarchive/speech05_14.htm (accessed 25.9.07).

Moffitt, T.E. (1993) '"Life-course persistent" and "adolescence-limited" antisocial behaviour: A developmental taxonomy', *Psychological Review*, 100: 674–701.

Montgomery, H. (2003) 'Childhood in Time and Place', in M. Woodhead and H. Montgomery (eds) *Understanding Childhood, An Interdisciplinary Approach*. Milton Keynes/Chichester: The Open University/John Wiley.

Moore, R. (2004) 'Intensive supervision and surveillance programmes for young offenders: the evidence base so far' in R. Burnett, and C. Roberts (eds) *What Works in Probation and Youth Justice: Developing Evidence-based Practice*. Cullompton: Willan.

Morgan, R. (2006) 'Editorial: historical perspectives', *Criminal Justice Matters* (CJM), 65: 3, 34.

Morris, A. and Giller, H. (1987) *Understanding Juvenile Justice*. London: Croom Helm.

Morrow, V. (2008) 'Dilemmas in Children's Participation in England', in J. Williams and A. Invernizzi (eds) *Children and Citizenship*. London: Sage, pp. 120–30.

Moss, P. and Petrie, P. (2005) 'Children – Who Do We Think They Are?', in H. Hendrick (ed.) *Child Welfare and Social Policy: an Essential Reader*. Bristol: The Policy Press, pp. 85–106.

Munby, J. (2004) 'Making sure the child is heard: Part 2', *Family Law*, 34: 427.

Munby, J. (2005) 'I'm a person, not a name or a number', *Newsletter*, Association of Lawyers for Children.

Muncie, J. (2004) *Youth and Crime: A Critical Introduction*, 2nd edn. London: Sage.

Muncie, J. (2006) 'Repenalisation and rights: explorations in comparative youth criminology', *Howard Journal*, 45 (1): 42–70.

Muncie, J. and Hughes, G. (2002) 'Modes of Youth Governance', in J. Muncie, G. Hughes and E. McLaughlin (eds) *Youth Justice*, London: Sage, pp. 1–18.

Munro, E. (2003) Quoted on the proposed Children Bill, in *The Guardian*, 28 November.

Murray, C. and Phillips. M. (2001) *Underclass + 10: Charles Murray and the British Underclass 1990–2000*. London: Civitas in association with the *Sunday Times*.

NACRO (2000) 'Persistent young offenders', *NACRO Briefing*, December. London: NACRO.

NACRO (2003a) 'The On-Side Project' (A-R Solanki), *Research Briefing 4*. London: NACRO.

NACRO (2003b) 'Looked after children who offend, The Quality Protects Programme and Yots', *Youth Crime Briefing*, June. London: NACRO.

NACRO (2006a) 'Prevention and youth offending teams', *Youth Crime Briefing*, March. London: NACRO.

NACRO (2006b) 'Working with Prevent and Deter', *Youth Crime Briefing*, December. London: NACRO.

NACRO (2006c) 'Managing risk in the community in the youth justice system', *Youth Crime Briefing*, September. London: NACRO.

NACRO (2006d) *Onside, Onside 2, Milestones: Nacro's resettlement programme for young people leaving Portland YOI*. London: NACRO.

NACRO (2007) 'Naming and shaming – publicity for children and young people involved in anti-social or offending behaviour', *Youth Crime Briefing*. London: NACRO.

National Audit Office (2004) *Youth Offending: the delivery of community and custodial sentences*, Report by the Comptroller and Auditor General, HC 190 2003–04. London: Stationery Office.

National Audit Office (2006) *Ministry of Defence: Recruitment and Retention in the Armed Forces*. London: Stationery Office.

NCB (2006) *Tell Them Not to Forget about Us*. London: NCB.

NCB (2007) *Developing Relationships between Youth Offending Teams (YOTs) and Children's Trusts Project No. 323*. London: NCB.

Norton-Taylor, R. (2006) 'Two-thirds of teenagers too fat to be soldiers', *The Guardian*, 3 November, pp. 1–2.

NSPCC (2006) *The NSPCC response to 'Making Sentencing Clearer'*. London: NSPCC.

NSPCC, Save the Children, Barnardos, The Children's Society, NCH (2005) *Room for Improvement: A Manifesto for Children*. London: NSPCC.

O'Brien, R. (2005) 'Translating a research intervention into community practice: the nurse family partnership', *The Journal of Primary Prevention*, 26 (3): 241–57.

Office of the Deputy Prime Minister (2005) *New Deal for Communities 2001–5: An interim evaluation*, NRU (Neighbourhood Renewal Unit) Research Report 17. Sheffield: Sheffield Hallam University.

Ofsted (Office for Standards in Education) (2007) *Food in Schools: encouraging healthier eating*, HMI No. 070016. London: Ofsted.

O'Halloran, K. (1999) *The Welfare of the Child, The Principle and the Law*. Aldershot: Ashgate.

O'Halloran, K. (2001) 'Adoption in the two jurisdictions of Ireland – a case study of changes in the balance between public and private law', *International Family Law*, 1–94: 43–54.

Olds, D. *et al.* (1998) 'Long-term effects of nurse home visitation on children's criminal and antisocial behavior: 15-year follow-up of a randomized controlled trial', *Journal of the American Medical Association,* 280 (14): 1238–44.

Olds, D (2005) 'The Nurse-Family Partnership: foundations in attachment theory and epidemiology', in L.J. Berlin, Y. Ziv, L. Amaya-Jackson and M.T. Greenburg (eds) *Enhancing Early Attachments: theory, research, intervention, and policy.* New York: Guilford Press.

O'Malley P. (2000) 'Risk Societies and the Government of Crime' in M. Brown and Pratt, J. (eds) *Dangerous Offenders.* London and New York: Routledge.

O'Sullivan, T., Hartley, J., Saunders, D., Montgomery, M. and Fiske, J. (1994) *Key Concepts in Communication and Cultural Studies,* 2nd edn. London: Routledge.

Ost, S. (2002) '"Children at Risk" legal and societal perceptions of the potential threat that the possession of child pornography poses to society', *Journal of Law and Society,* 29 (3): 436–60.

Painter, C. (2005) 'Managing criminal justice: public service reform writ small?', *Public Money and Management,* 25 (5): 307–14.

Palmer, E. (2003) 'Courts, resources and the HRA: reading section 17 of the Children Act compatibly with Article 8 ECHR', EHRLR, 3: 308–24.

Palmer, T. (1996) 'Programmatic and nonprogrammatic aspects of successful intervention' in A.T. Harland (ed.) *Choosing Correctional Options that Work: Defining demand and evaluating supply.* Thousand Oaks, CA: Sage, pp. 131–82.

Parker, S. (1994) 'The best interests of the child – principles and problems', *International Journal of Law, Policy and the Family,* 8 (1): 27–9.

Parry, R.G. (2006) 'Protecting the juvenile suspect: what exactly is the appropriate adult supposed to do?', *Child and Family Law Quarterly,* 18 (3): 373–96.

Parton, N. (2006) *Safeguarding Childhood, Early Intervention and Surveillance in Late Modern Society.* Basingstoke: Palgrave Macmillan.

Parton, N. (2008) 'The "Change for Children" programme in England: towards the "preventative-surveillance state"', *Journal of Law and Society,* 35 (1): 166–87.

Pearson, G. (2006) 'Disturbing continuities: "peaky blinders" to "hoodies"' *Criminal Justice Matters* (CJM), 65: 6–7.

Pecora, P., McAuley, C. and Rose, W. (2006) 'Effectiveness of Child Welfare Intervention: Issues and Challenges', in C. McAuley, P. Pecora and W. Rose (eds) *Enhancing the Well-being of Children and Families through Effective Interventions, International Evidence for Practice.* London: Jessica Kingsley.

Penna, S. (2005) 'The Children Act 2004: child protection and social surveillance', *Journal of Social Welfare and Family Law,* 27 (2): 143–57.

Petplan (2005) *Survey*. Guildford: Petplan Ltd.

Petre, J. (2007) 'Church told to defend youth "failed by Britain"', *The Daily Telegraph*, 7 July.

Pickford, R. (1999) *Fathers, Marriage and the Law*, JRF Findings Ref. 989. London: Family Policy Studies Centre).

Pinchbeck, I. and Hewitt, M. (1973) *Children in English Society: From the 18th century to the Children Act 1948*, Vol. 2. London: Routledge and Keegan Paul Ltd.

Piper, C. (1993) *The Responsible Parent: A Study of Divorce Mediation*. Harvester Wheatsheaf: Hemel Hempstead.

Piper, C. (1994) 'Parental responsibility and the Education Acts', *Family Law*, 24: 146–9.

Piper, C. (1995) 'Partnership Between Parents' in King, Kaganas and Piper (eds) *Legislating for Harmony: Partnership Under the Children Act 1989*. London: Jessica Kingsley.

Piper, C. (1996) 'Divorce reform and the image of the child', *Journal of Law and Society*, 23 (3): 364–82.

Piper, C. (1997) 'Ascertaining the wishes and feelings of the child: a requirement honoured largely in the breach?', *Family Law*, 27: 796.

Piper, C. (1999a) 'How do you define a family lawyer?' *Legal Studies*, 19 (1): 93–111.

Piper, C. (1999b) 'Moral Campaigns for Children's Welfare in the 19th Century', in M. King (ed.) *Moral Agendas for Children's Welfare*. London: Routledge. [Reprinted in Hendrick, H. (ed.) (2005) *Child Welfare and Social Policy: an Essential Reader* (Bristol: The Policy Press).]

Piper, C. (1999c) 'Barriers to seeing and hearing children in private law proceedings', *Family Law*, 29: 394–8.

Piper, C. (1999d) 'The Wishes and Feelings of the Child', in S. Day Sclater and C. Piper (eds) *Undercurrents of Divorce*. Aldershot: Ashgate.

Piper, C. (2000a) 'Historical Conceptions of Childhood Innocence: Removing Sexuality' in E. Heinze (ed.) *Of Innocence and Autonomy: Children, Sex and Human Rights*. Dartmouth: Dartmouth.

Piper, C. (2000b) 'Assumptions about children's best interests', *Journal of Social Welfare and Family Law*, 22 (3): 261–76. [Reprinted as 'Assumptions About Children's Best Interests: the risks in making assumptions about harm to children' in H. Hendrick (ed.) (2005) *Child Welfare and Social Policy: an Essential Reader*. Bristol: The Policy Press, 243–54.]

Piper, C. (2001) 'Who are these youths? Language in the service of policy', *Youth Justice*, 1 (2): 30–9.

Piper, C. (2004) 'Assessing assessment', *Family Law*, 34: 736–40.

Piper, C. (2007) 'The sexless child and accountable youth: shifting concepts?', Paper presented at the *Second International Symposium on Online Child Exploitation*, Centre for Innovation, Law and Policy, Law School, University of Toronto, 7 May.

Piper, C. and Miakishev, A. (2003) 'A Child's right to veto in England and Russia – another welfare ploy?' *Child and Family Law Quarterly*, 15(1): 57–69.

Platt, A. (1969) *The Child Savers: The Invention of Delinquency*. Chicago: University of Chicago Press.

PMSU (Prime Minister's Strategy Unit) (2007) *Building on Progress: Families*. London: Cabinet Office.

Pollock, L. (1983) *Forgotten Children: Parent-child Relations from 1500 to 1900*. Cambridge: Cambridge University Press.

Poole, T. (2007) 'The Reformation of English Administrative Law', LSE Law, Society and Economy Working Papers 12/2007, Law Department, LSE, London.

Poor Law Commissioners (1834) *Report from His Majesty's Commissioners Inquiring into the Administration and Practical Operation of the Poor Laws*. Reprinted 1905 as Cd. 2728. London: HMSO.

Pratt, J. (1986) 'Diversion from the juvenile court', *British Journal of Criminology*, 26 (3): 236.

Pratt, J. (2000) 'Dangerousness and Modern Society', in M. Brown and J. Pratt (eds) *Dangerous Offenders*. London and New York: Routledge.

Prime, J., White, S., Liriano, S. and Patel, K. (2001) 'Criminal careers of those born between 1953 and 1978', *Home Office Statistical Bulletin 4/01*. London: Home Office.

PR Newswire (on behalf of Switch) (2003) *News Release* 13 November. London: PR Newswire Europe Ltd.

Pryke, S. (2005) 'The control of sexuality in the early British Boy Scouts movement', *Sex Education*, 5 (1): 15–28.

Public Law Project (2006) *A brief guide to the grounds for judicial review*, Public Law Project Information Leaflet 3. London: Public Law Project.

Putnam, R. (1993) *Making Democracy Work*. Princeton NJ: Princeton University Press.

Quilgars, D. (2001) 'Child Homelessness', in J. Bradshaw (ed.) *Poverty: The Outcomes for Children*. London: Family Policy Studies Centre.

Qvortrup, J. (2001) 'School-Work, Paid Work and the Changing Obligations of Childhood', in P. Mizen, C. Pole and A. Bolton (eds) *Hidden Hands: International Pespectives on Children's Work and Labour*. London: Routledge/Falmer, pp. 91–107.

Qvortrup, J. (2005) 'Varieties of Childhood' in J. Qvortrup (ed.) *Studies in Modern Childhood: Society, Agency and Culture*. Basingstoke: Palgrave Macmillan.

Randall, J. (2007) 'Violent crimes are going up', *The Daily Telegraph*, 31 August, http://www.telegraph.co.uk/opinion/main.jhtml?xml=/opinion/2007/08/31/do3101.xml (accessed 25.9.07).

Raynes, B. (2006) 'Over-assessed and under-resourced', Paper presented at Reconstruct conference, London, 13 October.

Reece, H. (2005) 'From parental responsibility to parenting responsibly', *Current Legal Issues*, 8: 459–83.

Report of the Committee on Sexual Offences Against Children (1925). London: HMSO.

Report of the Matrimonial Causes Procedure Committee (1985). London: HMSO.

Respect Task Force (2007) *Tools and Powers to Tackle Anti-social Behaviour*. London: Home Office.

Roberts, J. and Devine, F. (2003) 'The hollowing out of the welfare state and social capital', *Social Policy and Society*, 2 (4): 309–18.

Roberts, K. (2005) 'Youth, Leisure and Social Inclusion', in M. Barry (ed.) *Youth Policy and Social Inclusion*. London: Routledge.

Rogers, C. (2006) *Implementation of Every Child Matters Green Paper*, Policy Discussion Paper. London: National Family and Parenting Institute.

Rose, N. (1985) *The Psychological Complex*. London: Routledge.

Rose, N. (2000) 'Government and control', *British Journal of Criminology*, 40: 321–39.

Ryan, J. and Schuerman, J. (2004) 'Matching family problems with specific family preservation services: a study of service effectiveness', *Children and Youth Services Review*, 26 (4) 347–72.

Salman, S. (2007) 'The story so far', *The Guardian*, Society Guardian, p. 1, 4 July.

Save the Children (2007) *Living Below the Radar: severe child poverty in the UK*, Briefing. London: Save the Children.

Sawyer, C. (1999) 'One step forward, two steps back – The European Convention on the Exercise of Children's Rights', *Child and Family Law Quarterly*, 11 (2): 151–70.

Sawyer, C. (2006) 'The child is not a person: family law and other legal cultures', *Journal of Social Welfare and Family Law*, 28 (1): 1–14.

Schiratzsk, J. (2000) 'The best interests of the child in the Swedish Aliens Act', *International Journal of Law, Policy and the Family*, 4 (3): 206–25.

School Food Trust (2006) *Eat Better Do Better, A revised guide to the Government's new food-based standards for school lunches*. London: School Food Trust, DfES.

Scottish Law Commission (1992) *Report on Family Law*, Scot Law Com. No. 135. Edinburgh: HMSO.

Scraton, P. and Haydon, D. (2002) 'Challenging the Criminalisation of Children and Young People', in J. Muncie, G. Hughes and E. McLaughlin (eds) *Youth Justice*. London: Sage.

Seebohm Report (1968) *Report of the Committee on Local Authority and Allied Personal Social Services*. Cmnd 3703. London: HMSO.

Sentencing Advisory Panel (2007) *Consultation Paper on Breach of an Anti-Social Behaviour Order (ASBO)*. London: Sentencing Guidelines Council.

Sheldon, S. (2001) 'Unmarried fathers and parental responsibility: a case for reform?', *Feminist Legal Studies*, 9 (2): 93–118.

Sherlock, A. (2007) 'Listening to children in the field of education: experience in Wales', *Child and Family Law Quarterly*, 19 (2): 161–82.

Shipman, A. and Shipman, M. (2006) *Knowledge Monopolies: The Academisation of Society*. Exeter: Imprint Academic.

Shute, S. (2004) 'The Sexual Offences Act 2003(4) New Civil Preventative Orders: Sexual Offences Prevention Orders, Foreign Travel Orders, Risk of Sexual Harm Orders', *Criminal Law Review*: 417–40.

Siman, S. (2007) 'Where do we go from here?', *Society Guardian*, 4 October.

Simon, J. (1998) 'Managing the monstrous: sex offenders and the new penology', *Psychology, Public Policy and the Law*, 4 (1): 1–16.

Sky News (2007) 'Yobs turning cities into no go areas', 24 July, http://news.sky.com/skynews/article/0,,91211-1276708,00.html (accessed 7.8.2007)

Smart, C. (1992) 'Disruptive Bodies and Unruly Sex: the regulation of reproduction and sexuality in the nineteenth century', in C. Smart (ed.) *Regulating Womanhood*. London: Routledge.

Smith, D. (2005a) 'The effectiveness of the juvenile justice system', *Criminal Justice*, 5 (2): 181–95.

Smith, D. (2005b) 'Contemporary Youth Justice Systems: Continuities and contradictions', in M. Barry (ed.) *Youth Policy and Social Inclusion*. London: Routledge.

Smith, D. (2006) *Social Inclusion and Early Desistance From Crime*, Report No. 12. Edinburgh: Centre for Law and Society, The University of Edinburgh.

Smith, D. (2007) 'Crime and the Life Course', in M. Maguire, R. Morgan and R. Reiner (eds) *The Oxford Handbook of Criminology*, 4th edn. Oxford: Oxford University Press.

Smith, D. and McVie, S. (2001) 'Theory and method in the Edinburgh study of youth transitions and crime', *British Journal of Criminology*, 43 (1): 169–95.

Smith, M. (2006) 'Early Interventions with Young Children and their Parents in the UK', in C. McAuley, P. Pecora and W. Rose (eds) *Enhancing the Well-being of Children and Families through Effective Interventions, International Evidence for Practice*. London: Jessica Kingsley.

Spargo, J. (1906, reprinted 1969) *The Bitter Cry of the Children*. Johnson Reprint Corporation: New York.

Spencer, N. (2003) 'Parenting programmes', *Archives of Disease in Childhood*, 88: 99–100.

Stainton Rogers, R. (1989) 'The Social Constructions of Childhood' in Stainton Rogers, W., Hevey, D. and Ash, E. (eds): *Child Abuse and Neglect*. London: Batsford and The Open University Press.

Stainton Rogers, R. and W. (1992) *Stories of Childhood: Shifting Agendas of Child Concern*. Hemel Hempstead: Harvester Wheatsheaf.

Stainton Rogers, R. and W. (1999) 'What is Good and Bad Sex for Children?' in King, M. (ed.) *Moral Agendas for Children's Welfare*. London: Routledge.

Stalford, H. (2008) 'The Relevance of European Citizenship to Children', in J. Williams and A. Invernizzi (eds) *Children and Citizenship*. London: Sage.

Stewart, J. (2001) 'The Campaign for School Meals in Edwardian Scotland', in J. Lawrence and P. Starkey (eds) *Child Welfare and Social Action in the Nineteenth and Twentieth Centuries*. Liverpool: Liverpool University Press.

Straw, J. (1997) Conference: *Good Practice Policing*, http://www.prnewswire.co.uk/cgi/news/release?id=15483 (accessed 26.10.07).

Sutherland, A., Merrington, S., Jones, S., Baker, K. and Roberts, C. (2005) *Role of Risk and Protective Factors*. London: Youth Justice Board.

Sutton, C., Utting, D. and Farrington, D. (Eds) (2004) *Support from the Start: Working with young children and their families to reduce the risks of crime and antisocial behaviour*. Research Report 524. London: Department for Education and Skills.

Taylor, R. (2007) 'Reversing the retreat from *Gillick*? *R (Axon) v Secretary of State for Health*', *Child and Family Law Quarterly*, 19 (1): 81–97.

Taylor, R. (2006) '*Re S (A Child) (Identification: Restrictions on Publication) and A Local Authority v W*: children's privacy and press freedom in criminal cases', *Child and Family Law Quarterly*, 18 (2): 269–86.

Teubner, G. (1993) *Law as an Autopoietic System*. Oxford: Oxford University Press.

Thompson, E.P. (1968) *The Making of the English Working Class*. London: Penguin.

Titmuss, R.M. (1938) *Poverty and Population: A Factual Study of Contemporary Social Waste*. London: Macmillan.

Tomaševski, K. (1999) Report submitted by the Special Rapporteur on the right to education Addendum Mission to the United Kingdom of Great Britain and Northern Ireland (England), *Commission on Human Rights, Fifty-sixth session*, 18–22 October.

Toynbee, P. (2007a) 'The public worry more about Spanish donkeys than child poverty', *The Guardian*, 30 March, p. 35.

Toynbee, P. (2007b) 'Young dreams', *The Guardian*, Society Guardian, 4 July: 1–2.

Tremblay C.H. and Tremblay V.J. (1995) 'Children and the economics of Christmas gift-giving', *Applied Economics Letters*, 2 (9): 295–7.

Tunstill, J., Allnock, D., Akhurst, S. and Garbers, C. (2005) 'Sure Start Local Programmes: implications of case study data from the National Evaluation of Sure Start', *Children and Society*, 19 (2): 158–71.

UNICEF (2007) *Child Poverty in Perspective: An Overview of Child Well-Being in Rich Countries*, Innocenti Report Card 7. Florence: UNICEF Innocenti Research Centre.

Utting, D. and Langman, J. (2005) *A Guide to Promising Approaches*. London: Communities that Care.

Utting, D. and Langman, J. (ed.) (2006) *A Guide to Promising Approaches*, 2nd edn. London: Communities that Care.

Utting, D. and Vennard, J. (2000) *What Works with Young Offenders in the Community*. London: Barnados.

Vaughan, B. (2000) 'The government of youth disorder *and* dependence?', *Social and Legal Studies*, 9 (3): 347–66.

Von Krieken (2005) 'The "best interests of the child" and parental separation: in the "civilising of parents"', *Modern Law Review*, 68 (1): 25–48

Walker, S. and Beckett, C. (2003) *Social Work Assessment and Intervention*. Lyme Regis: Russell House Publishing.

Ward, K., Sullivan, A. and Bradshaw, J. (2007) *Millennium Cohort Study*, Second Survey: Poverty, Briefing 10, http://www.cls.ioe.ac.uk/downloads/MCS2_Poverty.pdf.

Webb, B. (1926) *My Apprenticeship*. London: Longmans.

Webster, C., MacDonald, R., Shildrick, T. and Simpson, M. (2006) *Social Exclusion, Young Adults and Extended Youth Transitions*. London and Birmingham: Barrow Cadbury Trust.

Welshman, J. (2007) *From Transmitted Deprivation to Social Exclusion: policy poverty and parenting*. Bristol: Policy Press.

West, E. (1970) 'Forster and after: a hundred years of state education', *Economic Age*, 2 (5), http://www.ncl.ac.uk/egwest/pdfs/foster.pdf (accessed 16.10.06).

Wikely, N. (2006) 'A duty but not a right: child support after *R (Kehoe) v Secretary of State for Work and Pensions*', *Child and Family Law Quarterly*, 18 (2): 287–301.

Williams, J. (2005) 'Effective government structures for children?: The UK's four Children's Commissioners', *Child and Family Law Quarterly*, 17 (1): 37–53.

Williams, J. (2007) 'Incorporating children's rights: the divergence in law and policy', *Legal Studies*, 27 (2): 261–87.

Williams, J. and Croke, R. (2008) 'Institutional Support for the UNCRC's "Citizen Child"', in J. Williams and A. Invernizzi (eds) *Children and Citizenship*. London: Sage.

Williamson, H. (2005) 'Overview of Policy and Practice', in M. Barry (ed.) *Youth Policy and Social Inclusion*. London: Routledge.

Wilson, S. and Lipsey, M. (2007) 'School-based interventions for aggressive and disruptive behaviour: Update of a meta-analysis', *American Journal of Preventive Medicine*, 33 (Supplement 2), S130–S143.

Wintour, P. (2007) 'Time to stop knocking the young' and 'Miliband: "I want the buzz back in the manifesto"', *The Guardian*, 23 July, pp. 1 and 10.

Womack, S. (2007) 'British youngsters get worst deal, says UN', *The Daily Telegraph*, 14 February.

Woodhead, M. (1997) 'Psychology and the Cultural Construction of Children's Needs', in A. James and A. Prout (eds) *Constructing and Reconstructing Childhood*. London: Routledge/Falmer, pp. 63–84.

Worral, A. (1997) *Punishment in the Community*. London: Sage.

Wyness, M. (1997) 'Parental responsibilities, social policy and the maintenance of boundaries', *Sociological Review*, 45: 304.

YJB (Youth Justice Board) (2001) *Risk and protective factors associated with youth crime and effective interventions to prevent it*, YJB Research Note No. 5. London: YJB.

YJB (2002) *Intensive Supervision and Surveillance Programmes (ISSP): A new option for dealing with prolific and serious young offenders*. London: YJB.

YJB (2003) *Intensive Supervision and Surveillance Programmes: Key Elements of Effective Practice*. London: YJB.

YJB (2004) *Government Response to the Audit Commission Report – Youth Justice 2004: A Review of the Reformed Youth Justice System*, http://www.yjb.gov.uk/en-gb/News/ResponsetoReports.htm.

YJB (2006) *Common Assessment Framework: draft guidance for youth offending teams*. London: YJB.

Index

A v UK (1999), 203

acceptable behaviour contracts, 74, 172

accountability
  of children, 45–6
  of parents, 89–91, 100–2

Action Plan, for tackling exclusion, 71

active citizenship, 48, 76

actuarial justice, 111–12, 120

Addams, Jane, 37

adolescents, competing images of, 41–4

Adoption Act (1976), 147

Adoption and Children Act (2002), 14, 98, 147

Adoption (Northern Ireland) Order (1987), 147

adoption reform, 13–14

Adoption (Scotland) Act (1978), section 12(8), 147

adult/child boundaries, 33–4

'after care' duties, 138–9

Age of Legal Capacity (Scotland) Act (1991), 30, 31

age limits
  childhood definitions, 30–1
  for criminal liability, 31, 46

in relation to sexual offences, 41

Age of Majority (Northern Ireland) Act (1969), 30

Age of Majority (Scotland) Act (1969), 30

alcohol consumption, 8

anonymity rights, 209

anti-social behaviour, 172–3

Anti-Social Behaviour Act (2003)
  section 30(6), 155
  section 88, 181

Anti-Social Behaviour (Scotland) Act (2004), 206

anti-social behavioural orders (ASBOs), 5, 61, 208–9
  see also basbos

area-based rationing, 73

area-based targeting, 169

Armstrong, Hilary, 170, 212

assessment
  and the law, 137–40
  see also Common Assessment Framework; multiple assessments; needs assessment; risk assessment

Asset, 123, 125–9, 184

Auld, LJ, 141

Aynsley-Green, Sir Albert, 5, 9

Balls, Ed, 196–7
basbos, 17–18
Beeton, Mrs, 194, 198
best interests of the child, 12, 13, 81, 95, 145, 148
The Better Way of Assisting School Children, 93
Bingham, Lord, 156–7
Blair, Tony, 15, 65, 83, 163–4
Booth, Charles, 90
Booth, General William, 58, 60, 90
Botta v Italy (1998), 152
Boy Scouts movement, 88
Brooke, Annette, 59
Brown, Gordon, 63
Brown LJ, 210
Burnton J, 139
Butler-Sloss, Baroness, 103–4

Care Matters: Transforming the Lives of Children and Young People in Care (2006), 108
care proceedings, 148
Carpenter, Mary, 38
causal pathways, 121
CF v Secretary of State for the Home Department (2004), 153
change
    barriers to, 9–11
    legitimating, 11–13
Change for Children, 67–70
Charity Organisation Society (COS), 92–3
child
    as innocent, 20, 39–44, 88
    as moral actor, 151–2
    as offender, 42, 44–7
    regard to 'wishes and feelings' of, 23, 146–9, 151–2
    sentimental image, 36
    sexual abuse, 40, 41, 42, 43
    as a symbol of nostalgia, 19
    as victim, 35–9, 41, 42, 51, 87, 99–100
    see also community child; evil

child; good child; responsible citizen-child; Victorian child; worthy child
'child liberationist' approach, 22, 47–8
child policy see social policy (child-focused)
child pornography, 41
child poverty
    correlated with worklessness, 64
    government policy to reduce, 7, 64
    not considered a social problem, 12
    public misconceptions about, 67
    rates, 6, 7
child protection
    assessment, 124–5
    and control, 37–8
    in employment, 85
    from harm at home, 89–91
    legislation, 5
    partnerships, 205
    risk in, 112–13
    and the sexualised minor, 42
    see also safeguarding children
child welfare
    programmes, evidence-led practice, 167–8
    use of law to secure, 134
childhood
    birth and death of, 32–4
    concept/conception of, 32–3
    deficits, 6–9
        barriers to change, 9–11
        constructing the problem, 14–18
        legitimating change, 11–13
        see also child poverty
    giving children a, 20
    legal definitions, 30
children
    accountability, 45–6
    agency, 15, 48
    anxiety, 7

commodification of, 50
conceptualization of, 28–9
cruelty to, 37, 90
custody of, 91, 94–5
employment, 37, 84–6
expenditure on, 3–4, 136–7
feeding, 92–4
health indicators, 8
images of, 16, 32–52, 134–5,
   199–202
investment in *see* investment in
   children
invisibility, 37
keeping at home, 84–6
keeping as moral, 87
and the law *see* law
in need *see* children in need
negative attitudes to, 4–6
and the police, 156–7
poor life experiences *see*
   childhood, deficits
protection *see* child protection
responsibility, 45–6
   see also responsible citizen-
    child
rights *see* children's rights
school exclusion, 8, 149
suicides, 8
teaching *see* education
trouble in relation to, 16–18
truth about, 29–32
well-being *see* well-being
see also adult-child boundaries
Children Act (1908), 4, 45, 60
Children Act (1948), 4, 83
Children Act (1989), 4, 5, 14, 23, 31,
   50, 95, 97, 124, 135, 138, 149, 205
   section 1, 135
   section 1(1), 144–5
   section 1(3), 146
   section 2(1), 98
   section 2–4, 82
   section 3, 103–4
   section 8, 102
   section 11A–O, 102

   section 17, 112, 135, 136–7, 138,
    140, 143, 145, 147, 153
   section 17(1), 136
   section 17(10), 136
   section 20, 82, 139, 147, 205
   section 22(3), 142
   section 23(2), 139
   section 23(6), 139
   section 26, 140
   section 27, 142
   section 27(2), 142
   section 31, 82, 95, 103, 112, 135,
    145–6
   section 41, 148
   section 46, 147
   section 47, 112, 140, 147, 153
   section 61, 147
   section 64, 147
   section 105(1), 30
Children Act (2004), 50, 67, 70, 76,
   83, 128, 135, 142
   section 1, 154
   section 2, 154
   section 10, 137
   section 10(2), 68, 122
   section 10(2)a, 180
   section 10(2)d, 49
   section 10(4), 68
   section 11, 122, 137
   section 11(2), 69
   section 11(2)a, 68
   section 13, 69
   section 15, 77
   section 17, 137
   section 53, 147
   section 58, 203, 204, 205
Children at Risk Review, 63, 118
Children and Families: Safer from
   Sexual Crime: The Sexual Offences
   Act 2003, 41
Children and Family Court
   Advisory Support Services
   (CAFCASS), 69
Children (Leaving Care) Act (2000),
   138

children in need, 142
  expenditure, 136–7
  images of children, 16, 37
  investment and stigmatisation, 77
  and the law
    assessment, 112, 137–40, 153
    children's services, 140–2
    general or specific duties,
      142–3
Children (Northern Ireland) Order
  (1995), 146
Children (Scotland) Act (1995), 211
Children in Trouble (1968), 17
Children and Young People's Plan
  (CYPP), 69, 137
Children and Young Persons Act
  (1933), 38, 60
  section 1(7), 203
  section 39, 209
  section 44, 60, 210
Children's centres, 170, 185–6
Children's Commissioners, 154, 204
Children's Food Bill (2005), 59
Children's Fund, 20, 62, 63, 70–1,
  72, 174–5
  Strategic Plan Guidance, 175
Children's Hearings, 17, 155
The Children's Plan (2007), 77, 80, 94,
  181, 192, 194, 196, 211–12
children's rights, 21–5, 50, 149–54,
  159, 202–3, 209
children's services
  conditionality of, 76–7
  eligibility criteria, 124, 125,
    169–70
  involvement through Asset, 127
  joined-up, 20
  key outcome targets, 63
  and the law, 140–2
Children's and Young People's
  Services Plan, 137
children's trusts, 70, 73, 77, 127, 128,
  144
Choice and Diversity (1992), 49
Christianity, 29–30, 85

citizenship, 76, 207
  see also responsible citizen-child
citizenship education, 57
Citizenship Survey (2001), 100
civil orders, 61
class, construction of the innocent
  child, 88
Climbié, Victoria, 25, 35, 204
collectivism, fear of, 93
commerce, investing in, 58–60
Commission on Social Justice's
  report (1994), 64
'commodification' of children, 50
Common Assessment Framework
  (CAF), 122–3, 124–5
communitarianism, 45
Communities that Care (CtC), 176–7
community, in inclusion and
  investment policies, 208
community child, 48–50
complaints/grievance procedures,
  and the law, 140–1
conditionality
  of children' services, 76–7
  of help/support, 45
Connexions, 123, 169, 177
consent, 30–1, 88
consumers, children as, 50
context, risk/protection factor, 117
contractual governance, 73–4, 206
control, protection and, 37–8
Cooke Taylor, R.W., 86
Cotton Mills Act (1819), 85
crime see offending
Crime and Disorder Act (1998), 45,
  46, 61
  section 1, 206
  section 2, 206
  section 8–11, 206
  section 11, 206
  section 34, 47, 200
  section 37, 125
  section 38, 125
  section 65 and 66, 156, 179
Crime and Disorder Reduction
  Partnerships, 72

crime policy, 112
crime prevention, medical approach, 109
Criminal Evidence and Youth Justice Act (1999), 46, 61
Criminal Justice: the Way Ahead, 118–19
Criminal Justice Act (1991)
    section 57–8, 206
    section 68, 31
Criminal Justice Act (2003), 44
    section 226, 62
Criminal Justice Act (2004), sections 224–9, 111
Criminal Justice Committee (Finland 1976), 172
Criminal Justice and Public Order Act (1994), 206
Criminal Justice (Scotland) Act (2003), section 51, 204
criminal justice system, 31, 68
Criminal Law Amendment Act (1885), 88
criminalisation, 5
criminogenic needs, 120
cruelty to children, 37, 90
The Cry of the Children, 36
culpability, 31, 46; *see also doli incapax*
custodial sentences, indeterminate, 62
custody, of children, 91, 94–5
Custody of Children Act (1891), 91

dangerous threat, child as, 44–5, 51
'dangerous' young offenders, detention of, 62
Davenport Hill, Matthew, 45
defence, investing in, 60
delinquency, 116
democracy, investment in, 55–7
desistence, 115–18, 171
detention, 62
disabled children, 181
discretion, in relation to local

authorities' duties, 137
diversion, 45, 171–3
divorce
    children as victims of, 38–9, 99–100
    parental responsibility, 96–7
doli incapax, 25, 44, 46, 47
drug use, and delinquency, 116
dynamic risks, 120

early intervention
    effectiveness of, 194–5
    investment agenda, 21
    risk, 70–2
    scientific evidence, 130
    young offenders, 69
ecological triangle, assessment, 124
economics, investment in children, 19–20, 54–5
Edinburgh Study of Youth Transitions and Crime, 115–16
education, 91–2
    definition of child, 31
    interventions, 177–8
    investment in, 55–7
Education Act (1870), 56, 90, 91–2
Education Act (1944), 4
Education Act (1980), 59
Education Act (1996)
    sections 443–4, 206
    sections 579(1) and 312(5), 31
Education Act (2002), 147–8
Education Department, 91–2
Education and Inspection Act (2006)
    section 6, 69–70
    section 112–14, 144
Education (Provision of Meals) Act (1906), 11–12, 20, 58, 93
Education (Scotland) Act (1908), 93
educational managerialism, 49–50
eligibility criteria, for services, 124, 125, 169–70
emergency protection orders (EPOs), 205
emotional harm, of sexual abuse, 43

employers, cruelty to children, 37
employment, of children, 37, 84–6
empowerment, 49
European Convention on the
    Exercise of Children's Rights
    (ECECR), 24, 143
European Convention on Human
    Rights and Fundamental
    Freedoms, 23–4, 150, 152, 155,
    209
Every Child Matters, 20, 28, 67–8, 71,
    74–5, 101, 122, 123, 144, 150, 177,
    185, 191, 201; *see also Change for
    Children*
Every Child Matters: Next Steps, 111,
    123, 127–8
Every Parent Matters (2007), 101–2,
    108, 109
evidence-led interventions, 163–9
evil child, 87
exclusion *see* school exclusion; social
    exclusion
expenditure, on children
    by families, 3–4
    legitimating, 14, 195–8
    limiting, 73–5
    in need, 136–7
    school meals, 59
Extended Schools programme, 178

factory children, 37
family
    autonomy of, 12–13, 203
    conceptions of, 51
    disruption, and offending, 118
    expenditure on children, 3–4
    New Labour crime policy, 112
    role within society, 80
Family Law Act (1996), 99
Family Law Reform Act (1969), 30
family life
    right to respect, 152
    state intervention, 5, 13, 81–2, 87,
        89
family nurses, 187

Family Proceedings Rules (1991), 31
family risk factors, offending, 114
FAST programme, 190
fathers
    likelihood of seeking advice, 100
    parental responsibility, 82, 98–9,
        102
    rights over children, 94
    unmarried, 82, 98
feeding children, 92–4
Final Warning Asset tool, 126
Final Warning Schemes, 126, 156,
    179–80
Finnish Criminal Justice Committee
    (1976), 172
Finnish Youth Crime Committee
    (2004), 172
Food Bills (2004 and 2005), 59
Food Standards Agency, 59
*Framework for Assessment of Children
    in Need and their Families* (2000),
    123, 124, 137
*From Punishment to Problem Solving:
    A New Approach to Children in
    Trouble* (2006), 17

gender
    construction of the innocent
        child, 88
    performance on ISSPs, 182
gender issues, in parenting, 102
*Gillick v West Norfolk and Wisbech
    Area Health Authority and Another*
    [1986], 30, 96, 153–4
'good' child, 49, 51
'good' parent/parenting, 99, 107
Gravity Factor System, 126
Guardianship of Infants Act (1925),
    94, 95
Guardianship of Infants Act (1973),
    94–5

H v Wandsworth and others, 139
Hale of Richmond, Baroness, 96,
    151–2, 156, 158–9, 172

harm
    at home, protection from, 89–91
    see also emotional harm; parental
        harms; significant harm
health
    Every Child Matters outcomes,
        75
    indicators, 8
    interventions, 180–1
    investing in, 58–60
    reforms, 70
health services, access to, 180–1
Healthcare Commission,
    improvement review, 180–1
Herschell, Lord, 91
Hinduism, 30
Hodge, Margaret, 159
Holman J, 139
home
    mystical power accorded to, 86
    protecting children from harm at,
        89–91
Home Start, 185
home-school agreements, 74
homelessness, 6–7
hospital services, 180–1
Howard League for Penal Reform,
    153
Human Rights Act (1998), 23–4, 143,
    149, 150

'identification of anomalies', 149
images of children, 16, 32–52, 134–5,
    199–202
improvement review, hospital
    services, 180–1
In Re D (a Child) [2006], 151–2
In Re H (a Child) [2006], 152
incivility/ies, 61
inclusion see social inclusion
individual risk factors, offending,
    114
industrial schools, 20, 87
Industrial Schools Acts, 87
industrialisation, 33, 37, 87

Infant Felons Act (1840), 90–1
infant mortality rates, 8, 86
information, in risk assessment, 122
Information Sharing and Assessment
    Programme, 123
innocence, 36, 39, 40
innocent child, 20, 39–44, 88
Inspectorates, 144
Institute for Citizenship, 57
Intensive Supervision and
    Surveillance Programme (ISSPs),
    169, 181–2
inter-agency work/co-operation, 68,
    111, 128, 142
international conventions, 149–51
Internet, 41
intervention(s), 163–92
    blueprint for action, 190
    dosage, 187–8
    effective targeting, 109–10
    evidence-led, 163–9
    key programmes, 174–87
    local knowledge, 189
    multi-modal, 189–90
    pathways in relation to crime,
        116–17
    personnel and practice, 190–1
    targeting the subject, 169–70
    timing, 188
    see also early intervention; Family
        Intervention Projects; non-
        intervention; state intervention
investment in children
    change in rationale for child-
        focused policy, 25
    choices about the sort of, 19
    economic justification, 19–20,
        54–5
    education, 55–7
    effectiveness and utility of, 21
    health and nutrition, 58–60
    hurdles to, 11–14
    inclusion, 62–7
    in practice, 19, 75–8
    rights as a tool for, 24–5

risk management, 19
role of law *see* law
scientific justification, 55
sources of evidence to support,
    19
to ensure law-abiding adults,
    60–2
see also expenditure
Islam, 30
Isle of Man, 30

Jamie Oliver campaign, 59
*JD v East Berkshire Community Health
    Trust and others* [2005], 141
Jerrold, Douglas, 37
Johnson, Alan, 108
joined-up working, 20, 142, 191
*Joint birth registration: promoting
    parental responsibility* (2007), 98
Joint Youth Justice Unit, 201
Joseph Rowntree Foundation, 176,
    177, 183, 189
Judaism, 30
judicial review, 141, 144, 150
juvenile justice *see* youth justice

Key Elements of Effective Practice
    (KEEPs), 164

Laming, Lord, 204
late modernity, child in, 19
law, 132–59
    and the child, 30–2
    enforcing or denying duties,
        135–43
    as a giver of mixed messages,
        154–9
    images of children, 134–5
    legal criteria and concepts, 133–4
    local authority duties, 144–6
    role for rights, 149–54
    weight of child's views, 146–9,
        151–2
    see also legislation
Law Lords, 157–9

'law and order' agenda, 207–10
law-abiding adults, investment to
    ensure, 60–2
Lawrence v Pembrokeshire [2007], 141
legal capacity, age of, 30–1
legislation
    child-focused, 3, 4–5, 16, 83
    on-line exploitation, 40–1, 200
    as a strategy for furthering
        investment, 133
    see also individual acts
less eligibility, 82
liberationists, 22, 47–8
Lloyd Jones J, 138, 153
local authorities' duties
    enforcing or denying, 135–43
    explaining law's stance on, 144–6
Local Authority and Social Services
    Act (1970), 76
    section 7, 138
local education authorities, duties,
    69–70
Local Network Fund for Children,
    62
Local Safeguarding Children's
    Boards, 68–9, 77

McCann v Crown Court at Manchester
    [2002], 208
McGuire principles, 187, 190
Maloney Report (1927), 45, 87
managerialism, 49–50, 74
Masham of Ilton, Baroness, 40–1
mediation, parental separation, 97,
    99
medical approach, crime prevention,
    109
medical sciences, the child and, 29
medical treatment, consent to, 30–1
Messages from Research (1995),
    112–13, 164
meta-analyses, youth justice
    treatment programmes, 166–7
Milliband, David, 65
modernisation, 108

moral, keeping children, 87
moral actor, child as, 151–2
moral fears, for children and
    mothers, 85–6
moral guarantors, parents as, 102
moralisation, of children, 85, 92
Morgan, Rod, 107, 129–30, 173
mothers
    custody of children, 94–5
    encouraging to take
        responsibility, 102
    keeping at home, 84–6
multiple assessments, 122
Munby J, 39, 152–3

naming and shaming, 209
National Action Plan on Social
    Inclusion, 62
National Children's Bureau (NCB),
    6, 127
National Family and Parenting
    Institute, 124
National Health Service Act (1948),
    4
*National Service Framework for
    Children, Young People and
    Maternity Services*, 70, 123, 180
needs
    as problematic, 119–21
    see also children in need
needs assessment, 119, 137
negligence, actions for, 141–2
neighbourhoods, and desistance,
    115–16
net-widening, 173
New Deal for Communities, 64, 66,
    74, 183
New Labour, 15, 19, 45, 50, 60–1, 62,
    83, 108, 112
new localism, 189
new penology, 110, 120
new rehabilitationism, 165
New Right, 96
*A New Deal for Welfare: Empowering
    People to Work* (DWP), 183

Newcastle Commission (1861), 92
Nichols of Birkenhead, Lord, 138
No More Excuses (1997), 46, 48, 118
non-intervention, 81, 171–3
nostalgia, child as a symbol of, 19
'nothing works', 165
Nurse-Family Partnership
    Programme, 186–7
nutritional standards, 59

obesity, 8, 60
offender(s)
    categorisation, 111
    child as, 42, 44–7
    see also persistent offenders; sex
        offenders; young offenders
Offenders' Index, 119
offending
    approaches to managing future,
        61
    correlations between poor
        outcomes and, 109
    family disruption, 118
    pathways to, 113–21
    risk of, 110–12, 114–15
    see also anti-social behaviour;
        delinquency
On Side project, 189
on-line exploitation, legislation,
    40–1, 200
Onset, 128–9
opportunity-based policies, 73
Outcomes Framework (*Every Child
    Matters*), 67–8, 74–5, 101

paedophiles, 41
parental authority, 100
parental autonomy, 83, 203–7
parental harms, 99–100
parental partnerships
    with the state, 91–4
    state intervention in, 94–6
parental responsibility
    children's behaviour, 100–4
    for education, 92

encouraging, 102
fathers, 82, 98–9, 102
mandating, 103–4
new legal concept of, 95, 96
public notions of, 12
reconfiguration of, 83–4
remoralisation agenda, 78
undermined by responsibility to
    external agencies, 100
widening remit, 96–100
parental rights, 25, 94, 96
parental separation, mediation, 97,
    99
parental supervision, 120
parenting
    gender issues in, 102
    performance managed, 84
    science of effective, 107–10
    see also Nurse-Family Partnership
        Programme
parenting orders, 61, 102, 206
parenting programmes, 170
Parenting Support Guidance (2006),
    109
parents
    accountability, 89–91, 100–2
    duty to keep children moral, 87
    likelihood of seeking advice, 100
    as moral and social guarantors of
        children, 102
    as problems or partners, 80–4
    see also fathers; mothers
Parish Apprentices Act (1802), 85
Parliamentary Joint Committee on
    Human Rights, 83
parsimony principle, 136
pathfinder partnerships, 183
pathways to crime, 113–21
penal governance, risk-based, 120
penal welfare values, 211
performance managed parenting, 84
persistent offenders, 118–19, 171
physical chastisement, 203
police
    children and, 156–7

rule-based intervention, 171
police cautioning, 45
Police and Criminal Evidence Act
    (1984), 157
policies
    social inclusion, 21, 73
    youth justice, 210–11
    see also crime policy, social policy
'politics of adultism', 16
'politics of pathos', 36
Poor Law Amendment Act (1834),
    82
Poor Law Boards, 85
Poor Laws, 82, 134, 136
'poor' parenting, 107
post-modern childhoods, 32
poverty see child poverty
Powers of Criminal Courts
    (Sentencing) Act (2000)
    sections 25–6, 47
    sections 63–8, 181
Pre-Assessment Checklist, 124
Prevent and Deter, 72, 183–4
preventative intervention, 163
preventative state, 25
Prevention of Cruelty to and Better
    Protection of Children Act (1889),
    5, 89, 90, 91
Primary Care Trusts, 180
Prison Service establishments,
    rights-based judgments, 152–3
Prison Service Order 4950, 153
private life, right to respect, 152
Professional Certificate in Effective
    Practice (YJB), 167
Professional policy making for the
    twenty-first century, 108
Prolific and Priority Offenders
    Strategy, 119, 183
proportionality, 150
prostitution, 43
Prudent for Purpose (2002), 62
psychosocial disorder, crime as, 115
Public Service Agreements, 127, 181
punishment

by parents, 83, 203–5
and risk assessment, 111
punitiveness
and community values, 208
of investment, 76

Quality Protects programme, 127

R (Begum) v Headteacher and
Governors of Denbigh High School
[2006], 158
R (Howard League for Penal Reform)
v Secretary of State for the Home
Department [2002], 39
R (Kehoe) v Secretary of State for
Work and Pensions [2005], 158
R (on the application of K) v
Manchester City Council) [2006],
153
R (on the application of R) v Durham
Constabulary and another [2005],
156–7, 172
R (on the application of W) v Essex
[2003], 139
R (Rowley) v Secretary of State for
Work and Pensions [2007], 158
R v Islington Borough Council ex parte
Rixon [1998], 137–8
R v Royal Borough of Kingston-upon-
Thames ex parte T [1999], 140
R v Somerset CC ex parte Dixon
(1997), 150
R v Stanley and others v Metropolitan
Police [2004], 209
R v Tower Hamlets LBC ex parte
Bradford [1998], 140
R (W) v Lambeth LBC [2004], 82, 145
Rainer CtC, 176–7
rationing, 14, 73
Re G (Interim Care Order: Residential
Assessment) [2005], 140
Re L and H (Residential Assessment)
[2007], 140
Re S (Parental Responsibility) [1995],
98

Re S and W [2007], 145
Re T (Judicial Review: Local Authority
Decisions Concerning Children in
Need [2003], 141, 142
Re (W) v Commissioner of Police of the
Metropolis and another [2005], 155
reasonable, in relation to local
authorities' duties, 137
reasonable chastisement, 83, 203, 204
reasonable punishment, 204
recreation, 69–70
referral orders, 46–7, 61, 74, 206
Reform Acts (1832 and 1867), 56
reformable threat, child as, 45–6
rehabilitative programmes, 61
religion, 29–30, 85
remoralisation, 48, 65, 78
Report of the Committee on Sexual
Offences Against Children (1925),
43
Report of the Matrimonial Causes
Procedure Committee (1985), 96–7
research, evidence-led practice,
165–9
resilience, 117–18
Respect Action Plan, 102, 184–5
Respect agenda, 159
Respect Unit, 201–2
responsibilisation, 46, 96, 202
responsibility
of children, 45–6
individual, 16
see also parental responsibility
responsible citizen-child, 47–50, 56,
77–8, 199
responsible offenders, 46–7
responsible sex, 200
restorative justice, 61
Review of Child Care Law, 83
rights see children's rights; Human
Rights Act; parental rights
risk
in child protection, 112–13
early intervention, 70–2
of offending, 110–12, 114–15

perceptions of, 18–21
as problematic, 119–21
risk assessment, 107
and punishment, 111
tools, 121–9
risk management, 19, 67, 110–11
risk society, 18
Royal Commission on Secondary
Education (1895), 56

S v Miller (2001 SLT 531), 155
Sadler, Michael, 36, 86
Safeguarding Boards, 68–9, 77
safeguarding children, 17, 88–9
Save the Children, 7
School Boards, 91, 92
school exclusion, 8, 149
school meals, 11–12, 58–9, 92–3
School Standards and Framework
Act (1998), 74
science
dependence on, 198–9
early intervention, 130
of effective parenting, 107–10
investment in children, 55
Scotland
age of legal capacity, 30, 31
Children's Hearings, 17, 155
responsible offender, 47
Scott, Lord, 145
SEAL (social and emotional aspects
of learning), 177–8
Sedley J, 150
Seebohm Report (1968), 76
Select Committee (1882), 88
sentencing provisions, 44, 62, 111
seriousness of offending, court
orders, 111
services see children's services;
health services
'seven ages of man', 34
sex
age of consent, 88
responsible, 200
safeguarding children from, 88–9

sex education, 43
sex offenders, restrictions on, 43
sexual abuse, 40, 41, 42, 43
Sexual Offences Act (2003), 41
sexuality, as problematic, 40–1
Shaftesbury, Lord, 85–6, 90
Shakespeare, William, 34
Shelter, 7
significant harm, 112, 145–6
smacking, 83, 203–5
social anxieties, 33, 55
social capital, 65–6, 116
social causation, 121
social Darwinism, 58
social disadvantage, 8
social exclusion
Action Plan for tackling, 71
conditionality of help/support,
45
correlated with worklessness, 64
government commitment to
overcoming, 62, 65
key principles for reform, 212
terminology, 65
social guarantors, parents as, 102
social housing, 8
social inclusion
investment in, 62–7
philosophical roots, 66
policies, 21, 73
rights as a tool for, 24–5
'social investment state', 64
social policy (child-focused)
based on 'what works', 108
change in the rationale for, 25
child protection, 112–13
constructed for political reasons,
15
developments in, 50–2
ideologies and concepts
constraining, 13–14
social problems, 35
Social Purity Movement, 88
social selection, 121
Spargo, John, 38

special educational needs (SEN), 149
Spring-Rice, Sir Cecil, 49
state, parental partnership with, 91–4
state intervention
  in family life, 5, 81–2, 87, 89
  in parental partnerships, 94–6
stigmatisation, 77
Strategic Health Authorities, 180
Straw, Jack, 61
'submerged tenth', 90
suicides, 8
Supporting Parents (1998), 12
Sure Start, 62, 64, 169, 170, 185–6
Sure Start Children's Centres, 178, 185
Sure Start Local Programmes (SSLPs), 186
Sustain, 59

Tackling Anti-social Behaviour, 172–3
Taunton Commission, 92
Tea Act (1773), 14
Templeman, Lord, 206
Ten Hours Bill, 36, 86
third generation assessment tools, 120, 129
Third Way, 15, 45, 47, 56, 96, 194
threat, the child as, 44–6, 51
threshold tests, child protection, 112
trainable child, 49
trouble, in relation to children, 16–18

United Nations
  Convention on the Rights of the Child (UNCRC), 22, 23, 30, 147, 150–1, 154, 200, 202–3
  Declaration of the Rights of the Child (1924 and 1959), 22
  Standard Minimum Rules for the Administration of Juvenile Justice, 22
  Year of the Child (UN), 22–3
universal education, 56, 58, 92
urbanisation, 33

values, underpinning Third Way, 15
victim, child as, 35–9, 41, 42, 51, 87, 99–100
victim-offender mediation, 179
Victorian child, 35–8, 88
volunteering, within the community, 49
Votes are Power campaign, 57
voting, decline in, 57

wardship courts, 82
Webb, Beatrice, 90, 93
welfare *see* child welfare
welfare checklist, 23, 146, 147
welfare principle, 14, 60, 95, 144–6
well-being
  assessment, 124–5
  improving, 68
  industrialised nations, 8–9
  mixed indications of, 8
'what works', 108, 165, 168, 190
Widdecombe, Ann, 41
Working Together to Safeguard Children (2006), 124
worklessness, 64
'worthy' child, 43, 51

X (Minors) v Bedfordshire County Council (1995), 141

young offenders
  assessment, 125–9
  detention, 62
  diversion, 171–3
  early intervention, 69
Young People at Risk, 62
Youth Court, 31, 46
Youth Court Bench Book, 111
Youth Crime Briefing (NACRO), 172
Youth Crime Committee (Finland, 2004), 172
Youth Inclusion Support Panels (YISPs), 72, 113
youth justice
  evidence-led practice, 166–7

initiatives, 72
interventions, 188
investment agenda, 61–2
new discursive context of, 46
policy, 210–11
politicisation, 18
risk of offending, 110–12
system expansion, 173
welfare principle, 60
Youth Justice Board (YJB), 71, 72, 77, 113, 123, 164, 169–70, 184
Youth Justice and Criminal Evidence Act (1999), 209

Youth Justice – The Next Steps, 102
Youth Matters (2005), 17, 47, 49, 51, 57, 67, 73, 76
Youth Matters: The Next Steps (2006), 69–70, 74, 144, 150
youth offending teams (YOTs), 111, 127
Youthful Offenders Act (1854), 87
youth(s), negative constructions, 44–5

Z v UK [2001], 141
zero tolerance, 61